BUILDING DEMOCRACY
IN CONTEMPORARY RUSSIA

BUILDING DEMOCRACY IN CONTEMPORARY RUSSIA

Western Support for Grassroots Organizations

SARAH L. HENDERSON

Cornell University Press | ITHACA AND LONDON

First published 2003 by Cornell University Press

Printed in the United States of America

Library of Congress Cataloging-in-Publication Data

Henderson, Sarah, 1971–
    Building democracy in contemporary Russia : Western support for grassroots
organizations / Sarah L. Henderson.
        p.   cm.
Includes bibliographical references and index.
    ISBN 0-8014-4135-8 (cloth : alk. paper)
    1. Civil society—Russia (Federation) 2. Democracy—Russia (Federation)
3. Economic assistance—Russia (Federation) 4. Non-governmental organizations—
Russia (Federation) 5. Russia (Federation)—Politics and government—1991–
I. Title.
    JN6699.A15H46   2003
    300′.947—dc21   2003008022

Cornell University Press strives to use environmentally responsible
suppliers and materials to the fullest extent possible in the publishing
of its books. Such materials include vegetable-based, low-VOC inks
and acid-free papers that are recycled, totally chlorine-free, or partly
composed of nonwood fibers. For further information, visit our
website at www.cornellpress.cornell.edu.

Cloth printing   10 9 8 7 6 5 4 3 2 1

Contents

Preface

September 11, 1998, 11 A.M. About thirty activists from environmental and human rights organizations from across Russia had gathered in a slightly dilapidated building somewhere in the outskirts of Moscow, about forty-five minutes from the center of town. They were all affiliated in some way with either the Socio-Ecological Union or the Moscow Helsinki Group, two of the largest and best-known nongovernmental organizations in Russia. A few individuals stirred instant coffee or black tea in Styrofoam cups and engaged in desultory chatter with old colleagues or new acquaintances. Others sipped their beverages and stared off into space, lost in their own thoughts. These men and women were waiting to begin a two-and-a-half-day training seminar sponsored by the Moscow office of the National Democratic Institute (NDI), a U.S. quasi-governmental agency that provides training to political parties and grassroots organizations all over the world. The goal of the seminar was to help environmental and human rights organizations build coalitions with one another and to establish a common agenda for a national campaign. By the end of the training, NDI hoped that groups would return home with at least three plans to translate ideas into action.

After quick introductions, a U.S. and a Russian trainer speedily launched into a tightly organized crash course on grassroots activism. The weekend offered a whirlwind tour through the process of choosing, planning, and implementing a national campaign. Moving briskly, the trainers covered topics such as setting goals, identifying target audiences, designing strategies, studying previous successes, working with the power structure, and fund-raising. Participants listened to presentations, pored over case studies of "success stories," broke into discussion groups, and role-played various scenarios. In a surreal twist of information sharing, participants were given a translated brochure originally written by Jerry Brown and Mario Cuomo entitled "The Art of Forming Coalitions." It was not just U.S. culture and economics that had become globalized; now even U.S.-style politicking was being spread to the remote corners of the Earth.

I sat in the corner of the room, watching the faces and listening to the reactions of the activists to this foreign approach to grassroots activism. The legal right to organize independently from the state was a by-product of Mikhail Gorbachev's reforms, and so was less than a decade old. Most groups were laboriously making their way up a very steep learning curve, adjusting from Soviet definitions and standards of civic participation to the new era of quasi-democracy and free market capitalism. Some nodded sagely at the trainers' comments; others looked a little bewildered at the talk of strategies, coalitions, and campaigns. A few questioned the very utility of such a seminar. Although participants were passionate about their respective causes, many were quick to point out the numerous impediments that slowed their progress. The government did not care about their issues. The population was indifferent. Organizations had no money for activities. Russia was not the United States, and U.S. advice did not apply. Judging by the first hour, this training was going to be a hard sell. What did Mario Cuomo and Jerry Brown have to say that could translate into the Russian experience, anyway? Could a three-day seminar somehow distill the skills, traits, and customs embedded in Western-style civic activism? Was this training of any use to civic activists operating in such different political, economic, and social contexts?

By the end of the weekend, something had changed. The participants had developed tentative plans for several national campaigns. One group proposed a national referendum on nuclear power, another discussed a campaign to stop plutonium production, and still another designed a clean water campaign. Participants who two days previously had sat in stony silence, were now critiquing one another's ideas, offering suggestions listening to their colleagues. The participants were still a long way from implementing any of their plans, but they had already traveled some distance from their initial resistance to the Americanized idea of activism. At the end of the weekend, trainers and participants packed up their bags and shuttled back home, no doubt wondering if any of the plans hatched over the weekend would come to fruition.

July 30, 2002. Over my morning coffee, scrolling through search results of a Lexis-Nexis search on environmental activism in Russia, I read an article about the legislative battle over importing nuclear waste. In 2000, a coalition of public groups, spearheaded by the Socio-Ecological Union, the Moscow Helsinki Group, and other environmental and human rights groups hatched a plan to use a little-known 1995 law to force the government to consult the public via a referendum. By the fall of that year, they had collected almost 3 million signatures demanding the government seek public approval of its plans to store and process foreign radioactive waste. Although eventually blocked by the Central Election Commission, which disqualified enough signatures to leave the petition 50,000 names short, this was a significant attempt to carry off a Westernized national grassroots campaign on a political issue. Some of the groups I had observed four years earlier in Moscow were now the primary instigators of this referendum attempt. I thought back to that weekend and to the participants' efforts to hammer out ideas for a national campaign around the issue of nuclear waste. Many factors had gone into planning, shaping, and carrying through the referendum I had read about, but I wondered if any lessons learned from that conference had helped move this campaign along. Did the indirect coaching of Mario Cuomo and Jerry Brown, the training provided by NDI, and the monetary support provided by countless Western foundations, governments, and nonprofit organizations facilitate the emergence of this campaign? Could the West help these activists change the political landscape of Russia? Or is this Western strategy inappropriate and ultimately futile for organizations operating in a different political climate?

Once again, Russia is in the midst of a momentous transition; this time, it faces the task of dismantling socialist institutions and replacing them with ones conducive to democratic development and free markets. Russians have not had to weather this transition alone; since the early 1990s, Western governments, multilateral institutions, and international organizations have sent advisors, loans, and aid to assist in this most recent reconfiguration. In this book, I look at one slice of this transformation. I am interested in the development of civil society—the realm of activism situated between the nodes of state, family, and business, where citizens interact and form and join organizations. In practice, this means I am interested in everything from the Russian chapter of Greenpeace to the Stamp Collectors Society. I want to know what citizens were organizing about in the post-Soviet era, how they were organizing, and who they were working with to achieve their goals.

As I visited various organizations in Moscow in the late 1990s, I soon noticed that some groups were receiving substantial levels of support from a varied collection of Western donors. Foundations, governments, nonprofit organizations, and even groups such as Rotary International were contacting, exchanging information with, and providing financial assistance to these fledgling Russian groups in an effort to bolster civil society. How did external support, in an environment of domestic indifference, economic scarcity, and institutional fluidity, affect the ways these groups organized, interacted, and implemented their goals and strategies? I had read numerous articles about Western efforts to shape the course of economic reform, but until I arrived in Russia I was unfamiliar with this latest task—the redesign of civil society within the framework of support for democratization. Could Western money, advice, and assistance fertilize civic development, as it had economic development in other areas of the world?

My academic interests are a product of the political environment of my post-adolescent years. As a teenager, I had experienced the "Evil Empire" first hand. While still in high school, I spent four months in 1988 living in East Berlin. While my friends were thinking about their senior proms, I was shuttling back and forth over the Berlin Wall twice a day in order to attend school in the West. I became interested in the origins of the Cold War and enrolled in Russian language class when I returned to the United States and started college. Several months into my first year, however, the inconceivable happened—communism collapsed. Just one year earlier, I had spent 2–3 hours a day passing through a Byzantine border system, in a carefully orchestrated dance with security agents. Now I turned on the television set to see people dancing on top of the wall, spraying one another with champagne.

I became fascinated with the events unfolding in Russia, the country that had pushed Eastern Europe into reform. I watched Eduard Shevardnadze's predictions of a turn toward authoritarianism, the attempted coup of 1991, the initial efforts at economic reform and privatization. I spent a semester in St. Petersburg in 1992 witnessing the changes first hand and emerged from that trip shaken; Russia was heading deeper into instability, not away from it. Upon my return, I studied this process of transition, why it seemed to move in bumps and starts, lurching back and forth, rather than progressing steadily forward. I read mostly about politics and economics, but, as an idealistic young student, I was really interested in learning about changes at the grassroots level. I was interested more in what I saw as the power of protest than more formalized avenues of influence and elite patronage.

Six years later, in January 1998, I returned to Russia to spend a year researching my dissertation. By this time, Russia was well into its democratic experiment, it had survived privatization, and slowly but surely its citizens were forming organizations, getting involved, and trying in small ways to change the political, economic, and social landscape of Russia. In turn, donors were busy implementing programs to speed this process along. I tried to capture the significance of this process in several ways: I interviewed activists from nongovernmental organizations (NGOs) and program officers at various donor organizations, I worked for some of these organizations as a consultant, and I sent out surveys to certain parts of the civic community. I eventually branched out from Moscow, traveling to such far-flung areas as Murmansk, Irkutsk, Rostov, Nizhnii

Novgorod, and Tatarstan, meeting with and interviewing people in NGOs. I traveled from cities with populations of 6 million to villages of a few thousand. I endured long train trips, gritted my teeth through dicey plane flights, and trudged along icy sidewalks in search of information, organizations, and grassroots activity.

I met with a variety of reactions. Some people felt sorry for this bedraggled student so far from home. Others quickly intuited that I could not be of much help to their day-to-day struggles and brushed me off. Others went out of their way to facilitate my research for no reason other than to be helpful.

I also had to deal with my own reactions. I really enjoyed looking at an issue that addressed debates both academic and policy oriented. I was doing "practical" research that might be of some use to people outside of a narrow range of academic interests. But that realization also concerned me. Many nights, I woke up worried that a limited or negative portrayal of aid activities would end up as fodder in some U.S. conservative's crusade against "liberal" foreign policy agendas. I had gotten to know many of the activists, and respected the commitment demonstrated by a number of them. Some I got to know and like. Yet, I was not portraying all their efforts in a positive light. I had painstakingly gathered research to present an accurate assessment of foreign assistance; yet, would my research end up harming NGO development?

I had the opportunity to return to Russia for three months in fall 2002. I visited old acquaintances and colleagues in Moscow, and met new ones in cities such as Krasnodar, Ekaterinburg, Novosibirsk, and Vladivostok. I returned to see what had changed since my initial year of fieldwork and to explore new questions I had formulated about civic development in Russia's regions. I was initially nervous; how would my findings hold up after several more years of development? After three months and more than one hundred new interviews, I felt that the trends I had noted earlier had become more, rather than less pronounced, and that my assessment of the effectiveness of foreign aid was still accurate. Despite the tremendous responsibility I felt in portraying, interpreting, and evaluating the effects, positive as well as negative, of assistance, I also felt it was necessary to portray this development accurately, rather than through rose-colored glasses.

This book could not have happened without the assistance of literally hundreds of activists, program officers, and friends in Russia as well as in the United States. My fieldwork in Russia would never have lasted a year without the support of a wide array of friends, colleagues, and acquaintances. Douglas Conrad made the entire trip feasible by cutting through the substantial red tape I faced before setting foot for an extended period of time on Russian soil. Zoya Khotkina and Tatiana Troinova both played pivotal roles in assisting me with my survey; they encouraged me to continue with the project despite seemingly insurmountable obstacles. None of this would have been possible without the scores of activists who sat down and wrote out long, painstaking replies to my survey. To those who took the time to respond to my plea for information, thank you for sharing your stories, your struggles, your setbacks, and your victories. People at other NGOs responded to my requests for information by sitting down with me and sharing the history of their organizations' short but eventful lives. Many program officers at various donor organizations went above and beyond the call of duty when responding to my requests for an interview and talked frankly and openly of their struggles to foster NGO development in Russia. I also thank the Institute for International Education and the National Security Education Project of the Academy for Educational Development for their financial support of my field research in 1998.

The long and arduous process of writing was made much less traumatic by a wide array of friends and colleagues. I could not have completed the project without encouragement and feedback from Jeffrey Kopstein, Susan Clarke, Barbara Engel, Mark Lichbach, and Ann Costain. Numerous people weighed in with suggestions to improve the manuscript. Maureen Healey, Alice Henderson, Sarah Lindemann, Patrice McMahon, Sarah Mendelson, Sarah Polen, Mark Redhead, Adam Resnick, James Richter, and two anonymous reviewers for Cornell University Press provided valuable input. My two research assistants were indispensable in helping me make revisions: Valentina Fomenko provided crucial translating skills and Maxie Peterson spent a summer humoring my every research whim, indulging my requests for information on anything from trafficking in women to nuclear dumping. The Smith Richardson Foundation provided crucial financial support, which allowed me to rethink, rework, and research new parts of the project.

Many people never read the manuscript but helped me keep my sanity and patiently sat through my intermittent spells of distraction, ill humor, and occasional panic. Mara Sidney and Alana Jeydel provided support and encouragement at critical times. My family was always there, whether to listen to me talk about my research or to distract me during yearly vacations in the Canadian wilderness. And finally, my partner Doug has been there from start to finish. He met me at the airport when I stepped off the plane in Russia in 1998 and has followed the ups and downs of the project throughout the years. I thank everyone along the way. I truly could not have done it without your support.

Sarah L. Henderson

Corvallis, Oregon

BUILDING DEMOCRACY
IN CONTEMPORARY RUSSIA

Introduction

Imagine that a large number of civic groups in the United States received their primary sources of support from outside the country. How would this change the face of civic activism? How would it alter the dynamics of how civil society works? Doubtless, it would have serious implications for how civil society interacts with other civic actors, with society at large, and with the state. Yet large amounts of U.S. money have funded civic groups in other countries. This book assesses the degree to which Western assistance can facilitate the emergence of a civil society and, ultimately, democracy in countries where domestically such impulses are nonexistent or weak.

"Civil society" is a broad term that captures the wide range of voluntary organizations operating outside of the realm of government, business, and the family. In practice, it includes everything from social movement organizations (such as women's or environmental groups) to bowling associations, bird-watching societies, choirs, and professional organizations.[1] Since the 1980s, civil society's conceptual purchasing power has risen as events of the end of the twentieth century have vividly illustrated its force. It has been credited with fostering the downfall of authoritarian regimes in countries in Latin America, Asia, and, most dramatically, Eastern Europe, as formerly quiescent citizens spilled into the streets to demonstrate the power of mass action. Who can forget the televised images of thousands crowding into Wenceslas Square in Prague to cheer Vaclav Havel, the soon-to-be playwright-president? Or the shots of every-day, average German citizens tearing down the Berlin Wall with pickaxes? Or the seemingly improbable pictures of Russian babushkas grimly staring down tanks during an attempted coup in the early 1990s? "People power" became the mantra in explaining the rapid collapse of seemingly invincible authoritarian regimes around the globe.

Civic groups, however, provide more than good photo opportunities. They also often serve as crucial negotiating partners as states transition from authoritarian governments to democratic ones. They mobilize citizens to pressure departing state elites to negotiate. Often, civic groups substitute for fledgling or nonexistent political parties in the initial period of political reform and transformation. In countries that have passed the hurdle of democratic transition, civil society is considered an integral component to deepening the quality and substance of these fledgling electoral democracies, which are often in danger of political setbacks in their initial years.[2]

Even in stable, consolidated democracies, civil society helps democracies function effectively. Civic groups act as watchdogs on state power, convey citizen interests, and serve as mediators between private citizens and the institutions of the state. They also are nesting grounds for social capital, the habits of cooperation, solidarity, and public spiritedness that act as a civic glue against the dangers of the constant pursuit of naked self-interest. High levels of social capital help deepen democracy; low or eroding levels are a reflection of the decline in quality of meaningful democracy.[3] Civil society is crucial in terms of what it does—as a mediator among the state, the economy, and society, it collects, conveys, and articulates interests and generates the social capital necessary for binding citizens together in ties of trust and reciprocity. "Civil society," "people power," and "social capital" are all terms that have become intertwined with our conceptions of what prompts authoritarian breakdown and ensures democratic stability across a wide array of political settings. A civil society is now seen as a necessary, although not sufficient, condition for democracy.[4]

As authoritarian regimes have been replaced by fledgling democracies in countries in almost every geographical region of the world, this dramatic political transformation has been accompanied by an equally radical one within Western countries' foreign policy agendas—as an increasing number of countries struggle to establish viable political systems, various governments and international organizations have sponsored aid programs under the rubric of "democracy promotion" and, in particular, "civil society assistance" as a critical component of this task. Specifically, donors have identified nongovernmental organizations (NGOs) as vehicles for civil society development programs and have given thousands of NGOs around the world small grants, training, and other forms of technical assistance. Their actions have been motivated by the assumption that civil society is a crucial aspect of the transition to and consolidation of democracy.

This shift in political agenda in terms of focus, goals, and implementation represents a substantial foreign policy experiment. Western countries in the past have focused on promoting economic and social development; promoting democratic development, and civic development as a critical component of this process, through the allotment of foreign aid is relatively new terrain, and recipient countries have become laboratories of experimentation. The goal of promoting more stable democratic systems is perhaps chimeric; certainly, it is untested waters for many donors involved in the process.

As democratization trends have slowed or begun to reverse in many countries,[5] it is important to step back and assess the role that international forces have played in shoring up processes of democratization. This book aims to contribute to our understanding of the effectiveness of the external promotion of what has, until the 1990s, been perceived to be an internal process—the development of civil society. Can institutional incentives foster and even hasten civic development in countries that do not follow the West's civic model? Alternatively, to what degree does the growth of a civil society depend on a country's social, economic, and political environment? If we transplant Western civic practices to new soil, will that soil produce similar civic practices or ones reflective of the country's social, political, and economic peculiarities?

This book uses the Russian case to illustrate lessons learned from an aid strategy currently pursued by the West in over one hundred countries in Asia, Latin America, Eastern Europe, the former Soviet Union, Africa, and the Middle East. Focusing on foreign aid to the women's movement and the NGO sector in contemporary Russia, this work assesses whether Western efforts have helped, hurt, or been irrelevant to Russia's civic transformation. In doing so, it addresses larger theoretical issues concerning the role of international intervention in domestic processes of democratic development and illuminates much broader questions about the fields of democratization and comparative politics.

FUNDING DEMOCRACY, FUNDING VIRTUE

Until the wane of the Cold War, development goals for many countries and organizations were defined within the parameters of overcoming economic scarcity. Poverty hindered countries' trajectories toward increased economic stability; the task of aid in the post–World War II era was to uncover the precise mix of ingredients that would unlock the door to further economic success. Did developing countries need to replicate the West's progression, or could they take shortcuts or fashion home-grown solutions of their own? Since then, donor nations, organizations such as the World Bank, and other international and multilateral agencies have experimented with finding the appropriate mix of domestic variables, institutional incentives, financial aid, loans, and technical assistance to create increased levels of economic growth and, ultimately, political stability. Over fifty years later, donor agencies are still trying to find a perfect formula to overcome the burdens of economic scarcity.

Although the idea of the external promotion of development is not new, the inclusion of aid specifically targeted to the support of democracy is relatively fresh. Although the United States government has always rhetorically supported the ideals of democracy, actual policy positions formulated around the goal of democracy building were limited. Although the United States was a pivotal force in designing and implementing the Marshall Plan, it did not advance a coherent democracy program until the 1980s, during the Reagan administration. These forays consisted mainly of election-monitoring expeditions and judicial reform projects in Central America and were placed squarely within the ideological framework of fighting communism and the rhetorical flourishes of the Cold War.[6] This position quickly changed as the events of the 1980s superseded previously established foreign policy imperatives.

First, the global trend toward democratization, which started in southern Europe in the 1970s, swept through Eastern Europe, South Asia, the former Soviet Union, and Africa and finally trickled into liberalizing regimes in the Middle East, statistically created a much larger number of countries that claimed to be ruled by democratic institutions. Governments had to respond to this new world order and the implications that this created for foreign policy objectives. Also, the quick collapse of authoritarian regimes in the face of a relatively disorganized opposition fostered the belief that the institutionalization of democracy could be supported by the assistance of external forces even if domestic actors were lacking or weak.[7]

Second, the collapse of communist regimes in Central and Eastern Europe and in the former Soviet Union made not only the Cold War obsolete, but also a foreign policy structured around strategic imperatives of containing communism and the reach of the "Evil Empire." Suddenly, simultaneous economic and political transitions were underway in these same countries. Now that the U.S. government was no longer battling for the hearts and minds of susceptible left-leaning individuals, it could turn its attention toward a new, equally ideological task—winning the hearts and minds of individuals committed to democracy and capitalism. As foreign policy shifted away from counting missiles to counting voters, promoting democracy quickly became added to the U.S. government's list of national security interests. As expectations of a less conflict-prone world faded in the harsh realities of Bosnia, Rwanda, East Timor, and Kosovo, democracy building became the benign version of the project of nation building and, eventually, reassembling failed states.

This interest in democracy promotion was reflected in the creation of new government agencies to deal with the challenges of the post–Cold War era. In 1992, the British government funded the creation of the Westminster Foundation for Democracy to "provide assistance in building and strengthening pluralist democratic institutions overseas."[8] Two years later, the United States Agency for International Development (USAID) set up a new Center for Democracy and Governance for the explicit purpose of "promoting and consolidating democracy worldwide."[9] Part altruism, part national interest, U.S. aid targeting the promotion of democracy and governance initiatives rose rapidly. By the end of the 1990s, the U.S. government was spending almost $700 million a year on democracy promotion programs, distributed to roughly one hundred countries in Latin America, Eastern Europe and the former Soviet Union, Sub-Saharan Africa, Asia, and the Middle East.[10] Although this money pales in comparison to the money devoted to economic restructuring—in 2001, USAID devoted over $3 billion to traditional economic and agricultural development projects around the world— it is nonetheless a significant departure from previous foreign policy priorities.[11]

As the popularity of democracy aid rose, so did the faith in the connection between healthy civil societies and good governance. Civil society aid soon became an integral component of democracy aid. Civil society programs have continued to grow and in 2002 received the largest share of the democracy and governance portfolio—37 percent of USAID's $506 million budget went to civil society initiatives, an amount nearly double that in 1993.[12] USAID is not alone; efforts to fund civil society, either explicitly or through other defined key areas, have been highlighted by various Western governments, by multilateral agencies such as the World Bank or the United Nations Development Program, and by a host of private foundations such as the Charles Stewart Mott Foundation, the Ford Foundation, the MacArthur Foundation, and the Soros Foundation/Open Society Institute. Although there is no precise figure for the amount of money that goes specifically to strengthening civil society initiatives around the world, some estimate that the NGO development field is a $7 billion industry, with $2 billion coming from U.S. foundations.[13]

Like democracy aid, civil society aid is a product of the rapidly changing events unfolding in the late 1980s and early 1990s. The dramatic events of 1989 created a visual narrative of civil society in action and turned academic interest away from a focus on elite bargaining to the role of civil society in toppling authoritarian regimes and reconstructing repressive institutions into democratic ones.[14] The publication of works by Robert Putnam, such as "Bowling Alone" and *Making Democracy Work*, which look at the connection between civic associationism and democracy, brought the concept of social capital and civil society back into public discourse. These neo-Tocquevillian interpretations maintain that the strength and stability of liberal democracy depends on a vibrant and healthy sphere of associational participation; and donors adopted these arguments. Civil society aid has become a major component of donor strategies, not only to Russia, but also around the world. "Funding virtue"[15] has become part of the answer to the puzzle of fostering sustainable democratic development.

A CIVIC SNAPSHOT OF RUSSIA

In the early 1990s, donors quickly allotted significant sums of democracy (and economic) aid to the countries of Central and Eastern Europe and the former Soviet Union, although initially aid targeted toward NGO development was a small part of this assistance. The democratization of this area offered new territory for expansion; during 1990–94, funding from U.S. foundations grew fastest in Eastern Europe and the former Soviet Union, where it multiplied sixfold.[16] By the end of the decade, USAID had spent over $1 billion dollars on democracy promotion in Eastern Europe and the former Soviet Union, which was more than it had committed to Latin America, Sub-Saharan Africa, Asia, and the Middle East.[17] Within the former Communist bloc, Russia topped the list of aid recipients.[18] Its sheer size as well as in its strategic importance for the region ensured that it received a large share of funding, although smaller countries such as Ukraine and Armenia also garnered significant sums.

And in the 1990s Russian civil society was in desperate need of assistance. Although civic groups were numerous (over 450,000 by January 2001),[19] they were young; the vast majority of the NGO community was formed after 1990, following on the heels of legislation granting such organizations legal status. In addition, despite the enthusiasm of the emerging nonprofit sector, civic development was debilitated by a variety of factors. First, many of the individuals in these new groups had grown up with the practices of Soviet-era mass associations. They had relatively little knowledge or experience in acting as a voluntary sector within the framework of a democracy. Second, because previous civic traditions were steeped in the experiences of Soviet "forced voluntarism," the public was wary and distrustful of the concept of voluntary organizations. Finally, in a society where "checkbook activism" (or even checkbooks) was non-existent, groups faced a daily battle for survival. Given the ongoing economic crisis that waxed and waned over the decade following Russia's new statehood, many groups survived on the enthusiasm and charisma of the leader, who often worked tirelessly for little or no pay, when time permitted.

Thus, there was a real and obvious need for assistance; fledgling civic groups faced serious hurdles in their struggle to build voluntary organizations in the years following Mikhail Gorbachev's ascension to power. In response to these obstacles, funding from foreign agencies to the NGO community started to arrive in the early 1990s and specifically targeted constructing civil society. During 1992–98, USAID distributed approximately $92 million to civic initiatives and NGO-sector support projects. In 2000 alone, George Soros's Open Society Institute—Russia funneled more than $56 million to NGOs, universities, other civic minded organizations in order to create a lasting civil society.[20] During 1993–2001, the Eurasia Foundation distributed almost $38 million in grants to the non-profit sector in Russia.[21] During 1991–98, the MacArthur Foundation approved over $17 million in grants to support initiatives in the former Soviet Union.[22] The Charles Stewart Mott Foundation also was a significant player; during 1993–2002, the Prague office of the foundation made almost $10 million in grants to nonprofit organizations.[23]

Many organizations had idealistic expectations of how aid could build a vibrant civic community that would play an integral part in Russia's democratic reconstruction. As Don Pressley, a U.S. aid official, explained, "Civil society at that time was either nascent or nonexistent in most countries of the region. Most populations lacked the basic rights of a democratic civil society. . . . We decided early on that vigorous USAID support for local nongovernmental organizations would be a critical element of strengthening civil society in the region."[24] This interest in looking at civil society was "based on the premise that a strong civil society is desirable and makes democratic practices and traditions more likely to flourish."[25] Embracing the notion that power lies in empowering individuals at the grassroots level, donors such as USAID quickly made the concept of civil society into an important rallying cry, often within the overall project of democracy promotion.

Foreign assistance was extremely valuable to a civic sector battling upstream in a time of political, economic, and social chaos. Given that the concept of an independent NGO did not even exist until legislation in 1990 allowed citizens to freely organize, donors faced a steep challenge in designing and implementing grants and programs that would create a civil society. Donors channeled grants to the nonprofit sector and supplied such organizational basics as computer equipment, money for salaried employees, or office space. Grants were also given to fund domestic and international conferences on relevant issues or to support training and seminars to teach leaders practical skills for running an NGO. They sponsored publications and research and facilitated travel abroad. In addition, grants and assistance from the West provided a wealth of experience and opportunities not normally available to Russian NGOs. For many, foreign aid quickly became the primary monetary lifeline.

Given this world of potential opportunity, it was impossible to ignore the influence of Western aid to the civic community when I arrived in Moscow to begin my research. Conferences, round tables, and workshops on every conceivable theme piled up in triplicate—"How to Work with Local Government," "Fund-raising," "Managing Skills for NGOs"—the list was endless, and the Moscow NGO community was nourished on a steady diet of training sessions. When I visited the groups' premises, I learned that the office, computer equipment, and support for salaried employees were all financed by foreign grants. As I branched out to Russia's regions, I found this pattern repeated in other local NGO communities.

As a result, I expected to find clear and startling differences between groups that received foreign assistance and those that were struggling to survive on domestic funding alone. I expected to see differences in the groups' viability, capacity, governance, and networking capabilities. For example, given the benefits that grants provided in terms of office space, equipment, and salaries, I expected aid to make a large difference in the institutionalization and sustainability of organizations. I also expected civic groups to act differently; given that one of civil society's functions is to serve as a conduit from private to public, I expected groups that had received aid to be more likely to develop networks of accountability both to citizens and the state, crucial governance functions. Finally, because civic groups are the nesting points of social capital, I expected funded groups to be more likely to be embedded in dense networks of association with other civic groups. But as my year of field research progressed, I uncovered a much more complex and nuanced picture of the effects of foreign assistance on NGO development. Was aid, in fact, facilitating the emergence of what USAID officials had hoped for—a strong civil society?

A Tale of Two Civic Groups

Two groups involved in very similar activities came to symbolize for me the promise and problems associated with external funding. One group, which was loosely structured as a Committee of Soldiers' Mothers organization, a human rights organization dedicated to ending the war in Chechnya, was based in an industrial wasteland on the shores of the Volga River. Its office was located in a burned-out apartment building, its connection to the outside world maintained by a Stalinist-era telephone. Yet the office was nearly frantic with activity. Parents of soldiers wounded in the war with Chechnya called for information and stopped in to make inquiries; members and volunteers gathered for tea, gossip, and mutual support. Although the director worked with her own grim determination but with little or no pay, her tireless efforts yielded results in the local community. Her organization raised the funds to build a rehabilitation clinic for veterans of Chechnya, and she managed to staff it with solely volunteer labor. In addition, she had developed a working relationship with the local administration; after much lobbying, she and the local mothers convinced the administration to provide burial plots and head-stones in the cemetery for soldiers killed in the Chechen war.

A similar human rights organization in a nearby town was markedly different. This group was a rising star in the international human rights movement and had attracted substantial support from a variety of Western donors to implement its programs. With its grant money, it was able to rent an entire house for its activities. This organization also had several state-of-the-art computers, Xerox machines, and a small but dedicated paid staff. It had just hired a librarian to organize an NGO Resource Center, a room that housed brochures, pamphlets, newsletters, and books on various aspects of civil society in Russia. This was part of a larger men-toring project in which this organization served as a hub of knowledge and activity for other NGOs in the region. Its newsletters were expertly compiled, glossily printed, and smartly displayed. Yet the organization was strangely lifeless. Few people visited. The organization consisted of advo-cates without a visible constituency, an infrastructure without a base. It was an organization so reliant on foreign funding that it sought few alter-native means of financial or moral support.[26]

This pattern recurred repeatedly during my year of research in Russia and was still evident several years later, when I returned to Russia for a three month visit. Drawing on a variety of research methods, I found that the activities, goals, and structure of groups that receive foreign assistance differ substantially from those who rely primarily on domestic funding. Aid has made a tremendous difference in improving and increasing the short-term financial viability, organizational capacity, and networking skills among recipient groups. It has supported groups that doubtless would have failed to survive if left to their own devices.

This is only one side of a much more complex picture, however. Despite the enormous interest and good will among foreign assistance programs in fostering civic development, I found four strange and somewhat paradoxical effects of foreign aid. First, the goal of many Western agencies was to facilitate small grassroots initiatives. Yet Russian civic groups that had received aid tended to mimic the organizational style of the Western assistance agencies and implementing organizations operating in Russia, which are wealthy, centralized, and bureaucratized corporate NGOs. These groups were top-heavy with organizational infrastructure, and they connected that infrastructure poorly with concrete, practical activities aimed at the community.

Second, civil society theoretically is composed of grassroots, bottom-up organizations, but one of the most visible problems facing many of the funded groups was the lack of a grassroots constituency. Numerous organizations had offices, with state-of-the-art computers, paid staff, and glossy newsletters, but strikingly absent from these organizations were the people they claimed to represent. Russian NGOs targeted Western donors as the "voice that mattered," rather than the Russian population. Groups that had received funding tended to reflect the post-materialist values of the donor, such as concerns for gender equity, environmentalism, or respect for human rights, rather than the survivalist, materialist bent of many organizations that relied solely on domestic sources of financial support. As a result, the goals, agendas, and projects of NGOs that received assistance from Western organizations had shifted over time to reflect the agenda of the foreign assistance programs rather than objective domestic needs. In addition, Russian groups often lacked formal mechanisms of oversight, such as a board, or a system of checks and balances, or ongoing mechanisms for citizens to provide feedback or input. Organizations had no one to report to but donors and the occasional query from the domestic tax inspectors. In short, they lacked accountability.

Third, despite foreign efforts to spread the benefits of aid to a wide array of organizations, I noticed a fairly distinct civic elite, perhaps even civic oligarchy, within the NGO community. Rather than facilitating horizontal networks among groups, foreign aid strengthened the division of the civic community between the "haves" and the "have nots" and centralized resources in the hands of those organizations that had connections with the West. This further exacerbated already significant differences in civic development between Russia's centers and the regions, creating a hierarchy of NGOs based primarily in Moscow, who often work with designated affiliates or partners in the regions. Alternatively, a few strong civic organizations in the regions tended to monopolize scarce resources while hundreds of other NGOs subsisted as best they could on meager domestic rations. Funding created opportunities for some, while hindering others.

Fourth, although funded civic groups did have increased levels of contact with other organizations, few were engaging in activities that we might associate with "civicness." Instead of building networks and developing publics, groups consciously maintained small memberships, hoarded information, and engaged in uncooperative and even competitive behavior with other civic groups. In short, groups pursued individual, short-term gains rather than working for collective, long-term development.

Unfunded groups were not, of course, perfect paragons of civic virtue, the exhibitors of a completely opposite organizational culture. Overall, all civic groups were struggling to develop ties of accountability to the public, political society, the state, and one another. Many groups, funded and unfunded, tended to be small, relatively distrustful of others, and focused on guarding their civic turf. What was surprising, however, was that foreign aid was not necessarily ameliorating these problems; rather, it seemed to be exacerbating them, despite its intentions to the contrary. Although in many ways foreign aid has advanced NGO development in Russia, NGO development is not synonymous with civil society development,[27] and the development of one does not necessarily imply the advancement of the other. Civic trends within the Western-financed NGO community have developed in unexpected ways and with some unfortunate and unintended consequences, which can have negative and long-lasting effects on Russia's civic development.

EXPORTING CIVIL SOCIETY: PROMISES AND PROBLEMS

These observations are not new; in part, my research confirms a wide literature that has observed similar dynamics, not only in Russia but also in other recently democratized countries in Latin America and Africa. Despite the burgeoning enthusiasm for funding civil society projects, finding the magic bullet to reproduce civil society has been an elusive quest.[28]

Proponents argue that international actors can provide crucial moral support because they "create an atmosphere in which ideals are meaningful and worth striving for even though they are hard to attain."[29] Citing international actors' contributions in enhancing the resources, skills, and legitimacy of civil society organizations in the developing and formerly communist worlds, supporters such as Larry Diamond maintain "the prospects for democracy in the world will be much brighter if these many currents of practical engagement are sustained, refined, and widened."[30] In their overview of civil society aid in the Middle East, Africa, Asia,

Eastern Europe, and Latin America, Marina Ottaway and Thomas Carothers point out that the impact of civil society assistance has been "nothing short of dramatic."[31] Aid has kept alive thousands of NGOs that have gone on to lobby about, push, and mobilize over important political issues. In her assessment of U.S. assistance in rebuilding the economy, as well as the political and social infrastructure, of the Newly Independent States (NIS), Nancy Lubin argues that the most effective projects have been those focused on democracy assistance and particularly those that focused on small projects and partnerships—the cornerstone of civil society and democracy aid.[32] Other supporters are more subdued in their praise, asserting that democracy aid has been crucial in teaching activists and civil society actors important skills as well as democratic attitudes; however, all conclude that aid has done little to actually change how democratic institutions function.[33] All urge increased levels of financial support, citing that the limited nature of the impact had more to do with limited funding (compared to the amounts spent on economic aid) than intrinsic problems with the nature of the assistance.

This faith in civil society has spread; within the field of international relations, scholars have noted the increasing prominence of collaboration among NGOs from the North, South, East, and West. The development of these transnational networks has been critical in keeping organizations alive in countries ruled by hostile and antagonistic governments. These transnational social movements and organizations also pressure governments to adjust, rethink, or propose new legislation. No longer constrained by national borders, these "activists beyond borders" can create a boomerang effect; domestic social movements can bypass their own target states and appeal to international pressure to accomplish their goals.[34] Ultimately, they also have the potential to shape global political discourse and facilitate the emergence of a global civil society.[35]

This optimism has been met with cold doses of skepticism about the potential of foreign aid. Western aid encourages NGOs to develop ties of accountability to the donor, rather than to domestic constituencies. Even supporters of international and transnational civic networking, despite their optimism, acknowledge that joining a global civil society often comes at a price; organizations that had joined the international circuit "neglected their own communities."[36] A study of foreign assistance to Latin American NGOs concludes that groups tended to reflect the agenda and moral concerns of the donor.[37] Ottaway and Carothers echo this concern in a comparative overview of NGOs in Eastern Europe, Latin America, and the Middle East, stating that the survival of NGOs often "depends more on their ability to talk to and engage the donors than their ability to talk to and engage their fellow citizens."[38] Looking at the

Russian case, Valerie Sperling, Sarah E. Mendelson, and John K. Glenn warn that women's groups have become "ghettoized"; they are closer to their transnational partners than the constituents they are meant to represent or the governments they claim to be influencing.[39] This observation is not unique to women's organizations; it can also be made of other sections of civil society in Russia.[40] This trend leads us to question the legitimacy of donor-supported NGOs, given that it is not clear whose interests these groups represent.

The issue of audience raises questions about these organizations' long-term sustainability. If these groups are not representative of domestic constituencies, what will keep them alive once donor support is withdrawn? Writing on democracy assistance across regions, Marina Ottaway and Theresa Chung note that Western assistance tends to fund projects that are financially unsustainable after the funding ends and, as a result, make no lasting contribution to long-term development when aid inevitably dries up.[41] Diamond, despite his enthusiasm for democracy-building projects, acknowledges this question of the extent to which these are the civil societies of their own countries, and ultimately self-generating.[42]

Finally, although funding transforms activists into civic entrepreneurs, this also can encourage funded activists to value their own continued survival over cooperative group endeavors. Sperling, in her study of the women's movement in Russia, maintains that foreign aid, although instrumental in providing activists with a global language, has nonetheless fostered internal rivalries, jealousies, and overall divisiveness.[43] Pauline Jones Luong and Erika Weinthal, in their study of environmental NGOs in Kazakhstan, find that funding has led the NGO community to fragment as groups compete for funding opportunities.[44] James Richter also argues that, although foreign aid helps groups aggregate interests, it contributes little to groups' abilities to instill habits of cooperation, solidarity, public spiritedness, and trust.[45] The battle for lucrative sources of funding has divided the fragile civic communities.

My initial findings confirm these observations about civil society aid. Previous research also suggests that the problems arising from aid are not unique to Russia or to formerly communist countries.[46] Although the problems may be exacerbated, tamed, or personalized depending on how external projects mesh with local cultures, political structures, and economic challenges, findings suggest that external efforts to replicate the slow domestic processes of civic development are as problematic and idiosyncratic as ongoing efforts to facilitate economic and social growth in the developing world.

The literature is growing on the consequences, both expected and unintended, of the external promotion of democracy. This book further develops this area in three ways. First, previous research has tended to look solely at the effects of external funding on organizations or compared the same movement across national settings. I explicitly compare externally funded and domestically funded NGOs in the same country during the same time. In societies with few preexisting civic traditions, it is unclear whether all civic groups behave in ways that seem antithetical to the essence of civil society or whether externally supported NGOs actually structure themselves, act, or behave differently as a consequence of funding. Many of the problems associated with aid could simply be attributed to the nature of new, fragile civic sectors.

Second, we know something about the problems of aid, but how is this related to long-term civic development? Do shifting agendas, small constituencies, and internal jealousies and rivalries matter for civic development, and if so, how? I argue that funding has had a substantial impact on NGO development, but that this NGO development may undermine larger civic development.

Finally, I offer a framework for understanding why these civic side effects occur repeatedly in varying contexts. Previous explanations for aid success and failure have centered around two approaches. One argument, which was made vociferously after the financial collapse of Russia's economy in August 1998, contends that aid targeting economic reform failed due to corrupt agents on both sides. Those delivering and designing aid purposely looked the other way as crucial political and economic actors engaged in a wide array of counterproductive and even nefarious behaviors. Could this also be the case for aid targeting civic sector development? The other explanation, a culturalist argument, places primary responsibility of the aid failure on persistent Soviet legacies, attitudes, and norms that explain Russia's civic profile. In this scenario, the unintended consequences of aid can be explained away by internal cultural deficiencies. Although both approaches account for some of the unintended consequences of aid, I propose a neoinstitutionalist approach to the problem. Institutions, interests, and incentive structures impede successful collective action toward building a civic community by encouraging both donors and NGO activists to pursue short-term benefits over long-term development. Thus, the problems that arose were due to avoidable mistakes in the foreign aid process, rather than as a result of corrupt agents or internal cultural deficiencies.

Corruption

The critique that Western assistance to formerly communist countries has gone awry is not new; the bulk of this criticism, however, has concerned the politics of economic reform. Turning planned economies into free market ones proved to be more difficult than originally expected. Through the use of anecdotal stories about aid failure, single-country case studies, or macrolevel critiques of aid's failure to facilitate growth across the formerly communist countries, inept implementation, bad government, corruption, and crony capitalism have all been fingered as culprits in countries' problems with effectively implementing aid projects.[47]

Russia became the centerpiece of the heated debate over "what went wrong" in plans to transform these countries' economic systems with external assistance. Even before the collapse of the ruble in August 1998, policymakers and academics in the United States had begun to question the wisdom of foreign technical assistance and aid strategies designed to facilitate reform. Clifford Gaddy and Barry Ickes's article "Russia's Virtual Economy," which was written before but published after the crash, portrays the economy as an elaborate shell game, nurtured and sustained by Western aid and loans.[48] The fallout from the financial crisis merely added fuel to the fire and created a lightning rod for criticism of foreign policy approaches to the country. The battle for a capitalist, transparent, and democratic Russia was declared a lost cause, a high-profile failure of the Clinton administration's efforts to chart a new course in post–Cold War foreign policy.[49] It eventually became an issue in the 2000 presidential election race.

In particular, U.S. foreign policy choices were hammered on as inept, undisciplined, and inconsistent. Janine Wedel credits the failure of foreign aid for economic reform in the former Soviet bloc to a giant disconnect between East and West, "forged by the Cold War and exacerbated by the barriers of language, culture, distance, information, and semi-closed borders."[50] In this scenario, the fault lies with the arrogance of fly-in-fly-out advisors from prestigious U.S. universities and government agencies who had no experience with or knowledge of the real machinations of economic dealings in the former Soviet bloc. Stephen Cohen mercilessly critiques the Clinton administration for embarking on an arrogant ideological crusade to convert Russians to a highly idealized and unattainable version of free market capitalism and democracy.[51] The institutional design of reform was implemented by reckless individuals who took no account of culture or, as some argue, reality.

High-profile, highly placed Russians, in turn, took advantage of poorly institutionalized rules and regulations and bled the economy dry in a matter of years. Rather than checking the corruption, aid officials either ignored it by pretending it was not happening or argued that working with imperfect pseudodemocrats was preferable to the alternative—hard-line communists. At best, Western ignorance and lack of foresight accounts for part of Russia's dismal economic and political performance.

At worst, economic aid represents a conspiracy in corruption, in which donors tacitly agreed to look the other way when there were serious deviations from transparent, ethical behavior, in the belief that anything was better than a communist resurgence.[52]

Although the critique of economic aid is compelling, the dynamics of civic assistance were different. The players involved in civic reform were a completely different cast of characters than those involved in economic reform. The area of economic restructuring was a much higher-prestige area that attracted academic power glitterati looking to buttress their prominent careers with high-paying consulting jobs. Jeffrey Sachs, Anders Aslund, Milton Friedman, as well as members of the Harvard Institute for International Development, were all chosen as the fairy godmothers of capitalist reconstruction and were granted expensive magic wands to conjure up images of private entrepreneurship and free market economies.[53] In contrast, civic sector reform attracted a different clientele, perhaps because the money involved in civic development was much smaller than the large-scale projects of economic restructuring.[54] Certainly, early civil society projects were often bloated and top heavy with administrative costs and salary for short-term American consultants who knew little about Russia. However, over a period of several years, this segued into an approach that relied on program officers, grant managers, and long-term aid workers with a commitment to spending extensive time in the country. The program officers I interviewed who were involved in civic development were marked by their commitment to Russia and exhibited an extensive knowledge of Russian developments, past and present. In fact, many of them would answer my questions with a heavy sigh and the obligatory, "You have to understand that in Russia . . ." It was not that they did not care about their job or Russia. In fact, many were fluent in Russian and had arrived with a desire to help Russian civic development and then stayed on for several years looking for a way to make a difference. The charge that culturally insensitive Westerners were imposing cookie-cutter solutions on complex problems did not match my experiences in the field.[55] If anything, program officers seemed mired in the complexity of their own understandings of Russia.

I then turned to the behaviors of Russian NGO leaders themselves for an explanation. Did they share the same traits as the silver-tongued, well-heeled, and infinitely well-connected Russian architects of economic reform? Assistance for economic development has been heavily criticized for supporting cronyism within the halls of state power and for creating a class of well-paid domestic flunkies. Again, I found that NGO assistance was substantially different. Relatively few, if any, organizations were blatantly spending the money on a purpose other than that specified in the grant. Although grants provided a steady income for activists, it was not on a level comparable with the salaries of those involved in economic development. A grant might provide between $700 and $1,000 a month for salary and some office equipment, but it did not win entrée into the small circle of elites who were busy carving up the economic spoils of privatization among themselves. Civic activists were still driving half-dead Ladas and Volgas, not brand-new Mercedes. The explanation that is used to explain the failure of economic aid (high-powered Western consultant parachutes in to meet corrupt Russians) does not appear to apply to aid for civic development—the players involved were different; the money much smaller; and, most important, the Russian state, the sinkhole of the economic development story, was not involved.

Cultural Explanations: The Inexorable Weight of History

Alternatively, Russian political culture has been portrayed as the nemesis of successful aid efforts to promote civic development in Russia. In this scenario, foreign aid produces unintended consequences because it is unable to counteract the larger cultural environment within which it is working. Analysts need only point to Russia's repeated failed attempts at fostering democracy over the last two hundred years; Russians are historically prone to the "lure of the strong hand," culturally predisposed to authoritarianism, centralism, imperialism, and conformism.[56] Soviet political culture, rather than breaking with previous political traditions, has merely continued along the path established by the practices of Tsarist Russia.[57] In this rendering, Russians do not have the appropriate cultural pedigree or background necessary to support democratic values in the short run. Russia's lack of a "usable past" impedes its attempts to develop a viable future based on democratic values, and there are few "habits of the heart" that Russians can use to facilitate a new way of thinking.[58]

Nor are they likely in the short term to develop this sense of liberal bonhomie given the ongoing economic and political environment. Despite signs of an economic recovery in 2002, the economic record of the post-Soviet economy has ranged from unmitigated disaster to a holding pattern of stagnation. The Yeltsin administration began in an era of high expectations and hopes and ended in tales of political cronyism, corruption, and exploitation. Much depends on whether President Vladimir Putin can tame political and economic elites and channel high oil revenues into significant long-term economic growth. At best, post-Soviet Russia is a reflection of an emerging political culture of democratic procedures, norms, institutions, and values, as well as the residues of both pre-Leninist and Leninist political cultures. At worst, Russia's flirtation with democratic structures is merely a momentary lull in the inexorable pull of Russia's authoritarian past and future destiny. These dire predictions were in part supported by survey research. Early studies showed citizens supporting democracy as well as the concept of state control.[59] Later studies depicted citizens embracing values that at times could be interpreted as democratic and at other times as authoritarian.[60] In short, it was difficult to know what to make of the post-Soviet citizen.

Certainly, it would be foolish to not acknowledge that Russia's civic development will not, and possibly cannot, mimic that of Western countries. Chapter 2 discusses a number of impediments to civic development that can loosely be traced to a cultural explanation. However, culture is not stagnant; it moves, influenced by generational shifts, economic and political developments, and global trends.[61] Survey research has captured a variety of snapshots of citizen attitudes; whereas some studies demonstrate a cultural continuity thesis, others show that Russians, despite their authoritarian past, can be quite accepting of democratic ideals and beliefs.[62] Others argue that changes in cultural values can be traced back to the Soviet era, when strides in the Soviet economy throughout the 1950s, 1960s, and 1970s created seeds of eventual disillusionment with the regime.[63] Alternatively, Nicolai Petro argues that cultural continuity is a relevant factor, but that Russia has significant democratic impulses that are being revived, not authoritarian ones.[64] Although cultural continuity is a tempting thesis, often anything that cannot be otherwise accounted for is simply explained as a manifestation of Russia's ongoing fascination with authoritarianism and lack of experience with democratic institutions, beliefs, and practices.

In addition, the sheer number of emerging civic groups paints a different picture. If Russia's political culture spells doom for civic activism, then what explains the emergence of these new activists? Are they all statistical outliers? If culture is the primary impediment to civic development, then why are there so many glaring and obvious differences between groups that received outside funding and those that did not? A cultural explanation obscures the differences between the two groups of organizations, rather than highlighting them. My research acknowledges that, overall, civic development is path dependent—that is, it is patterned and shaped by historical legacies. Despite the undoubted power of these legacies, however, they are not determinant.

These two explanations—the politics of economic reform and the cultural legacies of communism—certainly explain portions of various actors' behavior and can be used to account for part of the paradox. Nonetheless, using these frameworks results in a piecemeal explanation at best. Neither provides a good fit with the experiences I observed on the streets of Russia.

Rather than witnessing widespread corruption, cultural insensitivity, indifference, or lack of support for democracy, I was confronted with an explosion of small grassroots attempts at individual activism and an engaged foreign aid community committed to encouraging this development. Yet the more the groups struggled to adopt the framework of civil society, the further some seemed to drift from functioning as one.

THE LOGIC OF COLLECTIVE ACTION

David Hume was perhaps the first to notice the paradox that confronts public-spiritedness: two reapers, both recognizing the benefits of working together to sow their collective fields, opt instead to lose their harvests "for want of mutual confidence and security."[65] This observation has been used countless times to explain the "tragedy of the commons" or the "prisoner's dilemma"; individuals often bearing no apparent malice or malevolence toward one another nonetheless behave in a way that produces suboptimal results for all those involved. It is in the collective interests of all, but in the self-interest of none, to contribute to the general welfare. Mancur Olson restates the paradox: contrary to the popular belief that rational, self-interested individuals logically will join a group to pursue common goods, in many cases it is in fact in their interest to take a free ride. The smaller the relative contribution to the cause, the less contributors can affect the outcome significantly, and the greater the incentive not to contribute.[66]

I argue that building civil society is a collective action dilemma, albeit one on a grander scale than most other projects that involve cooperation. Developing civil society within a fragile democracy is an admirable goal. Working together to build networks of civic groups would be beneficial to many Russian citizens because it would strengthen democratic tendencies as a whole in Russia by strengthening avenues of accountability among the state, the economy, and society, which are woefully lacking in Russia's contemporary landscape. In addition, it would help generate that all-important social capital, the civic glue of democratic culture. In theory, Russian NGO activists and Western assistance development specialists recognized the utility of and the need for a developed civic community. Yet the large number of individuals working both for Western foundations and within the domestic NGO community ensures that no one individual, by implementing a particular policy, and no one grant project can drastically alter the direction of civic development in Russia.

Developing civil society depends on the uncoordinated cooperation of many; the question, then, is how can people be induced to cooperate for long-term, large-scale benefit if it is not in their individual interests?

Olson suggests that the most important intervening variables are positive and negative "selective sanctions": the application or withholding of coercive and material resources to those individuals "who do or do not contribute to the provision of the collective good."[67] Positive sanctions increase the benefits of contributing and therefore induce the rational actor to participate. Negative sanctions make it too costly not to contribute and thus coerce the rational actor to take part in some collective action. Taxation, compulsory dues, membership benefits and privileges, fines, imprisonment, and the like are typical examples of both kinds of sanctions.[68]

This economically deterministic view fails to satisfactorily account for examples of seemingly altruistic and selfless behavior. It does not explain the many large-scale collective actions that take place in the absence of any substantial selective incentives. For students of communism and post-communism, the most obvious examples are the emergence of movements such as Solidarity in Poland in 1980, Charter 77 in Czechoslovakia, and other dissident movements that managed to garner popular support in the face of formidable disincentives for participation.[69]

Thus academics have made adjustments to Olson's characterization. One argument addresses rational actors' values—some participants may be altruistically inclined, others may get a thrill from participation, and others value that good so intensely that they are willing to engage fanatically to achieve it.[70] Alternatively, Edward N. Muller and Karl-Dieter Opp maintain that individuals may rationally believe that their contributions to large-scale rebellious collective actions really are indispensable.[71] Finally, new institutionalism argues that formal institutions can reduce "transaction costs," or the costs of monitoring and enforcing agreements, thus enabling agents to more effectively surmount the problems of shirking and opportunism.[72] In a "softer" institutionalist approach that borrows less jargon from economists, Robert Putnam has argued that norms of trust and reciprocity, or social capital, can facilitate spontaneous cooperation, overcoming the collective action dilemma in developing rich networks of civic associations.[73] Although the adjustments all vary in the degree to which theorists want to take account of such fuzzy factors as norms, feelings, beliefs, and culture, the lesson remains the same. For the most part, the best we can hope for is a marriage of self- and group interest; sanctions, incentives, and institutional design are all factors that can encourage or discourage this.

Defining the Dilemma for Russia

Applying this approach to the puzzle of constructing civil society in Russia is intellectually appealing. Russian citizens face domestic impediments to sustained, coordinated group action. In addition, the West's attempt to foster civil society, a grassroots bottom-up sector from the top down is an interesting attempt to solve a compelling collective action dilemma. How can we encourage actors to create a political system in which democracy becomes routinized and deeply internalized in the general society as well as among key elites?

Given this framework, a crucial aspect of understanding the dynamics of aid lies in evaluating the effectiveness of various solutions to the dilemma of building civil society. Is it possible to design sanctions and incentives to encourage groups to function as a civil society? Will groups that have received funding develop ties of accountability to the state, political parties, and their citizens? Can aid foster networks of mutual trust and cooperation and essentially purchase social capital? Or, more precisely, which aid strategies encourage civic behavior and which strategies encourage groups to defect from this project or pursue unexpected behaviors? The theoretical solutions to the problem of cooperation are numerous.[74] Yet making the leap from the theoretical to the actual, from talking about civil society to fostering civil society, is just as difficult and nebulous as any other efforts to externally promote development that has historically come from within.

The individuals involved in fostering civic development all face competing demands and pressures on their work. They must constantly make difficult decisions, weigh trade-offs, and define and pursue their interests.[75] Both Western funders and Russian activists must define the balance between working for a public good, civic development, and ensuring their own continued individual and organizational survival. The problem lies in the "rules of the game" itself; the game of funding involves a set of incentives and sanctions that encourages a separate pattern of behavior that undermines, rather than facilitates, civic behavior. Overall, Russia's distorted civic development can be explained by the interaction of three factors; institutions, incentives, and interests.[76]

Designing the Rules

As I discuss in chapter 2, in the wake of 1989 donors rapidly expanded their aid programs to include emphases on civil society building. Reflecting the influence of neo-Tocquevillian arguments, donors focused on promoting grassroots activism as an important component in building healthy democracies. They focused on NGOs, rather than on other forms of social organization and interaction, as the main indicator of the relative vibrancy of civil society. In addition, agencies consciously directed money toward groups that they felt could contribute to the larger processes of civic development and democratization. These tended to be categorized as advocacy organizations and were often drawn from the human rights, environmental, and women's movement. In effect, this singled out certain types of organizations at the expense of groups that provided more basic social services. This supply-driven vision of civic development, in which donors create programs while domestic NGOs respond to them, altered incentives for grassroots mobilization.[77]

The Calculus of Donors

This picture is further complicated by donors' own need for survival. As I discuss in chapter 3, U.S. foundations and public aid agencies operating in Russia both rely on an outside source for funding. Particularly for U.S. agencies, private as well as public, the U.S. taxpayer (or stockholder, for private foundations) is often the real constituent, not the average Russian. Consequently, funders are not free agents; rather, they are the expression and facilitator of U.S. interests as well as the monetary engine behind Russian civic organizations. In interviews, program officers repeatedly returned to the theme of accountability to their own home offices in the United States, which were constantly applying pressure on the field offices to implement particular programs designed in the United States to produce results. Donors, caught in the middle, recognize that they have two constituencies: the community they are supposed to serve abroad and their domestic source of funding. Thus, foundations' attention is divided between Russian needs and the politics of pleasing home offices.

As a result of this system of allegiances, Western donors, in turn, structure their programs to meet home requirements. Although aid in some ways is a business, the one major difference is that unlike businesses, the efficiency of agencies is not measured by profit; donors' developmental policies must be assessed through other, less obvious management techniques. As a result, the incentives for donors are to design grants that emphasize satisfying short-term interests rather than long-term goals; they need to produce results in order to keep their toehold in, or even increase their influence with, the home office. After all, they are but one of many claimants on the funds for implementing projects abroad. Thus, Russian grantees are encouraged to produce projects that generate quantitative results rather than qualitative progress.[78] There is little incentive for field offices to report failure, or to sanction grantees that have strayed from democratic principles. Rather, donors are often searching for ways to turn mediocre performance or even positive developments into stunning success stories.

The Calculus of Russian Activists

Last, funding is played out in a domestic environment that, for Russians, is marked by extreme uncertainty and scarcity. Although foreign donors have an interest in making their projects work, for recipients the stakes are higher; they have relatively few exit strategies. A grant from a donor far outweighs any amount of money that most private citizens, local governments, or domestic businesses could offer; the salaries provided from grants place NGO activists into a salary range that, although modest, is denied to many of their other, less fortunate Russian colleagues. Consequently, the calculations of NGO activists are driven by motives of survival in a risky environment. Despite their often very real desire to build civic community, the need to continue their own funding base also causes them to focus on producing results for the donor rather than necessarily making a substantial community impact. There are few incentives to be client driven or mission led. In addition, the material gains represented in a grant provide incentives for groups to engage in activities counter to the ethos of building social capital. The battle over scarce resources means that organizations often hoard information, duplicate one another's projects, and argue among themselves.

All of those involved in building civil society with the help of foreign funding are encouraged to go after short-term payoffs rather than building long-term results. The incentive structures for both grant givers and grantees create a system that often subverts the original goals and aims of the civic programs. As a result, grantees and grantors often work at cross purposes to achieve a constantly shifting target, civil society, despite their very obvious and real desire to make a long-term impact.

Aid to NGOs has not been a failure. It has played a crucial role in providing short-term financial and technical support to many NGOs, which will hopefully translate into longer-term sustainability. But, it has also created unintended negative consequences, which, if not addressed, can create long-term impediments to increased development. Just as the current incentive structure has encouraged behaviors that may undermine long-term civic development, the implication is that changing the rules and guidelines of funding can help correct some of the problems created in the first decade of this civic experiment.

RESEARCH DESIGN

My research questions the degree to which donors facilitated the development of a civil society in Russia. I chose to answer that question by operating within donors' definitional frameworks. Particularly in developing countries, NGOs (otherwise known collectively as the third sector or the nonprofit sector) have become increasingly identified as the primary building blocks of civic development. NGOs, however, do not represent the totality of civil society. Whereas civil society encompasses all formal and informal associations, including bowling leagues and bridge clubs as well as interest groups and charitable organizations, the third sector refers more specifically to the formal, functionally differentiated, and frequently professional nonprofit organizations that interact with state and market.[79] For many donors, this definition also excludes organizations that are political or religious in nature. Nonetheless, I chose to look at NGOs because foreign funders themselves have targeted the NGOs (rather than other entities) as the expression and signifier of civil society and because NGOs are recognizable entities that function as concrete measurable markers of civil society development. Thus, NGOs are benchmarks that provide a basis of comparison for further research, both between countries and within the third sector in Russia. Although they do not represent the totality of civil society, they represent a large chunk of civic activism.

I chose to look at women's NGOs as a case study for civic groups because they represent a significant portion of NGO activism overall. In addition, foreign donors themselves have targeted women's groups as an important component of civil society. USAID, the International Research and Exchanges Board (IREX), the Ford Foundation, and the Soros Foundation have all developed programs specifically targeting women's groups or have focused on women's organizations as crucial players in the larger task of fostering civic development. Given that aid to the civic sector is often distributed to organizations that belong to various social movements, such as the human rights movement or environmental organizations, engaging in an in-depth analysis of one of these sectors provides necessary and critical detail for a large and complex tale involving many players from a variety of countries, a wide array of resources, and a varied palette of strategies. I devote two chapters to the women's movement; the other sections of the book rely on interviews and information gathered from a larger selection of organizations within the NGO community as a whole.

I consciously chose to use women's organizations as a case study of the larger NGO community rather than to discuss gender and the women's movement for several reasons. First, there are already several excellent works on gender, feminism, and the women's movement in Russia.[80] These works, however, often are not placed in context with other social movements or within the larger realm of the civic community. In addition, previous work has tended to use a gender analysis because the subjects of their work, members of the women's movement, expressly identified themselves with a feminist/gendered perspective; however, the bulk of women's activism in Russia does not. In fact, many women's groups I interviewed took pains to tell me that even though they were women they did not primarily identify their activism with a gendered perspective. Although women's experiences certainly inform their identities, they are not determinative of all their actions. By taking a wide, rather than narrow, perspective of women's activism, I was able to observe a diverse microcosm of larger themes in the NGO community. In chapters 2 and 6, I explicitly discuss the larger NGO community in an effort to show where women's organizations diverge from and coalesce with larger trends in the civic community. In some situations, they serve as a mirror of NGO developments; at other times, they are a distortion of NGO trends.

I compare and contrast two types of NGOs: organizations that have received foreign aid and those that have remained isolated from the benefits of Western assistance. In addition, to avoid a Moscow-centric point of view, I examine these two groups of NGOs in a number of geographic locations; I conducted fieldwork in St. Petersburg, Pskov, Murmansk, Petrozavodsk (Republic of Karelia), Nizhnii Novgorod, Irkutsk, and Rostov-na-Donu. On a separate trip, I traveled to Krasnodor, Ekaterinburg, Novosibirsk, and Vladivostok. By talking with a variety of civic groups in this diverse set of locations, I avoided basing my conclusions solely on the experiences of groups in the capital, although my geographical reach could only go so far; Russia currently covers ten time zones.

Methods of Inquiry

Fieldwork in Russia requires conscientious detective work. It also demands of the researcher a studied determination to not let the constant chaos of life in Russia encourage her to take shortcuts and detours to unwarranted assumptions. In the midst of my year of fieldwork, the Russian economy collapsed once again, causing banks to freeze accounts, stores to shut their doors, and the population to queue up in long lines. At first, I did not know if I could access the finances to purchase food, let alone conduct research. The financial crisis also came as I was in the midst of receiving my first set of survey responses and preparing to send out another round. I wondered if this part of my research would just fall by the wayside. Subsequent trips to the regions in the winter, where hot water and heat was occasionally scarce, made me question my decision to leave Moscow to seek another perspective.

Despite these minor setbacks, I built a unique database, drawing on a wide array of research methods. My work, described in greater detail in appendix A, includes the following: survey data culled from 186 mail surveys received from women's NGOs across Russia in 1998; over one hundred personal interviews with NGO activists and women's group leaders; thirty-three personal interviews with representatives from various foundations and donor organizations; my experiences as a consultant for three foreign agencies working on civic development issues in Russia; a case study of the Ford Foundation's work with women's organizations; and a wide assortment of literature from various civic groups.

Each source portrays a different facet of a complex picture. No source, taken alone, provides enough evidence for my conclusions. Indeed, relying on only one methodology would have provided a distorted picture of Russia's civic development and the role of foreign donors in fostering it. Rather, the multiple methods I employed fit together to present an intricate depiction of the effects of international actors on the activities of Russian NGOs. From a qualitative perspective, the interviews and the workshops, meetings, and conferences I attended provided a plethora of leads for me to follow in my quest to understand the institutional impact of foreign aid on civic development. In keeping with Clifford Geertz's thoughts on the meaning of a wink, the various personal interactions I observed and participated in led me down a maze of mental alleys as I weighed the tone, inflections, stress, and meaning of various statements I gathered throughout my year of research.[81] They provided me with the hunches and the crucial stories that guided me through my thought process.

My work as a consultant provided me with an insider perspective on the rules of aid. Often donor agencies are treated as monoliths ineptly implementing programs that have little cultural resonance in domestic settings. My consulting experience, combined with interviews, allowed organizations and individuals to explain their behavior and rationale for decision making; this provided an alternative view of the motivations of donors and illustrated the complexity of the task with which donors were confronted.

Last, my survey research provided another crucial piece of my research puzzle. My impressions were generated from a variety of meetings, interviews, and observational sessions across Russia, but the survey provided the opportunity to collect systematic data on a wider array of groups beyond the cities I was able to reach in my travels. In addition, the quantitative tallies helped paint a picture that did not rely solely on my subjective interpretations of events.

OVERVIEW

Independent civic development is still in its infancy in Russia. In chapter 2, I maintain that Western aid did not start with a blank slate; rather, it was implemented within a Russian civil society defined by its past and shaped by its continuing struggles in times of extreme economic uncertainty. Further, civic groups faced a wide array of domestic impediments to collective action. Aid did not subvert civic development; however, this environment had significant implications for how civic activists responded to the incentives and sanctions of aid.

What were foreign donors' aims and objectives when they issued foreign assistance to Russian NGOs? Chapter 3 discusses the interests, goals, and aspirations of foreign donors in Russia. From the beginning, donors embraced a narrow vision of what constituted civil society and designed programs accordingly. In addition, donors had their own interests that they needed to protect. As a result, foreign aid offices often designed programs that reflected donor priorities in addition to objective Russian needs. Drawing on interview data, donor documents, and correspondence, I argue that short-term needs, rather than long-term development strategies, often dominated Western funders' plans.

Chapters 4 and 5 present a case study of the women's movement. They present two differing portraits of aid's impact. The surveys in chapter 4 tend to underline the abilities of foreign aid to facilitate NGO capacity; chapter 5, which relies primarily on interviews, presents an alternative interpretation of the benefits of aid.

Do the activities, goals, and structure of groups that have received foreign assistance differ substantially from those who rely primarily on domestic funding? Chapter 4 draws on the results of a mail survey I conducted among women's groups in spring 1998. Drawing on 186 survey responses from women's organizations, the chapter discusses the emerging divide that separates women's groups with access to foreign aid from those who rely solely on domestic support. I conclude that, although foreign aid has produced benefits in terms of ensuring short-term sustainability, providing physical and human capital necessary for running an organization, and fostering greater communication among the NGO community, aid has had relatively little impact on how groups interact with their populations or with the state.

Chapter 5 presents a more complex picture. It is a case study of the Ford Foundation's efforts to work with women's groups across Russia. This chapter draws on interviews with the foundation's grant recipients in seven cities. In each city, I interviewed women's groups that had received foreign aid from the foundation and women's groups that had not received aid. Groups that had received aid from the Ford Foundation did organize, talk, and act differently from groups that had not. But, these differences were not all entirely positive developments, nor did they necessarily contribute to long-term NGO stability and increased civic participation.

Chapter 6 returns to the theme of NGO development as a whole and recaps the emerging trends of foreign aid and civic development. Drawing on interviews, the chapter discusses the overall patterns of development fostered by the rules of foreign aid. Ironically, although aid can improve NGO capacity, it can simultaneously discourage groups from functioning as a civil society. I discuss three areas in which foreign aid realigns traditional civic development. By their nature, donor attempts to develop civil society are supply driven; despite efforts to be responsive to local needs, foreign aid supplies the projects and NGOs respond to them. This also encourages donors to take on roles that domestic groups should be filling themselves. The result is what I term "principled clientelism"; despite funders' self-proclaimed moral intentions, the outcome is the development of unequal vertical relationships between domestic groups and foreign aid. By fostering clientelistic relationships between the donor and recipient civic groups, foreign aid has weakened the nexus between the organizations and the society they supposedly represent. In some ways, similar to the dynamics of economic reform, aid is propping up a "virtual" civil society, a donor-driven civil society that claims to be much larger and more effective than it really is. Finally, I suggest ways that donors could redesign civic development in Russia in the hopes of reversing some of these trends.

Civic Traditions and Trends in Contemporary Russia: Impediments to Collective Action

For those following the transformation of an authoritarian Soviet Union into a democratic Russia, the transition has been strewn with economic, political, and social wreckage. The political prognosis has grown increasingly pessimistic since the heady days of *perestroika*; although Russia has established the institutional trappings of a democracy (elections and the transferal of power from one elected head of state to another), open transparent politics are neither "routinized nor deeply internalized."[1] Likewise, the economic shift from a command economy to one driven by market principles has also proved to be more difficult than expected; standards of living have plummeted while inflation, unemployment, falling productivity, and currency devaluation have undermined hopes of an economic miracle in the decade following the demise of the Soviet Union. The reasons behind these political and economic difficulties are numerous and complex; institutional legacies from the Soviet past, weak institutions, corrupt elites, perverse incentive structures, and an anemic political culture supportive of democracy and capitalism have all been fingered as reasons behind Russia's troubled transition.

Whereas Russia's checkered past in the management of these political and economic transitions has been reported copiously, its third transition, a civic transition, is often obscured, overlooked, or folded into discussions of general public opinion.[2] Russia is still in the process of developing an autonomous civil society, or "that arena of the polity where self-organizing groups, movements, and individuals . . . attempt to articulate values, create associations and solidarities, and advance their interests" autonomous of the state.[3] Previous patterns of interaction reveal few Tocquevillian civic tendencies; although Russia is not completely lacking in civic traditions, its immediate roots are located in a Soviet past in which voluntary organization was colonized by the state and thus dominated by state-run organizations. Stretching our focus back to Tsarist Russia reveals traditions of civic activism, but, again, an activism sanctioned by and carefully monitored by the state. The current context is also indeterminate; although civic groups have mushroomed rapidly in the 1990s, developing an institutional infrastructure supportive of a legally autonomous civic sphere, as well as the economic, political, and social supports to help it flourish, remains a challenge. Overcoming past and current impediments to collective action in the realm of civil society may be less dramatic than elite maneuverings or economic policy formulation, but it is just as crucial to Russia's process of deepening and widening its current democratic status.

If we were to take the pulse of civil society in Russia, what would our prognosis be? What is its emerging shape, and how do various civic actors define and determine their interests, goals, and strategies? What domestic factors have molded Russia's emerging civic sphere? How does it interact with other sectors of society, and do these other sectors support or undermine civil society? In sum, how institutionalized is civil society?

This chapter traces the emergence of an independent civil society and discusses the facilitators of and impediments to collective action in fostering civic development in the post-Soviet era. Since the Gorbachev era, Russia's third sector has grown from a rag-tag collection of forty or so small informal organizations to more than 450,000 as of early 2001.[4] Molded by the economic exigencies of the transition era, many voluntary organizations provide essential services and support to those struggling to maneuver in Russia's brave new world of economic decline and political and social fragmentation. A small but crucial collection of legislation passed in the 1990s carved out an institutional space for civic groups; law rather than the tentative toleration of a reformist state finally protects the autonomy of public organizations. This development has created an entirely new vocabulary for civic activists—"civil society," "third sector," "nonprofit organization," "nongovernmental organization"—as well as a new way of visualizing and creating linkages with the state, political society, other actors in the civic sector, and the private citizen. Given that the majority of growth has taken place in the 1990s, this surge in civic development is significant, both in its statistical presence as well as in its theoretical implications. As a channel for citizen demands and a transmitter of democratic culture and social capital, civil society is crucial to democratic consolidation.

Despite these strides, the fledgling third sector is experiencing a wide array of growing pains. Although the number of civic organizations is impressive, there is a large gap between the statistical presence of NGOs and the substantive reality of their operations; a much smaller percentage of groups carry out their activities on a regular basis.[5] Many NGOs exist on paper, but in reality their work is sporadic, driven by the personal dedication of a small core of enthusiasts who work when time and money permit.[6] Although the economic climate provides the impetus for organization, it simultaneously keeps groups from developing a stable presence. In addition, activists have relatively little experience in functioning as an autonomous civic sector within the framework of a democracy. Groups are tentatively beginning to act as a conduit from private citizen to public realm; as a whole, organizations are small, insular, and wary of outreach to both the public and the state. In turn, citizens know relatively little about the emerging nonprofit sphere or are ambivalent about joining organizations. Finally, for much of the 1990s the state, at the federal regional, and local levels has often been wary, as well as dismissive of the utility of nonprofit organizations. The Putin administration has been more proactive in its policies toward NGOs, although these actions have sent out mixed signals about its attitudes to the third sector. Civic groups' tasks are made more difficult by the reality of Russia's political situation; vacillating somewhere between democratic transition and consolidation, the state is alternatively both the facilitator and the impediment to greater institutionalization of civil society.

These problems originate from a tangle of past legacies and current constraints. Although the idea of a nonprofit, third, or civic sector is relatively new, the patterns and traditions of organization are not. Legal and independent organization is a development of the 1990s, yet civic groups were not created from scratch. Many groups still reflect the organizational practices and legacies of Soviet era, top-down "voluntary" organizations, and citizens are also more familiar with Soviet traditions and patterns of organization. In addition, the Russian government has done little to create a favorable legislative environment for continued development. Nor is civil society currently buttressed by the broader contextual essentials that provided the backdrop for Western civic development, such as a middle class, the rule of law, or a civic culture. Organizations are still operating within extremely fluid institutional structures.

When foreign assistance foundations arrived in earnest in 1992 to implement civic development programs, they were greeted with a vastly different looking civil society than the Tocquevillian ideal to which they were accustomed. In order to understand the effects of aid, it is crucial to understand the domestic context in which it arrived. Aid did not subvert civic development; there already were many domestic impediments to civic organization. And, given these impediments, aid played a crucial role in inadvertently reinforcing some habits and practices that could further discourage the functioning of a civil society within a democracy.

WHAT IS CIVIL SOCIETY?

Currently, it is nearly impossible to discuss the degree to which countries have established a flourishing democracy without mentioning the role of civil society. Civil society has become the entryway to larger discussions about the decay of tottering authoritarian regimes, the construction of new political institutions, and the vitality of established democracies. The anti-authoritarian movements in Latin American countries in the 1980s planted the seeds of this interest, which soon seemed to mushroom into fascination in the wake of the chaotic months of 1989. The rapidity with which old regimes across Eastern Europe fell in the face of public demonstrations and the near-spontaneous emergence of opposition movements and round-table negotiations lent credence to the concept "people power." This love affair with civil society was facilitated by the CNN effect—television stations broadcast images of crowds jubilantly dancing atop the defunct Berlin Wall and thousands marching through the streets of Weimar singing, "We shall overcome." These images were used to illustrate the rebirth of civil society, both as a physical force in toppling authoritarian dictatorships in communist-governed countries and as a theoretical concept intrinsic to democratic theory. The fall of the Berlin Wall both romanticized and expanded the meaning of the concept. Civil society was broadened to encompass anyone or any action involving some sort of opposition to an authoritarian state, whether it be organized labor unions in Gdansk, protesting citizens in Prague, angry babushkas in Moscow, or determined wall deconstructionists in Berlin. The experiences of the 1990s also caught academics by surprise and led them to retrain their analytical lens. Civil society superseded elite negotiations as a determinative factor in the collapse of authoritarian regimes, as a partner in the reconstruction of new ones, and as a crucial linchpin in those regimes' hypothetical future democratic consolidation.[7]

Although civil society plays a crucial role in a variety of political climates, it functions differently within the context of authoritarian regimes, transitioning regimes, and in democracies.[8] For example, in authoritarian regimes, civil society is rarely autonomous from the state, and the concept of a self-organized public sphere protected by law is often replaced either by top-down organization by the state in an attempt to coopt the development of political pluralism or by outright political repression. In this environment, almost any kind of political expression, however apolitical, is often viewed as an indicator of the presence of civil society. Dissidents such as Vaclav Havel advocated a new form of protest—choosing not to be active in state-led politics was interpreted as the "power of the powerless." Refusing to live the life of a cooperative communist was the only possible way to be subversive in a regime that defined acceptable modes of political expression. In addition, any increased nonstate-sponsored activity can often serve to delegitimize a regime or compel the regime to be more responsive to its citizens. Whereas in established democracies the elements of civil society become competitors for influence, in authoritarian ones unity among the opposition is critical to success.

In transitional polities, civil society, although often not granted legal independence, can garner de facto independence and gain leverage by bargaining for a role in designing the new system. Groups can provide an alternative to the old regime, mobilize voters during critical or founding elections, organize protests or rallies during negotiations, and hasten reforms. At the very least, civil society groups can act as a bulwark against state power; at their most influential, they can serve as a partner in democratic governance.[9]

The context of a consolidating democracy shifts and redefines the role of civil society. Civil society is protected and bolstered by a legal framework guaranteeing it a space relatively untrammeled by state influence within the public realm. The autonomy of civil society becomes no longer solely theoretical. Rather, that autonomy becomes institutionalized through the guarantee of individual rights and freedoms, the granting of legal status to freely formed independent groups, the establishment of a set of civil and commercial codes to regulate relations, and the presence of an independent court system in which groups can seek redress against an intrusive state.[10] This institutionalized civil society is also buttressed by a state apparatus that enforces the rights of civil society and by an economic system with sufficient pluralism to support the necessary degree of autonomy and liveliness of society. The sphere of civil society is often deepened by the presence of a variety of other larger socioeconomic factors, such as a middle class or a political culture that serves to reinforce the institutionalized elements of civil society.[11]

Finally, civil society functions differently within the framework of a democracy. The civil society argument is an amalgamation of different theories in which civic associations directly deepen democracy in a number of ways. Particularly in newly minted democracies, they are often the key purveyors of voter education as well as the source of information about the merits of democratic citizenship. Civil society enriches the political life of citizens by increasing their knowledge, skills, and sense of efficacy. It is the trading post of information, the arena in which citizens collect, exchange, articulate, and disseminate views, opinions, and positions. Associational life also stimulates citizen participation beyond the relatively passive process of voting, which at best only prods citizens out of their houses on a yearly basis. Civic groups also encourage citizens to articulate views, form goals, and work to achieve these goals within the political process.[12]

Civil society also serves as a crucial bridge between private citizen and public office. Groups gather citizens' interests and articulate their demands to political parties, local government offices, and state institutions of power. By acting as a watchdog for citizen interests, they also counteract the state and its potential to monopolize power through the control of ideas or positions by ensuring a plurality of ideas and pockets of influence.[13] At times adversary, supplicant, mediator, messenger, and partner, civil society reins in passions and widens public debate and communication.[14] More a midwife than an opponent to the state, civil society organizations theoretically keep channels of communication open, switching hats from opponent to ally to negotiator depending on the issue at hand.

Civic groups further contribute to the deepening of democracy in less obviously political ways by building social capital. In this view, civic groups perform crucial internal functions that have implications for democratic performance; they foster habits of cooperation, solidarity, public-spiritedness, and trust which are essential components of the social capital needed for effective cooperation among individuals.[15] Learning trust in these small, personalized local networks is crucial for creating the social capital that allows the development of trust and cooperation in the larger, more impersonal structures involved in modern democratic governance. They serve as incubators of a larger political culture supportive of democratic institutions.

Thus, civil society is crucial in all stages of transition. As the mediator between the state and private individuals, civil society can translate culture, values, and mores supportive of democracy in both directions. As Juan A. Linz and Alfred Stepan argue, "A robust civil society, with the capacity to generate political alternatives and to monitor government and the state can help transitions get started, help resist reversals, help push transitions to their completion, help consolidate, and help deepen democracy. . . . therefore, a lively and independent civil society is invaluable."[16] Although it is possible to develop a civic society in the absence of democratic political structures, the reverse is untenable; democratic tendencies cannot be cemented into consolidated democracies without a vibrant and fluid civil society. In other words, democracy becomes truly stable only when people come to value it widely not solely for its economic and social performance but intrinsically for its political attributes.[17] Although factors such as institutional design or functioning economic systems are also crucial for democratic consolidation, democracy fundamentally rests on the presence and quality of its civil society.

Turning this theoretical journey into a *fait accompli* is more challenging—theory provides the ideal; events define the possible. Independent organizations flourished in the wake of Gorbachev's reforms. However, Russia's political transition also forced civic groups to reposition themselves vis-à-vis the state and the population at large. It is still in the midst of defining itself within the current political institutions, which are caught somewhere between transition and consolidation.

How does Russian civil society measure up to the theoretical ideas just presented? In the following sections, I trace the emergence of a nascent civil society under Gorbachev, beginning in 1990 when the Congress of People's Deputies passed a landmark piece of legislation in which individuals were legally guaranteed the right to autonomous organization. This legislation marked the beginning of the emergence of a legally recognized, independent civil society. I discuss the challenges, new as well as inherited, that affected civic groups' abilities to further develop and grow.

THE (RE)BIRTH OF CIVIL SOCIETY?

Finding a starting point for the rebirth of civil society in Russia is difficult; in a country where independent organizations were not formally recognized by the state before 1990, assessing civic traditions can be a subjective process, depending on how we define voluntarism, independent activity, and civil society and interpret their presence. Although the tsarist autocracy sought to maintain control over voluntarism, it sanctioned charitable activities, and by the early twentieth century charitable societies were the most widespread form of voluntary associations in the Russian Empire and certainly the ones most tolerated by the autocracy. By the beginning of the twentieth century, more than six thousand charitable institutions were registered with the Department of Institutions of Empress Maria, the state agency responsible for overseeing private charitable initiatives. But in a country with more than 125 million people and covering 22 million square kilometers, this activity, although significant, was extremely limited in its scope and nature.[18]

The communist regime continued the tsarist policy of state control while championing different forms of associationism. Toward the end of the 1920s and into the 1930s, the state initiated the process of uniting smaller independent organizations into state-sanctioned mass associations. Charitable organizations soon were the objects of disapproval by the party structure; charity was declared "bourgeois and foreign," the problems that it aimed to ameliorate were declared "solved," and new difficulties were attributed to enemies of the people.[19] Although Nikolai Bukharin advocated the "unprecedented flourishing" of "all kinds of workers' and peasants organizations, press correspondents, and voluntary societies and associations," these groups were to be state sponsored because, as he argued, together with Soviet power, they "form a single system, which embraces, enlightens, and reforms the broad mass of toilers."[20] Citizens were organized into Soviet-sponsored mass associations to escort them from cradle to grave. Organizations such as the Writers' Union, the Soviet Foundation of Peace, hunters', anglers', and collectors' societies, and associations of disabled were all carefully orchestrated from above and declared "voluntary." Even the paying of dues to groups was not optional; all children and adults in the USSR were required to contribute to the Society for the Protection of the Environment, as well as to the Red Cross and the Society for the Preservation of Monuments.[21]

During the height of the Cold War, pessimists tended to interpret these activities as part of a larger Communist Party project to atomize and "flatten" Soviet society.[22] These efforts earned the Soviet system the moniker "totalitarian," and civic impulses were portrayed as carefully orchestrated and manipulated from above—and therefore not civil society. A strand of more recent scholarship also reflects this view that, because Soviet organization represented the purposeful destruction of what is now understood as social capital, civil society is an entirely new phenomena.[23] Theoretical norms of reciprocity, were, in the Soviet context, translated into a complex system of *blat* and patronage. (In this portrayal, Russia is continuing along a path more determined by its past than shaped by its new democratic vistas.)

Yet to dismiss Soviet society as totally devoid of civic impulses overlooks a multitude of literature that has taken pains to provide a more nuanced view of associational traditions. Some scholarship has countered this picture of a heavily atomized society with few civic traditions, portraying a "reawakening" of civil society, which had existed in the form of *obshchestvennost'* under the tsarist regime and withered during the Stalinist era, in the form of small underground groups in later generations. In addition, individuals such as Andrei Sakharov, Alexander Solzhenitsyn, and Roy Medvedev and the emergence of small organizations such as the Moscow Helsinki Group, the Human Rights Committee, and Group 73 in the 1970s belie the portrayal of an atomized indifferent society.[24]

Other recent scholarship has also countered the grim picture of an atomized society with a broad interpretation of civil society in the Soviet era that had pockets of independent activism that transcended the tiny dissident movement. An informal group sprang up in the 1970s in Akademgorodok, a community built outside of Novosibirsk, Siberia for Russia's scientific elite. Living far from the controlling arm of Moscow, music and ballet enthusiasts formed the Terpsichord organization and collected funds to bring artists to Siberia for performances.[25] Some have gone so far as to reinterpret the environmental movement as a movement of democratic resistance to the regime and as the real precursor to civil society.[26] Largely organized through state-created organizations, environmental groups were nonetheless populated by enthusiasts who advocated environmental improvements using nonpolitical methods. Although few people openly challenged the system, there were groups of individuals who used the atmosphere of relaxed tolerance to attempt to carve out some form of independent social and professional identity within a system that defined official models of behavior, ethics, norms, and identity for all.[27] Moreover, being in a state-controlled organization did not preclude some individuals from enjoying their experiences in them. Many activists I interviewed credited their experiences in the Pioneers and Komsomol as valuable education for their current lives as civic activists in non-governmental organizations. The desire for a civic outlet was not alien to people; it was often repressed or rechanneled into state-sanctioned forms of behavior.

Other scholars point to the economic strides that the Soviet Union made by the 1970s and argue that modernization theory had finally arrived in the Soviet Union; the growth created during the Soviet era created a population capable of later showing its dissatisfaction with the regime's inability to meet material needs.[28] The deepening economic crisis of the 1980s challenged the regime's abilities to maintain its provision of welfare benefits; strikes and popular demonstrations, although short-lived, were testimony to the argument that social compliance was contingent on the state's delivery of a consistent level of social welfare and social services.[29] Civil society, in this view, consisted of brief outbursts of public protest due to rising expectations.

These attempts to revise the previous grim picture of alienated citizens portray a realm of limited yet important activity. Certainly, intermediary organizations, associations, and voluntarist practices existed under both the tsarist and the Soviet eras. In both eras, however, organization was tolerated, rather than protected, by the state and activism was constrained to a small substrata of the population, often the intelligentsia.[30] In both eras, the state, rather than independent associationism, was the best watchdog of society. Although these reinterpretations certainly point to signs of nascent civil society and collective action, the continued existence of civic groups and autonomous organization was nevertheless subject to the good will of the state rather than the rule of law. Nor was this activity part of a broader groundswell of support, organization, or activity on a truly mass level.[31] The recent research reveals a more complex picture of civic associationism, but due to the lack of official state recognition this nascent civil society remained stunted until the arrival of Gorbachev.

Gorbachev's ascension to the position of general secretary of the Communist Party in 1985 created a new space for the concept of civic activism. Facing the realities of economic stagnation and a crisis in government legitimacy and surrounded by a wary hard-line elite, Gorbachev turned to social groups to develop and support allies for his vision of a reinvigorated socialism. Pointing to the need to unleash the creative activity of the masses, Gorbachev attempted to widen the battle for reform to the streets in an effort to circumvent the entrenched elites within the party. As with other areas of Gorbachev's agenda, his goal was not to develop a truly independent civil society but one that would remain under the sponsorship of and in service to the Communist Party. The project to reinvigorate civil society was part of the larger goal to bypass the hardliners and create grassroots support for the economic reforms while limiting this activity by refusing to legitimate it by giving it formal autonomy.

Gorbachev's struggle for reform unfolded in a variety of speeches, decrees, and eventual legislation over the following four years. Charitable groups, due to their ostensibly apolitical nature, received the first nod of approval from Gorbachev; in 1986, the Central Committee of the Communist Party and the Council of Ministries adopted a resolution creating the first charitable foundations since pre-Revolutionary Russia. These included, among others, the Soviet Children's Foundation, the Soviet Foundation of Culture, and the Soviet Foundation of Mercy and Health.[32] Although largely symbolic, this move legalized the idea of charity in the USSR and provided the first step toward further institutional development of a voluntary, state-sponsored sphere. In addition, the 1986 Statutes on Amateur Associations and Hobby Clubs proclaimed that "said associations bring together broad masses of the population with the purpose of satisfying the varied spiritual needs and interests of Soviet people in the sphere of free time and meaningful leisure."[33] Although this acknowledged the legitimacy only of state-sponsored voluntarism, it was a crucial step forward in that it widened and reenergized the concept of associationism.

In 1987, Gorbachev stepped up the pressure by introducing the concept "socialist pluralism" as the new framework for informal group activity in the Soviet Union. Gorbachev's call to respect socialist pluralism amounted to de facto toleration of the formation of some small nonstate citizens associations, or *neformalni* (informal) organizations, with charitable as well as political agendas.[34] Gorbachev acknowledged the need for the informal groups, arguing that they "exist because existing [official] organizations do not satisfy people in their activities, atmosphere, and methods." [35] For the first time, the Soviet state had acknowledged the presence of nonstate organizations and tacitly approved their existence.

Citizens responded to this call for a reinvigorated sphere of voluntarism. Soviet-era, state-sponsored organizations received a literal shot in the arm because of increased civic interest; for example, the All-Russian Society for the Preservation of Historical Monuments (VOOPIK), which in 1965 claimed 3 million members, had accumulated 19 million adherents a decade later and by the mid-1980s had more than 35 million members.[36] The informals also multiplied rapidly; by 1987, more than 30,000 informal groups, which were not affiliated, registered or controlled by the Communist Party had emerged. Within two years, that number had grown to 60,000.[37] The following year, the Russian Orthodox Church was permitted to resume charitable activities, a service denied them since the Revolution. Perceived as a tacit acknowledgment of socialism's failure to address many of the problems in Soviet society, Gorbachev's reforms provided the green light for the organization of associations dedicated to addressing problems previously ignored by Soviet authorities, such as alcoholism, homelessness, and the disabled.

Although the state originally had advocated for these developments, it greeted this increased activity with a mixture of policies designed to accommodate, coopt, and intimidate. Informal groups had to register with a formal party-sponsored social organization to obtain meeting space or legal recognition. The state still strictly regulated group demonstrations and rallies; it also tried to regulate this by passing a decree in July 1988 "on the procedure for organizing and holding meetings, rallies, street processions, and demonstrations."[38] Yet neither was Gorbachev consistently opposed to the process he had unleashed; rather, policies seemed to contradict one another. At times the state sought to coopt, at other times encourage and push, and at still other times quash grassroots organization. For example, while the state tried to control the nature of demonstrations, at the same time it was loosening other laws that impacted citizens' abilities to interact in the newly recognized informals as well as traditional state-sanctioned organizations. In 1988, the party began discussion about loosening official censorship and implementing new laws on the press that would accommodate certain publications. Thus, the latter half of the 1980s revealed a state deeply divided about the best way to control the forces it had released; it was suspicious of such activity, but the steps the state took to suppress such activity seemed to reveal the inevitability of its development. Nonetheless, without legal recognition from the state, these organizations were at the mercy of the state, depending on the broader political climate surrounding them.

This increased acceptance of organizations forming around social issues inevitably led to calls for greater political plurality; by 1987, groups with clear political agendas, such as the Perestroika Club, Memorial, Citizen's Dignity, and the Moscow Popular Front, advocated greater political liberalization.[39] The creation of the Congress of People's Deputies in 1989, which was accompanied by semicompetitive elections, also had an impact on civil society and the world of the informals. It drained civil society of activists; leaders left the civic realm to join the political sphere as deputies in the new congress. In this sense, the creation of the congress helped to more clearly articulate the growing development of a civil and a political society as two separate entities. In addition, it provided a new legislative forum through which to carve an institutionalized civic sphere, one protected by law rather than by the state's good nature.

The development of an independent civil society took another crucial step in October 1990. The Congress of People's Deputies passed a law on public associations, granting them legal recognition. Additional legislation in 1993 and 1995 further clarified their juridical status.[40] Most significantly, in 1995 Russia adopted a new Civil Code that laid the legal groundwork for noncommercial organizations.[41] The code outlined what information should be included in the organization's charter, the rights of members, some fundamental parameters for income-raising activities, and the legal process for liquidating foundations. In addition, on May 25, 1995, the State Duma passed the first law pursuant to the Civil Code further defining the legal status of public organizations. The federal law On Public Associations outlined the general provisions of a public association. Laws on charitable organizations (July 7, 1995) and noncommercial organizations (December 1995) soon followed.[42]

This legislation was critical for civic groups. Previously, formal civil society was a hierarchical, state-created system of mass associations and informal civil society a small assortment of organizations that depended on the good will and tolerance of a reformist state. Upon the passage of this legislation, organizations were recognized by the state as legal entities. They could now open bank accounts, rent offices, and have telephone lines. In a step that would prove problematic later on, certain types of NGOs undertaking business activities, such as charitable funds, as well as sports, disabled, and veterans' associations, were given tax advantages. In addition, other laws passed in 1990 granted state agencies, political parties, public organizations, labor collectives, and any Soviet citizen over eighteen the right to publish freely as long as he or she registered the publication with the appropriate state agency. This helped support the emerging civic sphere by allowing for freer flows of information.

What was the meaning of this increased activism? Certainly, the number of groups was significant, although this emerging social organization did not approach the level or scope of other nascent civic groups emerging in Eastern Europe at the same time. In addition, despite the explosion of informals in the late 1980s, these groups were unable to mobilize a larger public, as had other oppositions in countries such as Czechoslovakia and the German Democratic Republic; they were poorly connected to the public at large. Because of this, the initial informals, although significant in their appearance, also were never able to wrest control of the nature and shape of political discourse and the pace of reform. Although they were united in their opposition to the communist regime, they were unable to present an alternative to this rule. Finally, a broader movement was undermined by the nature of the groups themselves; often they were small, poorly organized, divided by internal rivalries, and unconnected with other groups.[43]

Thus, it is also important to not overestimate what this civic activism was able to do in the initial years of post-Soviet-era Russia. Although enthusiastic in the initial years of reform, it was weak and poorly connected with the political society, other groups, and with society at large. Still, its emergence was significant, and the legal recognition of civil society as a sphere that had state recognition and formal autonomy was an enormous step forward in the development of an autonomous sphere of civic activism.

INDEPENDENT CIVIC DEVELOPMENT:
SURVIVING THE TRANSITION

The 1990s was a decade of considerable development for groups within civil society. This section provides a snapshot of this civic activism. Despite the numerical proliferation of organizations, civic groups spent much of the decade following the collapse of the Soviet Union carving out a sphere of independent public activity protected by law. Redefining themselves as partners of and challengers to, rather than as solely subjects of, the state was a challenge. So was developing ties to individual citizens, who were often withdrawn into the problems of their own lives or poorly informed about the activities of the third sector. Doing all of this in a fluid institutional context defined by economic scarcity and constant political uncertainty was difficult. Despite the attempts to transform political, economic, and civic society, the broader political culture was slow to readjust and Soviet legacies still shaped the direction of civil society.

A notable aspect of civil society is its statistical presence; the number of civic groups exploded, increasing steadily every year. Estimates in 1989, before informals were granted legal status, placed their number at 60,000.[44] When civic groups were granted formal autonomy, they began the process of registering with the state and by May of 1993 8,479 NGOs had been registered nationwide.[45] By January of 1997, that number had grown to 160,000.[46] By January 1, 2000, 274,284 organizations had registered with the Ministry of Justice. By early 2001, that number had increased to approximately 450,000. Approximately 60 percent of this most recent figure consisted of independent civic associations; the remaining 40 percent were other types of noncommercial organizations, including political parties, religious organizations, labor unions, representatives of international organizations, and post-Soviet NGOs.[47] This translates into approximately 270,000 NGOs, a rapid increase from the late 1990s, when estimates placed the number of civic organizations at 58,000.[48] But this number is somewhat illusory. Many organization existed in name only and in reality were defunct or nearly inoperative; as few as 25 percent of registered groups were active.[49] In an effort to get a grasp on the number of organizations that actually operate with some regularity, the federal government has mandated that all NGOs reregister at the end of 2002. This will hopefully provide a more accurate picture of the shape of Russia's emerging civic sphere.

The economic free fall has provided the impetus for many citizens to organize. Although Russia's vast supply of natural resources, educated population, and developed infrastructure are positive indicators, Russia's economic status in the 1990s, for the majority of the population, can only be described as grim. Data from the first half of a decade of economic reform paint a picture of yearly declines in productivity of 12–15 percent, accompanied by inflation of anywhere from 22 to 900 percent in any given year.[50] In 1995, the GDP constituted 65.5 percent of the 1991 level.[51] Conditions improved somewhat by 1998, mainly in the forms of curbing inflation and stabilizing the ruble, but the financial crash of August 1998 plunged many citizens back into the realm of economic uncertainty. In a survey from the wake of the August 1998 financial crash, 37 percent of respondents felt that they could barely make ends meet and that there was not enough money for food; 60 percent of respondents rated their own material conditions as bad, or very bad, and almost one-half of all respondents declared their situation to be "unbearable."[52] In 2000, the Putin administration made economic development a central component of its overall package of strategic goals. Owing in part to advantageous oil prices, Russia achieved the level of economic development that had existed before the crash by summer 2002, prompting upbeat economic reports on declining unemployment and wage arrears coupled with encouraging growth rates. For many citizens, however, life was still financially more insecure than it had been in 1985, before the start of reforms. The Russian economy, in experiencing the ups and downs of an economic roller coaster, has spent more time moving downward than taking substantive steps back up.

The economic chaos was accompanied by the retreat of the state; federal, regional, and local governments were not equipped to handle the crisis. During 1991–95, state expenses for social issues, including welfare, public health, education, and culture declined 39 percent.[53] As a result, the once-guaranteed social safety nets were dismantled at a time when citizens needed their services more than ever. In the wake of the collapse of a command economy, the state was unable to fully provide the social services—free education, universal health care, pension plans, and other aspects of the Soviet cradle-to-grave social-welfare net—it had guaranteed under communism.

The severity of the economic crisis spurred many groups into activity; civic groups formed in self-defense to compensate for the state's failure to meet its responsibilities. Thus, the majority of voluntary organizations reflected the "materialist" concerns of economic and physical security.[54] To draw from my own survey research, for example, one group wrote, "[t]he crisis situation in Russia, first and foremost, makes it necessary to help us all live through this. This takes all strength, time, and hope for better times."[55] Some estimate that social welfare, or "social defense" organizations constituted up to one-third of all civic groups.[56] This social service sector includes charitable organizations for the poor in general, as well as interest groups representing particular segments of the population, such as veterans, the disabled, children, and pensioners. These groups usually form because the state has been unable to provide the promised social services and thus they act as surrogates for the state, providing services and support for those in need. One activist, in explaining her motivation, wrote, "I am concerned that people who have given their entire lives have been left to fend for themselves in old age. . . . They worked 10–15 hours per day and Sundays. The work was done on raw enthusiasm. For this work, they were paid wages, which more or less covered the expense of traveling back and forth to work and meager sustenance. But the future turned out to be even harsher. Something must be done to defend these people in their old age."[57] Another activist explained her rationale, "Unfortunately, life for the average person in

Russia has become worse. The government has isolated itself from the people. There is an active stratification of society on artificial terms into rich and poor. The brutal fight for power and money of the upper echelons of the power structure is morally corrupting society. Public associations are often the only salvation of the people."[58]

What united these otherwise disparate organizations was their common purpose—to survive the tidal wave of economic transition and dislocation. Surviving the transition became the dominant mantra for many organizations and magnified the struggle into one that embodied the principle of good versus evil. Discussing her activities in helping people who had fallen on hard times, one activist commented, "Generally, we deal with injustice, dishonesty, barbarity, and abuse of power."[59] That is quite a mission statement. Many of these organizations, although formally independent, were reconfigurations of old Soviet-era groups. Although the Soviet-era control of women's councils, professional associations, disabled societies, and others had faded, the organizational structures remained. They were sometimes filled by activists with Soviet-era mentalities but also with enthused citizens trying to make a difference. Soviet-era institutions and practices did not shrivel up; they were reconfigured, some more drastically than others, in this decade of intense change.

Not all groups, however, were concerned with immediate concerns of day-to-day survival; issue-oriented NGOs that ran the gamut of Western new social movement organizations also arose. During the 1970s, the human rights movement encompassed a handful of internationally known activists, such as Andrei Sakharov, Yelena Bonner, Anatoly Shcharansky, and Lyudmila Alexeyeva. They formed the Moscow Helsinki Group in 1976 to monitor the Soviet Union's compliance with the Helsinki Accords on human rights. Often operating from abroad, this small cadre survived primarily through Western support and press coverage. Yet by 1999, less than ten years after the legalization of voluntary associations, there were organizations in sixty of Russia's eighty-nine regions monitoring human rights.[60] Memorial, an NGO that started as an informal from the Gorbachev era, also expanded rapidly, developing many chapters in Russia's regions. Newer groups based solely in Moscow, such as the Center for the Development of Democracy and Human Rights, revolved around a younger generation of activists. As with the larger figures on NGO registration, however, numbers can be deceiving. Often, upon arrival in a regional city, a human rights organization can in reality be a single person, working out of the home in his or her spare time. Despite the impressive figures on human rights monitoring, the development of a human rights movement remains a slow process consisting of a few vocal citizens.

Environmental activism was also a significant part of this relatively small social movement activity. In addition to Soviet-era organizations, many new groups originated in the aftermath of the Chernobyl disaster in 1986. Russia's continued ecological problems resulting from its economic developmental strategies provided further impetus for people to organize. Environmental groups, such as the Socio-Ecological Union and Greenpeace became increasingly prominent at the national level. In 2000, environmental organizations managed to collect almost 3 million signatures on a petition demanding a referendum over government plans to finance Russia's failing nuclear industry by storing and processing foreign radioactive waste, although this initiative was eventually blocked.[61] Finally, as I discuss in chapters 4 and 5, the women's movement also moved beyond the rhetorical blandness of state-sponsored, Soviet-era organizations. They became active in issues such as combating domestic violence, stopping the trafficking in women, and protesting the continuing war in Chechnya.

These movements are small and stretched thinly across the vast expanse of Russia; it is important not to overestimate their strength, power, or influence on national level politics. In addition, many of these groups involved in new social movement issues reflected different concerns than their Western counterparts. In the West, these groups are usually labeled postmaterialist movements because they are concerned with quality-of-life and self-expression issues.[62] In Russia, these groups were molded by years of state-led economic growth, combined with current economic realities. Issues invoking postmaterialist themes, such as the environment, became materialist issues; that is, struggles for survival *are* quality-of-life concerns. Many of these groups, however, were often able to benefit from their identification with postmaterialist, Western issues and were supported primarily by external, Western sources.[63]

Geographically, concentrations of NGOs grew unevenly across the seven federal regions. Organizations in the Central and Volga regions proliferated; pockets of activism flourished in parts of Siberia, while the development of a civic sector in the Russian Far East lagged behind the rest of the regions. Civic development was concentrated in the larger Russian cities of Moscow and Petersburg. Provincial cities such as Yekaterinburg, Nizhnii Novgorod, Novosibirsk, Rostov Na Donu, and Samara also showed significant growth.[64] These larger cities were also often homes to the Westernized elements of civic development; smaller regional cities often exhibited a mix of newer groups as well as networks left over from Soviet forms of organization.

Tables 2.1 and 2.2 summarize the general cleavages of contemporary civic development, by issue focus and by function. Civic development

Table 2.1 Russian NGOs by Issue Focus[a]

Issue focus	Estimate (%)	Description and example organizations	Strengths	Constraints
Social welfare	30	Assist vulnerable groups in the population, such as disabled people, pensioners, orphans, homeless people, war veterans, and large families. *Example:* Perspektiva.	Attract the largest number of people to the nonprofit sector Working relationship with local government	Tend to be member-oriented self-help groups Lack of financial support, particularly foreign aid Susceptible to government cooptation Limited professionalism Poorly devised planning Absence of staff members Unclear internal hierarchy
Interests	24	Not a clearly defined program of activities; often serve as a forum for socializing, exchange of information, and mutual support *Examples:* bee keepers' and fishermen's societies	—	Receive almost no funding Mostly Soviet-era organizations
Environmental protection	10	Involved in issues such as the generation and safe use of nuclear energy, conservation, and clean up of local environment *Example:* Socio-Ecological Union	Close-knit community Well-networked with other NGOs, both domestically and internationally Working relationship with the state at the national level	Almost completely dependent on foreign aid

Arts and culture	10	Involved in the preservation and development of Russian culture through support of artists, dancers, museums, etc.	Receive business financing	Lack of financial support, particularly government financing
Human rights	10	Particularly well developed in the fields of social rehabilitation and the protection of the victims of repression, prison reform, refugees and forced migrants, consumer rights, and rights of people with disabilities. *Examples:* Committee of Soldiers' Mothers, Moscow Helsinki Group.	Working relationship with the state at the national level	Lack of information network Isolated from rest of NGO community Almost completely dependent on foreign aid
Women's organizations	1–10[b]	Involved in a wide array of activities from traditional areas of charity to Western feminist organizations *Example.* Independent Women's Forum	Well-networked with the international women's movement	Not recognized by local government Poorly organized work with volunteers Feminist wing almost completely dependent on foreign aid
Education and youth	7	No information available		
Sports	4	No information available		
Advancement of the sciences	2	No information available		
Professional organizations	1	No information available		
Health	1	No information available		

[a] Data from Paul Legendre, *The Non Profit Sector in Russia* (Moscow: Charities Aid Foundation, 1998); Maggie Christie, "Constraints on Russia's NGO Sector" (USAID/Russia, June 1996); Karen Greene, "Russian Women's Movements: An Overview" (USAID/Russia, June 1998).

[b] Estimates vary on women's groups. If we include only groups that defend women's rights and develop the women's movement according to Western feminist precepts, then the number is estimated at 1 percent. If we include the wider range of women's activism of more charitable/traditional themes, then the number is as high as 10 percent.

Table 2.2 Russian NGOs by Function[a]

Function	Estimate (%)	Description and example organizations	Strengths	Constraints
Self-help groups	30–40	Provide services to members, given lack of government intervention; involved most often in social welfare provision *Example*: associations of people with disabilities (over 70%)	Attract the largest number of people to the nonprofit sector	Limited professionalism in fields of management Poorly developed planning General absence of staff members Unclear hierarchy and system for decision making
Service organizations	20–30	Render services to resolve or assist in solving certain problems; generally not membership based *Examples*: rehabilitation for people with disabilities; shelters for the homeless; telephone hotlines; NGO resource centers	Attract qualified employees and sometimes volunteers Attract varied sources of financing Exhibit organizational infrastructure	Financial situation tenuous Potential for government cooptation
Interest groups	20–30	Movements, clubs, interest groups, professional associations, and scientific unions and institutes	No information available	
Advocacy groups	8–10	Provide for the defense of disadvantaged groups in the population; combine work of service organizations and human rights by helping people obtain what the government has promised but neglected to give them *Example*: Committee of Soldier's Mothers	Developing ties with local government	Rarely receives support from government or local business Almost completely dependent on foreign aid
Nongrant-giving charitable foundations	8–10	No information available		
Grant-giving foundations	<1	No information available		

[a] Data from Paul Legendre, *The Non Profit Sector in Russia* (Moscow: Charities Aid Foundation, 1998); Maggie Christie, "Constraints on Russia's NGO Sector" (USAID/Russia, June 1996); Karen Greene, "Russian Women's Movements: An Overview" (USAID/Russia, June 1998).

is not a monolith; thus I distinguish among the various forms of civic activism by outlining the relative strengths and weaknesses for each segment of civil society. The common thread connecting the two tables is the predominant focus on charitable and economic security issues.

CONSTRAINTS ON CONTEMPORARY CIVIC DEVELOPMENT

Surviving the political transition from the Soviet regime is merely one of a long list of constraints on Russia's civic sphere. This section discusses the impediments to civic development, as identified by Russian civic activists as well as Western donors: legality, economic viability, relations with society and the state, and broader institutional infrastructure supportive of a third sector. By explaining the weaknesses of civic development, we can understand how the incentives of foreign aid structure organizations' behavior, as well as evaluate the fit between Russian civic needs and aid's development strategies.

Legal Framework

Although legislation in 1990, 1993, and 1995 carved out a space for independent activity, winning official state recognition still involved following a maze of regulations. A crucial task for the emerging civic sector was defining its public space and then ensuring that it could survive within it. An important step in this, even before finding forms of support, is establishing legality. One of the first hurdles nonprofit organizations faced in the new era of legalized independence was registering. Working through the bureaucratic red tape of registration was an impediment to many groups; however, it was a necessary ordeal if a nonprofit organization wanted to open up a bank account, achieve legal status and recognition, and be eligible for funding and grants from outside sources. In the first years following legislation, however, no single system for registration existed. Often, there was no set place to register an NGO, although individuals could make inquiries at three different bodies: the justice department (in republic capitals, main *oblast'* towns and *krai* centers), the registration chamber or its affiliate, and the local administration (in the main *raion* centers).[65] Often, initially, the cost of registering an NGO differed from region to region. Nonprofit organizations needed to bring a large assortment of documents to begin the long process of achieving legal status, ranging from charter meeting minutes to copies of passport information. Public associations, a subcategory of nonprofit organizations, also had a dizzying array of choices to make. They had to choose a legal form of organization (public organization, movement, foundation, institution, or self-help body) and a territorial title (international, all Russia, interregional, regional, or local).

Throughout much of the 1990s, many civic groups themselves were unsure of the rules; a murky legal framework further blurred the line between legality and improvisation. Also, there was no clear process to monitor or regulate the activities of nonprofit organizations. According to Russian federal law, all public organizations must submit an annual report to the Department of Justice; however, the department did not possess a legal basis for issuing penalties of any type to negligent NGOs or the personnel to enforce this obligation. As organizations have rapidly multiplied, the government has responded by passing new regulations on the nonprofit sector. The federal Ministry of Justice issued a decree requiring all NGOs to reregister before July 1, 1999, in the hopes of finding out how many registered public organizations had collapsed or been dissolved in the previous five years.[66] In a further attempt to get an accurate portrayal of the number and nature of these new organizations, the government mandated a new registration process that required NGOs to get final authorization, not from the Ministry of Justice, but from the tax authorities. Registration fees became standardized, costing about 2,000 rubles ($65) for registration. Despite fears that reregistration would result in the persecution of non-Putin supporters, often the largest bias has been against NGOs which are far from their *oblast'* city center. Registration documents must be turned in to regional administration offices, and for groups that live out in the recesses of the *oblast'*, this trek back and forth to the regional center severely complicates the process.

Economic Viability

Once a group cleared the hurdle of legal recognition, they were faced with day-to-day struggles for survival. There were relatively few sources of domestic financial support for organizations. Although the economic conditions facilitated the emergence of organizations, they simultaneously constrained their abilities to continue work. In interview after interview, civic groups bemoaned their precarious financial status, wondering if they would have the time or energy to continue their work into the next week, month, or year. Although there are no definitive statistics on the budgets of nonprofit organizations, in 1997 the income of the nonprofit sector was estimated at $350 million.[67] Seventy percent of groups had a yearly income between $500 and 10,000. Only approximately 10 percent of all organizations boasted an income of over $100,000 per year, and these groups subsisted almost entirely on foreign grants.[68]

My own research with women's organizations confirms this overall trend in the NGO community. When asked about their budget dynamics,

40 percent of groups reported having no budget. For many groups, their financial resources waxed and waned, depending on what meager scraps of support they could wrangle here and there. One group simply wrote "1991–1994 without money. 1995–1996 assistance from the *oblast* administration. 1997–1998 grant."[69] One activist commented, trying to revive the tradition of public defenders, "Our work is based on the charity of all, sometimes we get small grants. For seven years the organization has existed on my own contributions."[70]

Finding money to support an organization was a difficult task, especially in a country that lacked a middle class capable of supporting "checkbook" activism. One woman physician, when asked why she did not give to nonprofit organizations, summarized the attitude of many—because she has not received her salary in many months, every day her work is a type of charitable gift.[71] Just 2 percent of the income for Russian NGOs originated from private contributions in 1998; in contrast, individual donations provided 90 percent of U.S. charities' budgets.[72]

Civic groups, then, had to find alternative sources of support. The three most frequent donors to voluntary groups were Russian businesses, foreign foundations, and various levels of the Russian government (although usually the local administration).[73] Again, women's groups reflect this trend. Although volunteer labor was a key resource for 62 percent of groups, in terms of material support foreign actors (36 percent), local businesses (32 percent), and local administrations (22 percent) remain key components of groups' abilities to stay afloat.

The means of the support varied; foreign donors often gave money and were the sources of relatively large amounts in Russian standards. In contrast, governments often provided in-kind support, such as free office space, telephone lines, and franking privileges. Businesses donated money as well as office supplies. These sources of support tended to favor certain groups over others. Many in the civic sector complained that businesses often championed the arts and cultural causes.[74] In contrast, the state tended to support Soviet-era organizations such as groups uniting youth or the disabled,[75] and Western foundations aided grassroots, Western-style social movements that ran projects with a clear, explicit connection to initiatives that were perceived to contribute to the development of democracy in Russia.

Organizations' lack of resources was compounded by the fact that there were few incentives for other segments of the population to donate time or money to voluntary organizations. In particular, there were few financial incentives for businesses to donate to NGOs; banks and businesses could only claim 3–5 percent of their profits as tax-free charitable donations.[76] If a firm decided to make a donation of furniture or computer equipment, the firm as well as the nonprofit organization had to pay value-added tax on the donation. This further detered groups from building ties with the community and businesses at large. NGOs' financial status was not improved by the tax reforms of the Putin administration in 2000–2002. In terms of taxes, nonprofit organizations are treated as commercial companies. As a result, they are taxed on such income-generating activities as the value of the services they provide (even if they are free), as well as on certain types of grants that do not meet Russian regulations. People receiving a service from an NGO are also taxed on the value of the service. In addition, what few tax incentives existed for charitable donations were eradicated. Thus, the whole labyrinth of tax legislation that has facilitated the emergence of a nonprofit sector in countries such as the United States is completely lacking in Russia.

Financial trends for the third sector began to change as Russia's civic sphere entered its second decade of growth. As the NGO community achieved greater longevity, local governments and businesses began to acknowledge their presence and provide more substantial support. In cities such as Novosibirsk, local NGOs successfully encouraged local administrations to sponsor small grant competitions. Often for sums as little as 500 rubles (around $160) and ranging up to 50,000 rubles, these grants demonstrate that regional administrations are beginning to take NGOs more seriously. Business has also followed suit; by the fall of 2002, corporate philanthropy was a term being bandied about with great frequency in Moscow by NGOs and foreign donors, who hoped that a new trend was developing into patterns of habit. A few businesses, particularly those run by the oligarchs, have upped their financial commitment to charitable deeds, perhaps mimicking the behavior of other robber barons-turned-philanthropists. Mikhail Khordokovsky, the President of YUKOS Oil Company, set up a charity program that addresses the areas of social support to the population, public health, cultural education, and other themes. The budget in 2003 for YUKOS philanthropy is $45 million.[77] Vladimir Potanin, head of the holding company Interros, also heads his own foundation and focuses on issues of education and support for a variety of social projects.[78] Boris Berezovsky, the oligarch turned political exile, donated $3 million to the Andrei Sakharov Museum, and also pledged $25 million for the establishment of a nonprofit foundation aimed at promoting civil liberties in Russia.[79] The Gargarin family, descended from Prince Andrei Grigorievich Gagarin, has a foundation based in Petersburg and aimed primarily at groups in that city.[80] NGOs such as ECHO and Charities Aid Foundation Russia have worked to establish community foundations that encourage giving from local business and community leaders.

While these developments are significant, it is also important not to overestimate their importance. Much of the excitement over corporate giving fades when one reaches the regions, where many NGOs are still trying to receive small amounts of often one-time support from local businesses. Despite the buzz over corporate philanthropy, it is far from being part of overall business culture in Russia's nooks and crannies. In addition, many beneficiaries of Russian corporate culture tended to be cultural. For example, in 1998, of the fifty-three festivals of theater, music, dance, film, and opera in St. Petersburg, only three were fully financed by the city government; private corporations supported the rest. Potanin of Interros donated $1.4 million to support the reconstruction of the Rostral Columns, a popular historical landmark in St. Petersburg, the largest donation made by a Russian company or individual since 1917.[81]

Partially as a result of these economic factors, maintaining an organizational structure was difficult; groups tended to be small, insular, and usually survived on the commitment of the founder. The average staff size for most nonprofit groups was one to three people, although most employees had other jobs to support themselves. Almost one-third of all NGOs had no paid staff, while an additional one-fifth could afford to pay only one person.[82] Anna Pastukhova, director of the Memorial Human Rights Society in Ekaterinburg, noted "we are in desperate need of professional staff. . . . We have lots of dedicated volunteers and activists, but our work cannot survive on enthusiasts."[83] My data on women's groups reflect this overall NGO trend; only approximately one-third of groups had the resources for paid employees (32.4 percent). As a result, organizations often ran on the grim determination of a few committed citizens, often working in addition to their normal daily responsibilities.

Facilitating Governance

Theoretically, a key function of civil society within a democracy is its ability to act as an intermediary between state and citizen. The intermediary role of NGOs is an important element not only in bringing the needs of the population to the attention of the government, but in creating pressure for the redistribution of power to society and reform of government policy. NGOs serve as checks on state power as well as conveyers of private interests. They can challenge the state through direct lobbying in order to promote their cause, protest government decisions, and demand policy changes. Civic groups can also supplement political parties by offering alternative channels for public participation and representation of social interests. This is particularly important when political parties are unstable; civic groups may substitute for political parties in the short run and help create such parties in the long run.[84] How did civic groups perform their governance functions in the Russian context?

Civil Society–Society Relations

The civic sector remained poorly connected with the public; in turn, the public was slow to recognize civic groups as a channel for their demands. Activists were wary of the public as well as of the concept of volunteerism. Many groups did not distinguish between active and passive membership; rather, the members were volunteers, and groups remained small. Most organizations, as one civic trainer commented, exhibited a "strong resistance to broadening out." Instead, they wanted to make sure that the few members they had were absolutely loyal.[85] In a survey of nonprofit organizations, 40 percent of volunteers were members of the organization, another 30 percent had founded the organization, an additional 20 percent of volunteers were also clients, and only 3 percent of volunteers were people "off the street" who were interested in the work of the organization.[86] This is due, in part, to the financial difficulties many people were experiencing; few people could commit to a cause when surviving day-to-day crises occupied a majority of their time. Also, as a Moscow survey shows, most people tended to rely on personal networks of family and friends to distribute assistance, and if they gave, they gave to a needy person on the street rather than to a charity.[87]

An additional factor is the legacy of Soviet forms of association; after years of Soviet voluntarism imposed from above, many citizens were at best simply ambivalent about the benefits of voluntary association and at worst suspicious of the motivations of voluntary groups. Citizens who had once been linked to one another through their participation in Soviet-sponsored organizations chose to remove themselves from civic activism in the new democratic era. In a survey conducted in Omsk, Krasnodar, and Stauropol in 1995, 90 percent of those interviewed had participated in some form of public activity in the Soviet era. Since the collapse of socialism, however, many citizens had deserted their former organizations. This same survey revealed that only 4 percent belonged to a voluntary organization.[88] Other data, although not as bleak, still portray a grim portrait. A 1998 Social Capital survey found that 80–90 percent of Russians did not belong to any voluntary associations.[89] World Values Survey Data indicate that Russia's organizational membership is 0.65 organizations per person.

This rate of associationism is low, even for formerly communist countries, which, as a bloc, have the lowest rates of organization among democratizing countries, having a membership mean of 0.91 organizations per person, compared to 1.82 for formerly authoritarian countries (such as South Africa, Argentina, and the Philippines) and 2.39 for older democracies (including Japan, Australia, and Finland). In addition, Russia ranks poorly compared to its former satellite countries; only four of these countries trail behind Russia, with Bulgaria bringing up the rear with an average organizational membership mean of 0.35.[90] While all previously communist countries are struggling with redefining what it means to be active citizens, Russia trails behind most and is barely ahead of a few fragile formerly communist democracies.

More damaging, however, is the increasingly evident trend that citizens do not trust the idea of voluntary associations. A 1998 survey reports that only 4 percent of the 1,000 Russians surveyed trusted Russian charities, while 65 percent agreed with the statement that "charities are an artificial face for dirty tricks."[91] Alternatively, roughly one-half of those interviewed thought public organizations were organized to advance the political or secular priorities of their leadership. Although some of Russian society's distrust of civic organizations originated out of memories of enforced Soviet participation in "voluntary" activities, this distrust was magnified by a series of scandals in the early 1990s, in which the Mafia or other criminal operations formed nonprofit organizations as fronts to import and export alcohol, cigarettes, and so on. For example, during 1992–95 the National Foundation for Sports became the biggest importer of alcoholic beverages in Russia, providing for 80 percent of imports to Russia.[92] In addition, the financial pyramid MMM, which absconded with millions of people's savings, called these people's investments "charitable donations."[93] Businesses, as well, were wary of giving; one business leader commented that donations would "more likely help . . . somebody else to patch up the holes in their budget."[94]

A more benign explanation is that Russians know relatively little about the activities of the third sector in Russia—a May 2001 survey indicates that 55 percent of Russians said they had never heard the term "civil society."[95] Another Russian polling firm found that 74 percent of Russians could not name a single charity.[96] In a survey of the public in eight cities in central Russia, when asked, what is a "noncommercial organization?" many responded (1) "there is no such thing as a noncommercial organization today, only commercial organizations exist," (2) "it is a type of illegal activity," (3) "it is an organization established by people who wish to get or save money without paying taxes," or (4) "an organization created by people who have been given a special mission by God."[97] Perhaps it would be more accurate, however, to state that the public is not sure what to think of nonprofit organizations; in the same survey that measured people's trust in the nonprofit sector, rather confusingly, 75 percent of respondents totally or partially agreed that nonprofit organizations were doing helpful work. Voluntarism and philanthropy are difficult concepts to distill in a society where such acts were traditionally considered ways for the Western upper and middle classes to assuage their guilt and not necessary in a society in which class distinctions were supposedly eradicated. In addition, in a society in which few businesses turn a legal profit, it can be difficult to explain the difference between a nonprofit organization and one that is unable to turn a profit.

Civil Society–State Relations

Civil society is crucial because it serves as the mediator between society at large and the state. At times opponents, watchdogs, supplicants, and allies, groups have been in the process of reformulating their relationship with a government that, over a decade previously, would not acknowledge their presence. Although Russia possesses the institutional trappings of a democracy, its performance has been alternately lackluster, progressive, clientistic, corrupt, Westward-looking, and nationalistic. Going from the federal to the regional and municipal level, the variation in quantity and quality of good governance increases drastically. As a result, civic groups across Russia had extremely varied experiences with local, regional, and federal offices of authority.

A large challenge for civic groups was simply learning to interact with various state officials and to exercise pressure to advocate a particular cause. One Western civic trainer who spent several years working with local NGO activists on developing advocacy skills commented that initially "NGOs don't see they may have a role in the change themselves; they don't have the ability to see who has the power to do something, they don't know the right person to go to."[98] Learning this skill is difficult, and sometimes NGOs do not come up with the "right" answers that Westerners expect to hear. After working with groups in Nizhnii Novgorod, the civic trainer was nonplused over some NGOs' reasoning. "One idea the civic groups had was, because voters get upset that parties and candidates spend so much money on elections, that the parties and candidates should hide the funds they spend! Of course, the normal answer is that they should be open!" Alternatively, when brainstorming over ideas of holding elected officials accountable, another group had a different solution. "One group decided to propose a plan to hold office holders accountable for the promises they make. They proposed a bill to be passed. What constitutes a promise? When is it to be accomplished or fulfilled?"[99] Civic groups have had only about ten years to digest ideas about why they are theoretically important for democracy; as a result, many groups were still navigating what it meant to establish relationships with local governments, particularly ones that were corrupt, clientelistic, or inefficient.

Nonetheless, in ten years civic groups rapidly progressed through a steep learning curve. NGO efforts were much more successful in establishing working relations with government at the regional and municipal levels, although this varied tremendously from region to region and defies easy categorization. Whereas many NGOs tended to see the local administration as a potential source of financial support, often receiving office space or small amounts of operating funds, others negotiated with local administrations to provide social services to local populations. For example, in November 2000 the Volga Federal Administrative district conducted a $1 million grant competition for NGOs and municipal structures to promote innovative and effective social programming.[100] Municipal governments in Novosibirsk and Irkutsk also distributed budget money to NGOs on a competitive basis.[101] Although the budget amounts are small, they indicate that some local governments, in turn, acknowledged the benefits of working with NGOs.

These few success stories tend to be the exception rather than the rule, and many factors beyond NGOs' control shaped how they interacted with the state. As the number of local administrations that operated using corrupt, opaque, clientelistic methods proliferated, NGOs themselves were faced with the danger of cooptation. Alternatively, they understand that local authorities could seriously hinder their work should a confrontation arise and thus tried to maintain friendly, or at least civil, relations. Even in areas where satisfactory relations between NGOs and government existed, local government officials might be quick to understand the benefit of working with NGOs only at election time. In turn, local activists saw little value in linking their organizations' identities to the fate of political parties, often preferring to remain neutral during elections and advocating their cause with officials after elections occur.[102]

Accustomed to state indifference during the Yeltsin administration, state–civil society relations took a new turn when President Putin expressed an interest in bringing together NGOs for a nationwide conference. The hypothesized reasons for this are numerous; some charge that Putin was uncomfortable with the idea of a civil society supported externally by Western foundations and thus sought to find ways to foster a civil society more reliant on domestic sources of support.[103] Others think that he was in search of new channels of support for his continuing reforms and to increase political support for his presidency.[104] Still others perceived this as a further step in efforts to co-opt civil society and to silence opposition. Regardless of the reasons behind this move, Putin charged key members in the administration with identifying and developing contacts with key NGOs. Known as the Civic Forum, the conference brought together over 5,000 representatives from various NGO sectors from all over Russia in November 2001. In the space of two days, the Civic Forum held seventy round tables grouped under twenty-one topics of discussion, including the war in Chechnya, the rights of pensioners, prison and military reform, and the state's responsibility to nurture civil society.[105] This conference was the first time that government officials and NGO representatives from throughout Russia had met to discuss the development of civil society in Russia.

The reaction to these state-led efforts among the NGO community and other political figures was mixed. Some felt that the conference was expensive lip service to the concept of civil society. Gregory Yavlinsky, head of the Yabloko faction, noted, "If the authorities were willing to listen to the rights-protectors, they would have given them an hour of open air on a state TV network. However, they do not listen to the right-protectors, their reports are not read, their congresses are not attended, but they are invited to the Kremlin to a forum. Is this a dialogue?"[106] Discussing the tactics of the Putin administration in general, Alexei Yablokov, head of the independent Institute for Ecological Politics in Moscow, felt that "We are allowed to participate, and play our role, but we are never allowed to win. That is the hallmark of the Putin era."[107] Civic associations were politely tolerated, mainly because of their perceived lack of real political power.

Others put a more sinister spin on events and portrayed the Kremlin's efforts to meet with civic groups as part of a larger plan of coopting the organizations. The Civic Forum was just one more step in the Kremlin's overall plans to muzzle opposition, in addition to other activities, such as the takeover of NTV, Russia's only nationwide independent television station; this was just part of a larger policy to strengthen the state at the expense of democracy. Financier Boris Berezovsky, newly converted to democratic values, opined that "The kind of dialogue that the government tried to impose on society by convening the Civic Forum is absolutely unacceptable. Society must be in opposition to the government, not try to ingratiate itself with it."[108] A state-organized civil society, in this view, would be inherently contradictory.

The conservative right wing also weighed in, charging that civil society itself, as a Westernized concept, was inappropriate for Russia's Eurasian culture and was part of a larger problem with the Putin administration; too focused on pleasing Western powers, Putin was busy selling off

Russian power and prestige to remodel the country into something that it could not, and should not, reflect—Western values and ideas.[109] Vladimir Zhirinovsky weighed in, approving of the top-down rature of the conference, in that "In Russia, everything comes from above. Revolution comes from below."[110]

Groups out in the regions also tended to have their own views. In my own interviews with activists in the fall of 2002, many groups located far from Moscow, frustrated from working with intransigent local governments, felt gratitude at this federal-level acknowledgement of their importance. Many thought that this in turn would signal to local administrations to take NGOs more seriously. Others felt that the conference was an encouraging step forward for a federal government that had previously been weak, disorganized, or uninformed of civic sector activities. The danger, rather, lay in ensuring that a small number of NGOs did not assume control over a large and diverse body of civic organizations.[111]

Recognizing groups' apprehensions and fears of state cooptation, President Putin acknowledged in his opening speech that "there were fears that the state is out to establish control over civil society and make it controllable." He continued, "I think everyone understands—representatives of the government do too, believe me—that civil society cannot be established at the state's initiative, at the state's will, much less in accordance with the state's plans."[112] Although it remains to see if state verbal commitment to the idea of civil society lives up to its actions, this nonetheless marks a significant departure from former President Yeltsin, who devoted an entire section of his presidential address to the construction of civil society but in practice made no such overtures to the third sector.[113] The state once again made an important but, at this point, merely rhetorical commitment to the concept of civil society and followed through with a conference. Whether it was motivated by desires to coopt, control, work with, or simply learn more about the civic sector, the fact that the administration was willing to devote the resources and the time to organizing this conference indicates that civic groups were perceived to be a potentially influential voice.

Institutional Infrastructure

Civil society cannot exist in a vacuum; by definition, it is a creation and reflection of the society within which it is embedded. As one critic notes, "Present day Russian society is a quasi-civil society, in which structures and institutions, while having many of the formal attributes of the structures of civil society, perform the opposite functions."[114] Russia had the trappings of a market economy, the appearance of a democratic political infrastructure, a population that sometimes embraces the basic values

embodied in liberal democratic political theory. Under the Yeltsin administration, however, this development was a mixture of fiction and truth;
in reality, the economy was a shambles, the Yeltsin administration more
characterized as a kleptocracy than a rationalized bureaucracy, and the
population increasingly estranged and disconnected from its own political and economic institutions. The Putin administration has shown a
strong desire to clean things up, reestablish centralized authority, and
push through ambitious economic programs. What this will mean for civic
groups is unclear; will they be regarded as a force that can move Russia
forward or will they be victims of the larger drive to enforce tax legislation, political accountability, and obedience to Moscow directives? Despite
encouraging economic trends, the framework and structure, which facilitated the emergence of a civil society in the West, was still weak and
poorly established in the East.

The capitalist bourgeoisie was a significant factor behind the growth of
a civil society in the West; the potential of this same class for demanding
and maintaining a civil society has formed the basis of arguments that
promote the development of a civil society in the East and South.[115]
Russia's economic performance presented a mixed picture. One of the
hopes arising during the initial years of economic reform was that it would
produce a middle class; however, the larger economic indicators, after
noting the rollercoaster-like ups and downs of economic performance,
painted a picture of a steady decline.

GDP fell, year after year. Shock therapy, promised to last only a year,
was endured for a decade. Privatization turned into asset stripping and
was often facilitated by the state, which could not afford to pay pensions.
Foreign investment brought money in, but exported even more out.
A stabilized ruble, one of the few accomplishments to come out of the
years of reform, capsized in 1998, declining 45 percent from July 1998 to
January 1999. It seemed that a broader economic infrastructure supportive of civic society was not on the horizon.

On the other hand, prior to the economic crash in 1998, some estimates tentatively placed the middle class at 20–25 percent of the working
population. In addition, a fairly large proportion of the population
possessed the sociocultural attributes (high levels of education and professional qualifications) of a middle-class existence, if not the economic benefits.[116] Once again, in 2002, the economic prognosis for Russia
is looking rosier. The economy is growing, the ruble is stabilized, and
foreign investment is returning to the country. Economic stability is key
to providing a nurturing environment for civic groups, although it
remains to be seen if the growth of 2002 can be continued into long-term
macroeconomic stability.

Strong political institutions are also an important part of the broader context within which civic groups are embedded. The popular U.S. view of civic development is that civil society is often the antidote to strong states, when, in fact, strong states can be good for civil society. Coherent and clearly articulated political institutions can help organize and artic-ulate citizen interests, whereas a weak state can encourage citizens to opt out of political participation or to perceive civil society as an alternative to political society rather than as an avenue for participating in it.[117] Strong states are useful in other ways that are not antithetical to the devel-opment of democracy; strong states are able to design, implement, and enforce a hierarchy of laws and policies necessary for the smooth func-tioning of fledgling democracies. In this sense, efforts to strengthen state capacity and to channel and articulate citizen interests, whether through the development of civic organizations or through clearly articulated political parties, can represent a step forward from the legacies of the Yeltsin administration.

Once again, Russia stands at a crossroads. One of the defining legacies of the Yeltsin administration was weak political institutions. Political parties were numerous but poorly defined, short-lived, colloquial rather than broad-based, and not clearly linked with an articulated constituency. Power was attached to the person holding the office rather than to the office itself. And state capacity to implement and enforce much-needed legislation was limited. Despite fears that Putin's agenda is to centralize state power in ways reminiscent of the Soviet Union, an alternative inter-pretation is that these changes are also strengthening state institutions in ways that may have payoffs for the strengthening of civil society in the long term.

CONCLUSION

Given the troubled prospects for civic development in Russia, it is no surprise that Western governments, foundations, and nonprofit organizations identified areas in Russia's emerging civic sector that needed aid, material as well as moral. I do not argue that foreign aid sub-verts the development of an otherwise healthy, vibrant civil society in Russia. There are many domestic impediments to collective action. Civic activists face an uphill battle; they must fight against Soviet legacies, eco-nomic hardships, and their own inexperience in running viable inde-pendent civic organizations. Aid did not land in a utopia, nor were Western agencies starting from scratch; rather, they were imposing rules and institutions on a society that tended to distrust civic groups, a civic community that was inward looking and resource poor, and an environment marked by extreme uncertainty.

However, for many groups, the economic hardships provided the very incentives to act collectively. Because many groups assumed the duties of the retreating state, citizens who received assistance trusted them out of necessity; they were the only ones who could provide assistance to a part of the population in need. Can aid expand on these small initiatives and help provide material incentives for civic groups to act in ways that develop informal norms of trust and reciprocity, which are so necessary for making democracy work? Can Western strategies for civic development be imported into a country with radically different social and institutional legacies?

Chapter 3 describes the aims and aspirations of various foreign donors in their plans to foster civic development in Russia. But just as Russian civic development is defined by domestic impediments, so too is aid entangled in its own web of allegiances, institutional legacies, and structural design. The design of aid has a substantial impact on the direction and scope of its efforts in Russian reform.

Constructing Civil Society:
Foreign Aid and NGO Development

As Russian NGOs spent the 1990s struggling to develop a viable nonprofit sector, a panoply of Western donor organizations arrived in earnest to offer technical, monetary, and moral support. Major donors included government agencies of Western countries (primarily the United States, Germany, the United Kingdom, and Norway) as well as multilateral organizations (such as the European Union, the United Nations, and the World Bank). These efforts were supplemented by the work of a wide array of Western nongovernmental and non-profit organizations, ranging from large foundations (such as the Open Society Institute, the Ford Foundation, the MacArthur Foundation, and the Charles Stewart Mott Foundation) to international nonprofit organizations (such as the Eurasia Foundation IREX, World Learning, and the Institute for Sustainable Communities). A mélange of factors, including the end of the Cold War, the Third Wave of democratization, the rise of "people power" against authoritarian regimes, donor fatigue with traditional approaches to development, and a general wariness of the state as the locus of aid strategies led many organizations to reformulate their strategies to include NGOs as the carriers of substantial political, economic, and social benefits. This shift also expanded the parameters and mission of development strategies to include a broader goal beyond economic success—facilitating civil society and, eventually, democracy. In the Russian case, the 1998 economic collapse and subsequent fallout over economic aid strategies encouraged many donors to increase their rhetorical support of aid to civil society, as opposed to the state.

The task confronting donors working in Russia, as well as in other democratizing areas, was formidable. Conventional wisdom held that a country's genetic cultural code often had long-lasting implications for the relative health or weakness of its civil society.[1] Given the pull of what seemed to be intrinsic internal characteristics, how could civil society be promoted by external actors? In addition, how could donors take what they knew about the theoretical contributions of civil society to democratic stability and implement these concepts out in the field, often in placcs with vastly different histories from the primarily Western countries that had served as models of civic evolution? This raised a whole host of practical questions: What areas should be targeted to promote civil society? Who should be the focus of these programs—society at large? the middle class? civic organizations? If civic organizations, which ones? Once the donor has targeted an area of activity, what are the best strategies to foster the goal of civic development? How is "success" measured in efforts to facilitate civil society? This extensive list of questions demonstrates the difficulty of the task. Although economic development had a proven track record of effective strategies and disastrous projects, civic development was relatively unchartered territory. Mapping a strategy that could be used in multiple countries and varied contexts, let alone one country and one context, was more an experiment than a tested blueprint.

In addition to resolving these theoretical questions, donors faced enormous challenges specific to the Russian environment. Some donors maintained that Russian civil society had been held "hostage to a totalitarian regime," and worried about how historical trajectories would impact current civic practices and trends.[2] Other donors focused on current domestic constraints. The most immediate objective was simply to teach Russian civic activists the skills and tools needed to learn how to run an organization: formulating a mission, defining goals, targeting a constituency, identifying and organizing specific programs, and navigating the complex and new legal environment that governed the third sector.[3] Many groups did not have the money to buy paper, let alone the technology, such as computers, fax machines, and copiers, that could expand their impact. In addition, NGOs were inexperienced in functioning as a civil society within the parameters of a democracy and were poorly connected with local governments, other NGOs, and the public. Furthermore, donors were confronted with the challenge of teaching civic groups not only a new language, but also a new way of thinking and acting. Attempting to build an NGO sector alone was difficult, and facilitating the emergence of more esoteric concepts such as civil society and social capital in a decade was a Herculean task. Yet many donor agencies arrived with a plan in the hopes that supporting NGOs would foster the institutions of civic society and, for some donors, would eventually lead to the institutionalization of democratic culture and practices.

Western NGOs employed a variety of "solutions" to stimulate civic development and provided opportunities to civic groups that they, in their existing financial status, could not afford on their own. They supplied trainers and training on a variety of topics related to civic development and the nonprofit sector. They sent leaders of civic groups abroad for international conferences and trips related to their interest area. They financed the translation of the necessary books from English into Russian, paid for research, and supported the organization of domestic conferences for NGO activists. They funded basic infrastructure costs, such as office space, salaries for employees, computers, Xerox machines, and organizational newsletters. They created resource centers for NGOs in the regions in order to develop small magnets of information across areas larger than the continental United States. On a less tangible level, Western program officers scattered in offices across Russia provided moral support, encouragement, and advice to Russian civic leaders.

Intentions rarely result in perfect outcomes, however. Aid is never a neutral endeavor. The key to understanding the effect of aid lies in the convoluted trail of how aid happens:[4] Through whom does it flow and to whom does it go? Under what circumstances? And for which goals? The answers to these questions determine the nature of what recipients finally receive and how they respond to it. More important, however, the answers to the questions are factors that shape aid's ultimate success or failure.

In this chapter, I outline the goals, motivations, and strategies that donors have employed to foster civil society in Russia. I emphasize two aspects of civil society aid: the institutional design of aid and the structure within which donor organizations are embedded. How donors define civil society affects who receives aid. Highly influenced by neo-Toquevillian visions of social capital and civic development, donor agencies consciously directed money to advocacy groups that they felt could facilitate the larger processes of social and political transformation. This vision of civic development focuses almost solely on NGOs and singles out organizations that are considered to contribute to "good" civil society, often overlooking organizations that do not directly contribute to democratic political development.

Donors' own interests and needs further complicate this picture. In addition to reflecting altruistic impulses and facilitating democracy, civic development is also a business—a multimillion-dollar industry that employs numerous academics, consultants, and practitioners whose careers depend on supplying justifications and rationales for continued civic aid. Western NGOs involved in distributing civil society aid survive by providing advice, training, and support to organizations in democratizing countries such as Russia.

As a result, many donor NGOs working in Russia owed allegiances in two directions. Previous research has emphasized the issue of "multiple accountabilities," often focusing on the relationship between recipient NGOs and their Western donors.[5] Less attention has been paid to the fact that Western donor organizations, in turn, face two constituencies: the community they are supposed to serve abroad and the sources of their own funding. Consequently, agencies and organizations implementing projects in Russia were not free agents. Rather, they were the expression and facilitators of home-office interests, their own donor priorities, and the material engine behind Russian civic organizations. Donor organizations working in the field were divided between meeting Russian needs and pleasing home offices.

These divided allegiances had two major effects on the design and implementation of grant programs. First, Western donors working in Russia structured their programs to meet home-office priorities, requirements, and demands. Second, the incentives were for donors to design grants that emphasized satisfying short-term interests in the hopes that they would fulfill long-term goals; they needed to produce results, "success stories," in order to keep their toehold in, or even increase their influence with, the home office. Russian civil society had been profoundly shaped by its past legacies and current environment; aid to the civic sector was similarly shaped by donor priorities as well as by battles and disagreements that often reflected the need to ensure organizational survival.

FUNDING CIVIL SOCIETY

In chapter 1, I discuss the general shift toward funding civil society as a new development focus in the post–Cold War world, both as an end in itself and as part of a broader strategy aimed at promoting democracy in developing countries. This interest in NGOs and NGO development is not new; rather, NGOs have merely increasingly broadened their mission and purpose as donors adjusted their own development priorities and definitions. In the 1970s, many donors shifted their development strategies to emphasize priorities such as participatory development, community development, and local development and as a result granted increased funds to both international and local NGOs.[6] As a result, NGOs skyrocketed, both in their number and in their prominence in the field of development. The number of international NGOs increased by 25 percent in the 1990s and membership to these groups exploded; on the domestic level, grassroots organizations multiplied rapidly.[7] Lester Salamon, commenting on this explosion of NGOs and grassroots organizations, refers to this phenomena as an "associational revolution" at the global level that "may constitute as significant a social and political development of the latter twentieth century as the rise of the nation state was of the nineteenth century."[8] Although this prediction is somewhat hyperbolic, nonetheless in the world of development, NGOs became increasingly popular with Western governments and international agencies as a low-cost, high-impact method of effecting wide grassroots level change in less developed countries.[9]

Whereas NGO projects in the 1970s related to health, agriculture, and population, for example, in the 1990s the growing focus on civil society and democracy radically altered the way that donors viewed NGOs and their merits in fostering development. Previously viewed as important partners in alleviating poverty, NGOs were now perceived as agents of civic development and strengthening democratic institutions.

In turn, donors began to set up specific departments and programs aimed at promoting the development of civil society abroad, hired staff that was interested in civil society development, and began to focus in earnest on responding to the changing world of the 1990s.[10] USAID's newly created Democracy and Governance Program developed programmatic emphases on establishing the rule of law, encouraging good governance, strengthening political processes, and, last but not least, supporting civil society.[11] USAID staff designed an NGO sustainability index to gauge the strength and continued viability of civil society in Central and Eastern Europe and in Eurasia.[12] In a similar vein, the World Bank, which had increasingly championed NGOs as agents of development, in 1995 also adopted civil society language by renaming NGO liaison officers "civil society specialists."[13] In addition, the United Nation's Development Program (UNDP), which had always seen NGOs as crucial to strengthening self-reliance at the community level and as partners in development projects, also adopted the language of the "civil society" argument; in 1996, the UNDP, like the World Bank, also renamed its NGO Unit the Civil Society and Participation Unit as part of a resolution to increase the participation of civil society in the work of the UN. This shift in program priorities, although partially only symbolic, also signaled that donors were talking about development in new ways that put previously undervalued priorities, such as civil society, at the center of development initiatives.

Foundations also followed donor agencies in adopting the rhetoric of civil society. The Ford Foundation renamed its Governance and Public Policy Division the Governance and Civil Society Division and in 1998 sponsored a major international study of civil society in twenty-two countries, which focused on the role of civil society in processes of democratization.[14] Both the Open Society Institute (OSI) and the Charles Stewart Mott Foundation established civil society programs within their larger donor activities; OSI eventually expanded into more than fifty individual countries to promote "open societies" around the world. Other groups, such as CIVICUS, were formed with the express purpose of "strengthening citizen action and civil society throughout the world."[15] Civil society became the lens through which donors viewed development, and development expanded to include levels of democratic stability. In some ways, it became *de rigueur*.

This shift in the discourse to the relationship among democracy, development, and civil society was also enormously influenced by the social capital argument. That is, in explicitly citing the Putnam effect (more horizontal associationism breeds social capital, which in turn facilitates democratic performance), development agencies assumed that investments in both social capital and civil society were necessary to achieve democracy and, by implication, development.[16] The World Bank took the social capital argument to heart; in 1996 it launched a Social Capital Initiative and by 2002 was funding ten social capital projects in an effort to define and measure social capital, its evolution, and impact.[17]

The collapse of communism in Eastern Europe and the former Soviet Union, in addition to providing the impetus for donors to shift priorities, also opened up a whole new geographical area into which development specialists could expand. All these countries were going through transitions that were substantially different from ones that had come before; the economy and society had not been so much underdeveloped as "misdeveloped." Rebuilding, rather than simply adding to, previous economic, political, and social structures was a task that would require substantial financial commitment from donors, who often had little or no experience with the region prior to the 1990s. The development industry in Russia in the 1990s was rapidly expanding, with donors arriving daily in search of new opportunities, new challenges, and perhaps a small bit of fame and fortune. For those donor agencies involved in the increasingly popular mission of NGO development, Russia was the largest stop within the constellation of former socialist states. Organizations, such as IREX or Project Harmony, that had been active even during the days of the Soviet Union, running various cultural and academic exchange programs, were soon joined by innumerable government agencies, foundations, and nonprofit organizations that worked specifically on civil society issues.

MAJOR DONORS

The United States has a large presence in Russia, both as a facilitator of the larger process of economic reform and in terms of its commitment to funding democracy and governance initiatives.[18] In 1990, the U.S. Congress passed the Support for Eastern European Democracy (SEED) Act and, soon after, the Freedom Support Act for Russia and the ex-Soviet republics in order to facilitate the process of simultaneous economic and political transitions.[19] U.S. government agencies quickly established strategic goals for Russia: economic restructuring and growth, democratic transition, and social stabilization.[20] Slotted under the larger goal of democratic transition, civic programs were the vehicle through which to foster, in USAID language, "Increased Better-Informed Citizen's Participation in Political and Economic Decision Making."[21] By 1993, various agencies of the U.S. government had managed to fund several large multiyear projects designed to facilitate the construction of civil society in Russia.[22] Large, multimillion-dollar projects were doled out to some of the heavy hitters of the development industry, many of whom had no previous experience in Russia. U.S. government-funded organizations, such as World Learning and Save the Children, were two of the first arrivals in this brave new world of externally supported civic development. By the mid 1990s, the U.S. government was also the largest provider of civil society assistance and in 1995 accounted for 85 percent of all civil society assistance, sponsoring 335 out of 440 civil society projects.[23]

Although various U.S. government agencies, such as the State Department and the United States Information Agency (USIA), were involved in Russian NGO projects, the bulk of civic aid was channeled through USAID, which maintains a mission in Moscow. The USAID/ Russia mission spent over $92 million on civic initiatives and NGO sector support projects during 1992–98.[24] This aid was considered temporary rather than long term; USAID hoped to facilitate civic growth and then leave when that task was accomplished. Originally, USAID optimistically predicted that they could accomplish their civic building tasks by 1999; that date was revised to 2002. A new target date was later set for 2010 although as of fall 2002, USAID was no longer predicting an exit date. It is possible that USAID might never reach its strategic objective of "increased citizen participation," but it has tried to quantify its efforts by establishing the NGO sustainability index, which gauges the strength and continued viability of the region's NGO sectors. Analyzing seven dimensions of the NGO sector, the index scores recipient countries on a scale of 1–7, with 1 as the most positive score. In 2001, Russian civil society was rated 4.3, which placed it behind many countries in Eastern Europe, ahead of those in Central Asia, and still in need of further assistance before the Moscow office's work was done.[25]

USAID is rarely involved in distributing money directly to the Russian civic sector, although the USAID/Russia mission occasionally gives grants directly to Russian NGOs.[26] Rather, they direct money through Western quasi-governmental organizations, such as the Eurasia Foundation, to implement programs to foster civic and political development.[27] In addition, USAID contracts projects to a variety of U.S. NGOs and universities.[28] In 2001, its principal contractors, grantees, and agencies consisted of a mix of quasi-government agencies, such as the Eurasia Foundation, IRI, and NDI; major nonprofit organizations, such as the Institute of Soviet-American Relations (ISAR, currently Initiative for Social Action and Renewal in Eruasia), IREX, and World Learning; and Russian organizations such as the Sakharov Center and the Moscow Helsinki Group.[29] Given that many Western organizations are implementing USAID-funded programs, the agency casts a long shadow over Western initiatives in Russia.

Other governments also implement projects, either through their embassies or through their own development agencies. The British government, through the Department for International Development (DFID) and the Westminster Foundation for Democracy, funds projects to facilitate civil society, human rights, an independent media, trade unions, and women's groups, among other goals.[30] The Canadian International Development Agency (CIDA) targets civil society under its Good Governance portfolio. In addition, under the aegis of the Civil Society Fund, the Canadian Embassy in Russia grants up to $100,000 to organizations working on projects that encourage "the emergence of an effective civil society in Russia."[31] The Swiss government sponsors a program for the consolidation of civil society and promotion of human rights in the Russian Federation. The European Union (EU) has also been a major multilateral donor with an interest in civic initiatives. Through the Technical Assistance to the Commonwealth of Independent States (TACIS), the EU focuses on civil society through its Democracy Programme. Even the World Bank has arrived on the scene; in 2002 it began a small NGO development program in Russia. Although none of these programs matches the scope and effort of USAID efforts, they are among the larger government donors active in promoting civic development.

Private foundations, such as the Charities Aid Foundation, Charles Stewart Mott Foundation, Ford Foundation, and OSI are other crucial donors that are involved in civic initiatives. These foundations usually issue grants to Russian civic groups directly from their field offices.[32] Similar to USAID, they also grant money to Western nonprofits seeking to implement projects involving Russian NGOs. Again, the amount of money does not match USAID commitments, but it nonetheless makes a visible difference in the lives of many Russian NGOs. From 1993, when it opened an office in Moscow, to 2002, the Charities Aid Foundation Russia gave out over $6 million in grants.[33] From 1991 to 1998, the MacArthur Foundation approved over $17 million in grants to support initiatives in the former Soviet Union.[34] The Mott Foundation distributed nearly $12 million from 1994 to the first quarter of 2002.[35] In 2000 alone, George Soros's Open Society Institute—Russia gave more than $56 million to organizations in order to create an "open society"; over $4 million went to civil society projects, while the rest went to NGOs under a variety of programs, such as women's programs, youth programs, media, and so on.[36] Ford Foundation is also a significant player; from 1999 to the first part of 2002, the Moscow office of the foundation made more than $6 million in grants to Russian nonprofit organizations.[37] These private foundations, unlike government agencies such as USAID, are not constrained by congressional oversight and often have more long-term commitments to maintaining a presence in a particular country. They also can be more flexible with their grantmaking.

Another active force in the campaign to construct civil society are Western and international NGOs involved in civic development issues specific to Eastern Europe and the former Soviet Union, as well as to the developing world in general. These organizations often maintain a central office in their home country, in addition to supporting a network of field offices in their target countries. Organizations active in Russia, such as the Eurasia Foundation, IREX, Save the Children, Institute for Sustainable Communities, and many others receive large multimillion-dollar grants from government agencies and private foundations to administer grant competitions, workshops, and training to foster "citizen participation." Some of the larger programs have been implemented by the Eurasia Foundation,[38] IREX, World Learning, and Save the Children's Civic Initiatives Program (CIP).[39] As NGOs themselves, they are both the dispensers of aid and fellow supplicants, dependent on larger donors to sponsor their funding efforts.

GOALS

When justifying their activities in Russia, many organizations have consciously adopted the neo-Tocquevillian argument connecting democratic stability with the health of the domestic civic sector.[40] In this view, ordinary citizens are engaged in a wide variety of crosscutting forms of civic participation, working diligently to ensure that a reluctant government becomes responsive to its citizens. Adjectives such as "vibrant" and "flourishing" are attached to the term "civil society" to express that not only the presence but also the number and nature of civic organizations have a direct effect on political outcomes. CIVICUS refers to the need to facilitate the emergence of a "rich and diverse array of organizations," particularly in "areas where participatory democracy [and] freedom of association . . . are threatened."[41] The goal of the CIP is "to support the creation of a vibrant, diverse, self-sufficient nonprofit sector in order to facilitate the development of a strong civil society and a lasting culture of democracy in Russia."[42] Thus, the way in which individuals relate to one another and their society, and not the attitudes of political elites, for example, explains the degree to which democracy is successful.

While accepting the Tocquevillian rationale, donors have also narrowed their conceptions of what organizations make up civil society. Civil society is a broad term that is used loosely to refer to a whole host of organizations, ranging from women's groups, to PTA associations, to choirs, bird-watching associations, and bowling leagues. But when discussing civil society, donors have consciously singled out NGOs as the most visible symbol of the absence or presence of a civic community, even though NGOs do not represent the totality of civic organizations. Whereas NGOs had become increasingly popular in the 1960s and 1970s as a relatively inexpensive way to deliver development services to populations in need, the events of the late 1980s and early 1990s reframed donors' views of NGOs and their function so that they have become the embodiment of the Tocquevillian vision. For example, the USAID/Russia point person for civic development justifies the agency's civic program in the following way: "USAID/Russia believes that a vital civil society is essential for promoting democratic reform. Effective NGOs contribute to the development of civil society by helping citizens solve community and social problems; by lobbying government at all levels on behalf of citizens' rights and concerns; by promoting an awareness of those concerns among public decision-makers from the media, government and business; and by pressing for transparency in government and business practices."[43]

In other publications, USAID officials argue that "the hallmark of a free society is the ability of individuals to associate with like-minded individuals, express their views publicly, openly debate public policy, and petition the government. 'Civil society' is an increasingly accepted term which best describes the non-governmental, not-for-profit, independent nature of this segment of society. In countries with fragile democratic traditions, the freedoms so necessary to building and sustaining an active and independent civil society often are little understood, temporarily curtailed, or simply denied."[44]

Similarly, the Westminster Foundation for Democracy (established in March 1992 by the British government to provide assistance in building and strengthening pluralist democratic institutions overseas) also made a neo-Tocquevillian case for the need to focus on civil society. It maintains that: "The development of civil society enables wider citizen participation in influencing social, cultural and economic policy, an alternative to the ballot box as well as a means of involvement between elections. A strong and vibrant third sector provides the required foundation and framework for open democratic society. . . . Lack of civil society and democratic institutions can leave a country more vulnerable to the whim of whichever group may have climbed to the top of the power ladder." The foundation goes on to justify the focus on NGOs because:

> NGOs play a key role in creating civil society. Their focus on mobilizing resources, providing services, undertaking research and public education while also providing advocacy for membership organization and people's associations gives NGOs an unparalleled liaison role between civil society and government. Effective NGOs contribute to civil society development by pressing for transparency in government and business practices; by helping citizens become involved in solving local problems; by lobbying for the government on behalf of citizens and promoting awareness of these concerns locally, nationally and internationally.[45]

Other organizations echo this belief in the Tocquevillian connection between civil society and democracy and in the nonprofit sector as the symbol of civil society.[46]

Some organizations do not explicitly connect civil society to more open politics, although they focus primarily on NGOs and connect the importance of grassroots initiatives to larger socioeconomic developments. Mercy Corps International's civil society program aims to "demonstrate the importance of civil society in creating a more enabling environment . . . for sustainable development." Thus, the organization focuses on NGOs in order "to increase their level of participation in local decision making, promote accountability and transparency, and establish the opportunity for dialogue, consensus building, and peaceful change."[47] The Initiative for Social Action and Renewal in Eurasia (ISAR) "promotes citizen participation and development of the NGO sector in countries of the former Soviet Union in their efforts to create just and sustainable societies."[48] These donors share, however, an assumption that NGOs are synonymous with, rather than a part of, civil society. NGOs were thus invested with even greater responsibility than they were previously; in addition to being partners in development projects, they also in the 1990s became visible indicators of the presence of civil society and, as such, crucial components of a country's process of political development.

This donor focus on civil society has been further narrowed by the concentration on a certain slice of NGOs—advocacy NGOs, which are groups that represent some aspect of the public interest.[49] These are the groups that donors believe are able to perform the vital external functions of civil society, such as aggregating and conveying citizen demands to the state and holding the state accountable to the promises it makes to its population. Advocacy NGOs can potentially foster long-term change by pushing for needed legislation, increasing citizens' knowledge, and enriching the sometimes sparse world of political opposition in newly established democracies. As a result, funding tends to be directed toward groups that support human rights, the environment, women, and so forth because, donor agencies argue, these groups are able to articulate citizens' interests, increase citizen participation, and provide impetus for better government performance.[50] But this narrowed focus tends to overlook significant portions of civil society: social and socioeconomic organizations, such as churches and labor organizations; social and cultural clubs, such as sports clubs, nature clubs, and music societies; informal groups based on social identity, such as rural associations; and the large class of NGOs in Russia that try to provide social services, such as volunteer health clinics, charitable societies, and so on.

In developing target areas within civil society, donor agencies have chosen to focus on NGOs that they think can foster long-term change. This has tended to favor Western-style social movements that advocate human rights, gender equality, and environmentalism and organizations that are devoted to fostering greater NGO development—organizations not representative of the predominant focus of overall civic trends in Russia. This focus has helped to marginalize the majority of the sector which cannot easily fit into this "democracy framework."

METHODS

Donors do not simply distribute aid to needy organizations in need of a helping hand; rather, aid is carefully diced, spliced, and divided into a variety of topical programs that in some way are related to civil society. Programs under USAID, TACIS, the Eurasia Foundation, the Mott Foundation and the Soros Foundation, for example, have specific civil society programs and give grants to NGOs that work specifically on building civil society. Grants might fund, for example, the creation of an NGO resource center to strengthen the abilities of NGOs to exchange information and network with one another, or sponsor seminars for NGOs on anti-corruption projects or transparent budget processes.

However, NGOs also receive technical assistance from a variety of other programs that are not explicitly civil society initiatives. Each donor has a unique division of labor within its own organization and runs programs that can affect NGOs without being part of a designated civil society portfolio. Often, donors focus on particular sectors of civil society or a particular issue; thus, they often target movements, such as environmental organizations, human rights groups, or women's organizations. Organizations such as ISAR often work with environmental groups, whereas the Ford Foundation has a program for human rights advocacy and the OSI has a Gender program that targets women's groups (although it also has a specific Civil Society Program, as well). For many of the donor organizations, NGOs can receive funding through a varied palette of portfolios, and groups with a specific issue focus can qualify for a grant under either programs designed specifically to foster civil society or programs tailored for their specific movement. Thus, NGOs in Russia are targeted by a wide array of development programs, some that fund them for specific civil society projects and some that fund them as part of another, related goal (e.g., fostering environmental awareness or preventing ethnic conflict).

Finally, donors also support initiatives to foster the development of other institutional supports that facilitate civil society, such as programs that promote the rule of law by sponsoring judicial training programs to encourage the growth of a cadre of impartial judges. The Soros Foundation sponsors a project that awards small loans to start up independent presses in the hopes of facilitating the emergence of an independent media in Russia.[51] In 2002, the Eurasia Foundation launched a large program with YUKOS Oil, in the hopes of sparking indigenous funding sources.[52] CAF-Russia has been working to encourage corporate philanthropy. This chapter discusses aid activities of the first two types: projects that are part of a specific portfolio designated toward the creation of a civil society and projects that are aimed at NGOs to further a thematic issue, such as human rights, the environment, or women's rights.

Despite the variations in the rubrics under which civic groups are funded, the greater commonality is that donors ultimately decide programmatic emphases and recipients respond to them. Even though donors try to address local needs, nonetheless, civil society development is primarily what Marina Ottaway has referred to as "supply driven."[53] Russian NGOs do not receive financial assistance merely because they are deserving; rather, they must also fit their activities within larger programmatic priorities set by donors.

STRATEGIES

Donor agencies active in Russia had to design and implement programs that could replicate the extensive, drawn-out evolutionary process of civil society building in just a few years. A donor's list of Russian NGO needs in the 1990s often included: establishing a legal framework and helping NGOs learn and navigate the new system of rules, helping NGOs achieve economic viability, teaching them organizational know how, fostering NGO–community relations, teaching them to network with other NGOs, developing NGO ties to the state, and developing a broader infrastructure to support the NGO sector. In focusing on these various tasks, Western organizations tended to use four strategies to foster civic development: providing technical assistance, funding partnerships, distributing small grants, and supporting resource centers.

Technical Assistance

One of the first tasks that donors tackled was teaching fledgling NGO activists the skills needed to run a nonprofit organization. Although many Russian activists were enthusiastic, even charismatic, they had relatively little (and usually no) experience running an independent, nonstate organization. Most groups were unaware of the complex legal terrain of registration. Words that were second nature for NGO leaders in the West were unknown in Russia. "Fund-raising," "mission statement," "strategic planning," and "coalition building" were all foreign concepts. Broader concepts such as "civil society" were even less understood; the term had not been necessary just three years previously. After 1992, Western NGOs, such as Counterpart International (as part of Save the Children's CIP), World Learning, IREX, NDI, and IRI offered a dizzying array of seminars, training, and workshops on a variety of themes. Charities Aid Foundation Russia still maintains an NGO School, which provides seminars covering a wide range of subjects.[54] As Russian NGOs gained experience, many of them launched their own training seminars.

Strategic planning, management and organization, restructuring, social marketing, outreach, volunteer recruitment, and fund-raising were all popular themes for various workshops for Russian NGOs in the early years of development (1992–96).[55] In later years, donors focused on long-term strategies, such as developing advocacy skills, learning to work with local government, developing a constituency, and coalition building. This training was extensive; Save the Children's CIP alone estimates that it held 1,200 training events on NGO management, social marketing, and computer skills, as well as providing more than 2,000 individual consultations to NGOs.[56] As part of the training process, Western NGOs distributed material to Russian NGOs on legal issues related to NGOs, taxation and accounting, working with local government, public relations handbooks, directories of NGOs, and examples of model legislation.[57]

At first, many of the trainers were flown in from Western countries for short visits. Groups, such as NDI or IRI, that had a Moscow office sent their mainly U.S. staff around the country, developing workshops for NGOs. Lasting for as little as a few hours or extending into a long weekend, these workshops often had only hours to try and distill a lifetime's worth of teaching. At first, there was little Russian material available. Large chunks of U.S. nonprofit lore was translated into Russian and handed to activists, despite the large differences in the two countries' political evolution. As I mention in my preface, Jerry Brown and Mario Cuomo, prominent U.S. politicians, made their literary debuts in scores of concrete meeting halls. Publications on fund-raising by the U.S. interest group Emily's List also made the transatlantic trip.

However, by 1995, donor organizations were making some efforts to indigenize their efforts. Johns Hopkins University launched a Train the Trainers program. This grant focused on training the leaders of the Russian NGO community, in the hopes that these leaders, in turn, would train more Russian activists. Unfortunately, however, this consisted of flying Russian activists over to Baltimore for six weeks, which also required fluency in English. Finally, donors began to support NGO resource centers (discussed later), partially with the idea that leading Russian NGOs could take over the training that Western donors had initiated.

Partnerships

Particularly in the early years of foreign involvement (1992–96), aid was often directed toward large-scale partnership programs between U.S. and Russian nonprofit organizations. The justification behind this was similar to the idea of training, but this time organizations would learn by doing. The purpose of such a strategy was to allow Russian NGOs to pair up with a much wealthier Western counterpart in order to learn valuable skills from their more knowledgeable partner about running an NGO. USAID funded programs such as World Learning's NGO Sector Support Program (NGOSS), CIP, the Institutional Parterships Program (IPP), Sustaining Partnerships into the Next Century (SPAN), and Partnerships, Networking, Empowering, and Roll-Out Program (PartNER) were designed to pass on skills from experienced Western NGOs to their less knowledgable counterparts in Russia. Reflecting on her experience as deputy director of the World Learning Program Margot Mininni explained that:

> Partners acted as sounding boards for ideas and strategies and provided legitimacy and prestige to struggling groups. . . . Western partners played a useful role in prodding groups to devote time to organizational development, since

local groups were often so overwhelmed delivering services that they were reluctant to spend time thinking about how to improve their organizational infrastructure. The concepts of clear financial management, long-range strategic planning and comprehensive fund-raising strategies were even harder for local groups to master, and partners proved to be essential consultants. In other cases, the most valuable role of the partner was simply being there as the young organization navigated the new environment.[58]

In addition to these large-scale, federally funded projects, partnerships flourished on a more informal level through a variety of grassroots programs throughout the world. U.S. projects, such as the sister-city model, facilitated the exchange of thousands of individuals. Local chapters of the Rotary Club, the League of Women Voters, and other civic groups often sponsored cultural exchange trips. Less institutionalized and usually less expensive than government-funded partnerships, these smaller projects, when successful and sustained, often allowed groups to develop relatively close relationships that endured through the decade.

Small Grants Programs

NGOs, however, could not live off of advice alone. A large focus of aid efforts were through the distribution of grants that were given directly to Russian NGOs to implement particular projects or programs. Ranging from sums of money as small as a few hundred dollars for a one-time project, such as sponsorship of a domestic conference or the publication of research, to more long-term institutional support consisting of several hundred thousand dollars, direct funding often provided organizational basics, such as computers, fax machines, and photocopiers. They covered salaries, travel money, and other staff-related costs. For many organizations, this source of aid was their lifeline; it was often the one source of relatively reliable financial support that could guarantee organizational survival for at least the duration of the grant. The Eurasia Foundation, ISAR, the Soros Foundation, the Ford Foundation, the MacArthur Foundation, and the OSI were all involved in distributing this type of assistance.

Small grants were rarely awarded outside the parameters of an open grant competition organized along a particular theme. NGOs could qualify for a large number of grants, but only if they fit their mission within the confines of the grant priorities. IREX provided financial assistance to women's organizations, but only to those who submitted successful applications under one of three programs: support of crisis centers for women, promoting the empowerment of women in order to combat trafficking in women, and support of organizations launching antitrafficking campaigns.[59] The Eurasia Foundation provided small grants to

NGOs but within certain themes, for example, to fight corruption. Whereas the ISAR Moscow office funded mostly environmental organizations, the ISAR Far East office (until 2002) concentrated on NGO development, focussing on women, youth, or citizen's rights.[60] Although organizations such as the Eurasia Foundation had other programs that gave them wider lattitude in the themes under which certain NGOs can qualify—for example, an NGO could receive a grant if they wrote a good proposal that explained how their work would advance NGO development—nonetheless these donors set the funding theme and the Russian NGOs responded to it.

Donors were flexible in shifting program emphases. Their programs were not static, and they made efforts to respond to changes within the NGO community. Thus, as donors got to know the NGO environment better in Russia, some shifted funding priorities toward organizations that provided social services, in addition to funding priorities for such Western issues as gender, the environment, and human rights.[61] As the following section discusses, one of the most popular grant projects among donors in the late 1990s has been the effort to support resource center projects.

NGO Resouce Centers

Finally, donors focused their efforts on NGO resource centers. The genesis of this funding trend grew out of earlier partnership programs, such as the World Learning Program and CIP, which were started in 1992–94. Building on the experiences of working with a select group of NGOs in the regions outside the urban centers, donors began to promote the idea of funding resource centers in earnest in 1998, when the Eurasia Foundation funded twenty-five organizations across Russia.[62] Resource centers became popular as donor agencies sought to further indigenize the development process by "going local" and spreading their money beyond the larger cities to the regions. Resource centers were conceived as a further step in guaranteeing the long-term sustainability of the Russian NGO sector. Donors supported regional organizations that served as hubs of information sharing with local NGOs, many of which were small, poorly connected to one another, and badly in need of advice and assistance. Resource centers also quickly became the local providers of NGO training, continuing to provide seminars to other NGOs in the region on such topics as working with local government, fund-raising, accounting, and even grant writing.[63] Many also housed NGO resource libraries for local NGOs, in case they wanted to find out about legislation, other NGO activity, or grant opportunities. Often, as one of the few NGOs with a fax, photocopier, scanner, and computer, resource centers were also a source of technology for poorly informed local NGOs. These centers were diverse in size and mission, ranging from large organizations of full-service centers that reached out to and enabled the work of satellite centers across wide geographic areas to strong, issue-oriented NGOs that provided a few basic resources to other NGOs in the local community. NGO resource centers, ideally, will continue to offer seminars to other NGOs on management training, act as innovators, and catalyze the development of local NGO associations. The Eurasia Foundation, the Ford Foundation, the Soros Foundation, Save the Children, and World Learning all financed resource center projects, and in 2001 IREX signed a contract with USAID to implement the project Promoting and Strengthening Russian NGO Development (Pro-NGO). This work continues USAID's commitment to funding resource centers for another three years, and assists NGO resource centers in Siberia, southern Russia, and the Volga regions.[64] In an effort to turn over more decisionmaking to these NGO hubs, resource centers are now allowed to make small grants to NGOs in the surrounding areas.

NEW TRENDS

As civic development has changed in Russia, so have donor priorities and demands. In the early years of funding, the programs tended to be top heavy in favor of spending to support the Western staff, and startup costs were substantial. Foundations and projects that had a field office in Russia spent a significant amount of their budget supporting their office, employing a mixed Western and Russian staff, and flying in experts from the home office for trips out to the field. This employed U.S. staff both abroad in the Russian office and at home in the U.S. office. For example, IREX's SPAN project, which gave grants to foster twenty-five partnerships between Russian and American NGOs, employed ten staff people to manage it; six people were working on the project in the IREX Moscow office while four people were needed back at the Washington, D.C., office.[65]

The costs of bringing over a Western nonprofit organization and paying Western workers a comparable salary drained a substantial amount of money from budgets meant to target third-sector growth. Western nonprofit organizations paid Russian employees approximately $1,000 a month in metropolitan areas such as Moscow, but an American working abroad cost from $25,000 on up. In addition, Americans who did not speak Russian required the hiring of English-speaking Russians to translate. Furthermore, grants had to be submitted both in Russian and in English for the home office. In the beginning, this was seen as a necessary sacrifice.

These practices in the first half of the 1990s, when many large scale civic projects were getting off the ground, mimicked, to a lesser degree, the practices of larger, more expensive economic development projects—substantial salaries, hefty overhead, and fly-in consultants with little or no experience of Russia. The CIP, a consortium led by Save the Children, but also including Johns Hopkins University, Counterpart, and others, won a $30 million contract on September 30, 1994 to facilitate NGO development in Russia. Five months into the project (and a year after originally bidding on it), the four foreign representatives in Moscow were still working out of the luxury Aerostar Hotel, perfecting the program design. None of the consortium representatives spoke Russian, and they budgeted nearly $10 million dollars of the project to go to consultants in management fees and general administration costs.[66] Johns Hopkins University, which ran a training program (Train the Trainers) as part of CIP, flew English-speaking Russian activists to Baltimore for six weeks for civic training, also in English.

The reduction of USAID's Russia budget, as well as accumulated experiences in the region, led to some changes. Although budgets tended to be top heavy in the early years, organizations later made efforts to further localize their efforts by hiring more Russian staff. In addition, they avoided or scaled down large partnership programs that kept the predominant chunk of the budget in Western hands. In hiring Western program officers to staff the field offices across Russia, the donor agencies stressed hiring Russian speakers with a knowledge of and experience with the Russian NGO sector. Donors further indigenized their programs by posting Russian-version websites for their organizations. Donors such as the Eurasia Foundation provided online manuals written in Russian distilling advice on writing successful grants, and providing contact information for donors that work on NGO development in Russia.[67] As discussed previously, funders focused on spreading grants by courting civic groups in the regions, as opposed to supporting groups based solely in Moscow or St. Petersburg, and worked on more traditional issues that provide social services to needy or underprivileged clientele.

Recognizing that many NGOs had become almost completely financially dependent on Western aid, donors turned their attention to encouraging groups to find alternative sources of domestic support for when Western aid moves on to another cause, another country. Fostering domestic philanthropy became a targeted area for donors. For example, the Eurasia Foundation signed a cooperative agreement with YUKOS Oil to encourage small business support and community development in Russia. The Charities Aid Foundation Russia started a program to foster local philanthropy in Russia and began a program to encourage help from Russians who were living abroad.[68] In addition, donors took a few initial steps to broaden their view of civic participation by expanding their focus beyond NGOs, and a few concentrated on grant programs to foster voluntarism and citizen participation outside organizational membership.

THE CHAIN OF ACCOUNTABILITY

Despite efforts to try and keep up with the quickly changing environment of NGO development in Russia, donor NGOs that work in Russia are not free agents. They themselves are often intermediaries, implementing projects or grants that they have applied for and won or have been allotted. As a result, they have to report to a home office back in the West. This is particularly true for Western nonprofit organizations implementing USAID projects (see figure 3.1). They are embedded in a "wedding cake" structure of accountability and must report to at least two, and sometimes three, higher sources of funding. For example, a Western NGO working in the field on a USAID project is accountable to the USAID/Russia mission as well as to its own home office. The USAID/Russia mission and the home office of the implementing NGO are, in turn, accountable to the USAID/Washington, D.C., office. The Washington, D.C., office is, in turn, accountable to Congress. Although the chain of accountability for field offices of private foundations is less convoluted, nonetheless they too are subject to pressures of accountability to the home office (see figure 3.2).

Accountability manifests itself in a variety of ways. One of the largest issues is money—Western intermediary NGOs are responsible for multimillion-dollar budgets. As a result, their attention is divided between meeting Russian needs and responding to home-office concerns. Donor organizations spend numerous hours writing up reports, justifying decisions, and explaining rationales to a home office thousands of miles away, to a program officer who only rarely makes spot visits to Russia and often has little knowledge of the challenges that the field office faces in implementing its programs. But because the home offices supply the money, many decisions made by the field offices have to be cleared with and documented by the home office.[69]

Complicating this chain of command is the enormous amount of competition among Western nonprofit organizations to receive grants from a foundation or to implement contracts from an agency of the U.S. government. The business of aid is a crowded field; although it disburses large sums of money, the demand to implement such projects is always higher than supply. On the one hand, these Western groups are donors providing assistance to Russian NGOs; on the other hand, they themselves are always searching for new funding sources. Thus, groups such as the Institute for Sustainable Communities and IREX, both of which imple-

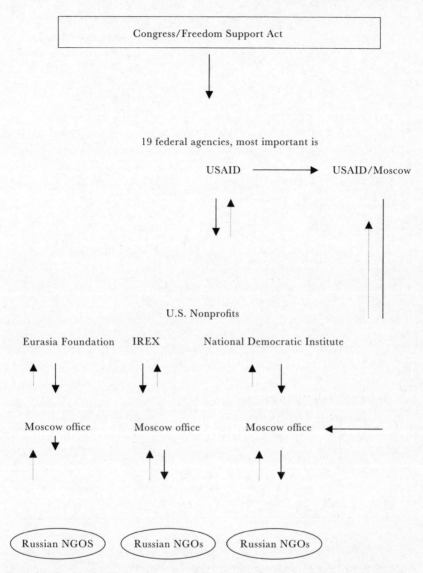

Figure 3.1 Tracing the Chain of Accountability for U.S. Government–Funded Projects.

ment USAID projects, are potential competitors, bidding against one another on tendered projects. Civic aid is an industry that supports thousands of organizations around the world, competing for relatively small pots of money.

Thus, like any other business, Western donors need to demonstrate past successes in order to ensure future projects. Unlike businesses, however,

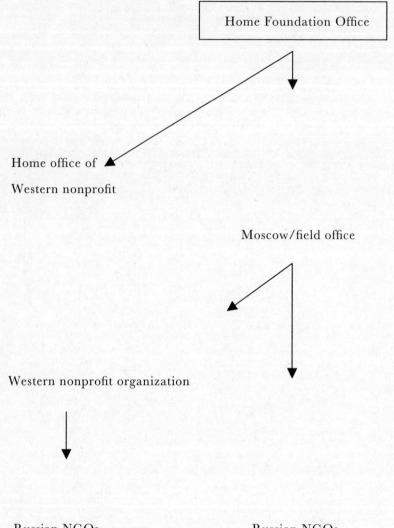

Figure 3.2 Tracing the Chain of Accountability for Foundations.

the success of development agencies is not measured by profit but through other, less obvious management techniques. Measuring success- ful civic projects is a difficult task: how can an organization demonstrate that it has furthered civil society in Russia? Often, donors rely on provid- ing anecdotal "success stories" that highlight a particular organization's activities, which have resulted in some notable achievement. Alternatively, donors collect numerical data on a program's activities as a method of measuring impact. This, in turn, puts pressure on the field office to deliver the goods to the home office in order to increase the home office's credibility and competitiveness for future funding. Thus, they rely on Russian NGOs recipients to supply a steady stream of numbers—the number of newsletters distributed, journals published, people serviced, and so on. "Results" are often quantified, and are rarely framed or presented in terms of the overall impact of the project. It is a confusing chain of command in which Western nonprofit organizations working in Russia, which are seemingly autonomous, are nonetheless caught in a web of accountability. Long-term goals of fostering civic development can become sidetracked by the need to constantly write up reports, find quickly gathered, measurable data in order to provide a snapshot of impact, and find ways to demonstrate that the work is valuable, necessary, and deserving of future funding. Even timely spending matters; as one person pointed out, "shoveling money out on time sometimes becomes as important as spending it wisely."[70]

DONOR PRIORITIES

Donors have to learn how to speak to multiple audiences, only one of which is the Russian NGOs. For many funding agencies, the U.S. taxpayer (or stockholder, for private foundations) is often the real constituent, not the average Russian citizen. Much of aid to Russia, if government funded, revolves around the justification of U.S. efforts to Congress and, less directly, to the U.S. citizen. As a result, many funding efforts designed to bring about civic development in Russia must also reflect U.S. interests and concerns in order to receive approval from an increasingly conservative Congress. A belligerent Congress and the looming apathy of the U.S. taxpayer have an indirect, although extremely crucial impact on defining to whom, how, and why aid gets distributed to the civic sector.[71]

As the decade of the 1990s progressed, Congressional attention began to wander elsewhere. Despite all the rhetorical support for free market reforms, democracy, and civil society, USAID/Russia was protecting a steadily shrinking budget since the peak funding years of the early 1990s. Lisa Petter, the official charged with overseeing the civil society/participation portfolio for Russia, likened the experience to "going from a loaf of bread to a muffin."[72] As a result, USAID/Russia, as well as other implementing agencies, spent much of their time ensuring that they could produce "results" to document and send back to Congress to, at worst, protect their shrinking budgets, and, if lucky, win an increase for the next year's budget. As Petter succinctly stated, "people in DC say we're an inch deep and a mile wide." Because of this suspicion, "we [USAID] have to watch the money."[73] Their reputation is constantly at stake. That someone else is ultimately providing the financial support for the programs fundamentally shapes the ways in which donors working in the field must design these programs.

Thus the need to ensure continued funding often affects priorities out in the field. In a memo from the Washington NDI to regional offices, Thomas O. Melia, the Vice President for Programs, cautioned NDI personnel first and foremost on their interrelations with USAID because "NDI's work is these days about 80 to 85 percent financed by grants or cooperative agreements from USAID." He reasoned, "It is important for NDI to work well with AID not only because it provides money to us, but because how well they do, and how well they approach their work . . . inevitably affects our own work. This is why it is important for us to maintain, to the maximum extent possible, cordial and productive working relations with the U.S. Government officials . . . even when we may have a differing analysis or priorities." The memo concluded with suggestions to local staff on how to work collegially with the local USAID mission.[74]

This need to take into account donor priorities influences where funding goes, who gets funded, and how those funding decisions are made. Aid to Russia's civic sector does not go to the most needy areas; rather, there are cities that have been designated important funding locations. Organizations receiving USAID money to carry out work in the civic sector are pressured to focus grant making on various cities because they are perceived as friendly to U.S. investment, and, as one program officer complained, "so they [USAID] can justify increased funding to Congress."[75] Similarly, the NDI and the IRI work in an array of USAID-approved target regions that are perceived as friendly to U.S. interests.[76] On the one hand, it makes sense to focus money on areas that are experiencing increased economic development; higher levels of development might be accompanied by other factors that can support civic groups in the long run, such as a middle class or a greater interest in corporate philanthropy. On the other hand, many regions in Russia are overlooked because they have no (or few) patrons in the United States. One activist who had spent quite some time working with Mongolian NGOs complained about the situation: "No one will give money to Mongolia because no one in the States is there to represent their interests to USAID."[77]

This desire to please the home office often means that the home office plays a big role in influencing programs proposed by the field offices. One program officer for IREX, commented on their Moscow office mandate: "it's written by DC [the home office] and you don't mess with that."[78] Particularly for USAID projects, the need to justify continued money from Congress affects which topics are addressed in Russia. For example, certain areas in need of aid are ignored for fear of raising controversy in Congress. One program officer complained that "basically USAID won't touch anything to do with gays or birth control. Once I wanted to do a program with juvenile delinquents but even that was deemed too controversial."[79] Similarly, when NDI wanted to do a civic advocacy training with the Committee of Soldiers' Mothers, the Washington office, according to the program officer in charge of the training, "got very nervous about the Committee. They thought they were too controversial."[80]

Sometimes, the home office of a development NGO is willing to step on the field office's toes to avoid offending the primary donor. When the IREX/Moscow office began implementing two partnership programs (IPP and SPAN), they became entangled in bitter infighting with their own home office as well as with the USAID/Russia mission. All the decisions for grant making for the IPP project were made back at the U.S. office, despite the existence of the Moscow office with a Russian-speaking staff. For the SPAN project, the IREX/Moscow office was allowed to pick the grant recipients; however, USAID/Russia then rejected all of their choices. John Snydal, a program officer at IREX, complained, "then they [USAID] added two bad projects because they were already well connected with USAID!" USAID then faxed all of the information to interns back in Washington, who then read all of the information that the IREX/Moscow office had already covered and faxed back questions. Reflecting on his time with IREX, Snydal felt that "bad decisions were made on the part of the home office and a lot of money was wasted." But, IREX mistakes never came out into the light, he felt, because "the Washington office is willing to sweep things under the rug because of the fear of damaging their own relationship with USAID and future funding." Reflecting on the issue of accountability, he asked, "[w]here does responsibility rest? In the end, IREX is always blaming USAID, USAID always blames the State Department and Congress, and so it goes."[81]

EMPHASIZING SHORT-TERM RESULTS

Because donors are rarely free agents, they spend a lot of time reporting on their activities to their home office. For example, of the twenty-one Western NGOs implementing USAID funded projects in Russia in 1998, over 50 percent had to write monthly reports back to the USAID office; another 25 percent wrote quarterly reports detailing their various activities, successes, and progress. In a survey distributed by USAID/Moscow to their implementing agencies, 25 percent of the respondents reported that USAID micromanaged their activities.[82] Accountability is time consuming and pulls these organizations away from serving their Russian NGO constituents. In addition, implementers often have so many projects going simultaneously, that even routine reporting turns into larger paper traffic jams.

It also creates enormous pressure on field offices to focus on the product created from the money. As a result, analyses tend to focus on numbers, which are easy to measure and count. As organizations active in Moscow work to ensure their own increased funding, they focus on projects that can produce quantitative results; this, unfortunately, does not often encourage donors to focus on measuring qualitative impact.

Thus, donors often stress fulfilling short-term goals and emphasizing projects that can produce numbers for the reports to the home office, rather than long-term civic development. Snydal discussed the proliferation of similar grant projects that could produce numbers for the home office: "After a while, every project starts to look the same—there are seven components of a 'successful' grant—seminar, round table, publications, newsletter, training, conference, database."[83] These are all exceedingly fundable projects because they produce concrete results and reach a specified audience (150 people trained, 500 journals published, 50 documents collected). This ensures, at least on paper, that links are being forged—people show up to conferences; they send their newsletters to physical entities. In addition, this allows donors to count that, as a result of foreign assistance, five hundred Russian NGOs have received assistance, which in turn has an outreach impact of 5,000 Russians, providing usable data for their own report back to the home office.

Donors working in Russia are caught in the middle; they are both patrons and supplicants, altruists and entrepreneurs. These opposing pressures in turn impact what gets funded, who receives help, and how that aid is delivered. There is constant pressure to find a magic bullet; donors out in the field attempt to provide that bullet by conjuring up "success stories" and statistics for the home office. Donors are constantly assessing their performance and sponsoring independent evaluations of their work, but evaluations often focus on whether the grantee met the requirements of the project, not on the impact of the work funded.

CONCLUSION

The collapse of communism created a resurgence of interest in the concept of civil society and its connection to democracy. This renewed interest was not only manifested in the scores of books, articles, and papers within academia; civil society became a new funding mantra for donors interested in expanding traditional development programs in new ways. Yet the task of fostering civic development was untested waters for many, and the challenge of designing and implementing programs to replicate a complicated, extended process of historical development using externally funded shortcuts is still in the experimental phase. Many donors did reach consensus, however, on funding NGOs and focusing on providing training, partnership programs, small grants, and support to resource centers as vehicles to greater civic development. Donors are still in the process of assessing which crucial mix of aid strategies produces the intended results.

This task is further complicated by donors' own needs and priorities. Aid is not a crude reflection of Western imperatives and interests; however, aid is filtered through a large number of Western players who have their own agendas and interests that they try to secure and balance along with Russian needs. As a result, donors often have to please two groups that might not have compatible goals. Although field offices have a wide degree of latitude in serving Russian needs, ultimately they owe allegiance, and accountability, to their own home office. Granting millions of dollars in aid to Russian NGOs, they are the conveyers of economic assistance. Yet, as agencies working under the approval of a home office, they must also constantly rejustify their continued relevance. Although their mission statement may entail bringing democracy to Russia and the countries of Eastern Europe, legitimating that mission is the task that ensures their continued funding, either from the home office in the United States or alternatively from USAID and, ultimately, Congress.

Donors working in Russia are also caught in a web of allegiances, alliances, and relationships that shape their own decisions about grant making and grant giving. The elaborate process needed to convert Western altruistic impulses into an impact on a Russian civic group is complicated and convoluted, involving multiple transactions and agreements that reflect Western desires to "do the right thing," self-interested funding motivations, and Western perceptions of what the Russian civic community needs.

The next two chapters present a case study of foreign aid and the women's movement. This allows a closer look at the behavior of foreign donors, as well as the behavior of Westernized and non-Westernized Russian NGOs, and allows us to further unravel the strands of the relationship between foreign aid and domestic civic development.

Women's Organizations and Foreign Aid

Given the hurdles facing Russian civic groups and donors' efforts to alleviate them, what has aid been able to foster in its short time in Russia? How and to what degree does foreign assistance affect civic development? What does aid "purchase"? Do groups that have received foreign aid behave differently than groups that are shut off from contact with Western and international donor agencies? Is aid able to ensure organizational survival, encourage a set of goals and activities, or inculcate patterns of cooperation and mutual assistance? As discussed in chapter 3, aid provided an influx of technical expertise, financial assistance, and moral support to emerging civic organizations.

The women's movement is a fitting case study for exploring the larger impact of foreign aid. Donors, in their efforts to foster civil society, often focus their aid sectorally, on specific types of NGOs. Sectors such as the human rights movement, the environmental movement, and the women's movement were all initially targeted as important islands of activism within the larger sea of NGOs. For example, USAID has targeted women's groups as part of their Women and Development program, as well as through their focus on funding crisis centers for women to combat domestic violence.[1] Through further funding from the U.S. Government, IREX runs the Regional Empowerment Initiative for Women program, which addresses the issue of trafficking of women.[2] Other Western countries have echoed this focus on women's issues. The Canadian International Development Agency (CIDA) has a separate gender equality portfolio in their Russia program. The Westminster Foundation for Democracy (funded by the British government) also has a program devoted to women and women's political participation.

Private foundations have also added a gender focus to their programs targeting NGOs. In 1997, the Open Society Institute (OSI) created a Women's Program to work on the issues of violence against women, women's human rights and participation in public life, women and education, Romani women, and women and health.[3] In fact, the OSI is one of the strongest supporters of women's NGOs in Russia; in my own research, out of 186 women's organizations, thirty received support from the OSI. Throughout the 1990s, the Ford Foundation sponsored a variety of projects in Russia aimed at facilitating the emergence of a women's movement in Russia; twenty-two groups in my survey reported that they had received a grant from the foundation. In addition to being targeted by programs under the rubric of gender, women's groups qualified for grants outside of specific gender portfolios; many received grants for civil society projects. For example, the Eurasia Foundation had no specific gender program, but twenty-six organizations competed for and won grants to implement programs with an alternative programmatic emphasis. Although the OSI, the Ford Foundation, and the Eurasia Foundation were some of the most frequently cited sources of external support, women's groups also received aid from other private foundations,[4] Western governments,[5] and smaller nonprofit organizations.[6]

Funding of women's NGOs has been due, in part, to the desire to bolster women's sagging status in Russian society in the wake of serious economic hardships brought about by the transition to democracy. Women were often the first fired and last hired in the initial years of economic dislocation, and they often lacked significant political representation of their interests. Western donors also justify their programs as an effort to foster Western-style gender equality, not only in Russia but also as a programmatic emphasis in the developing world in general. For example, the Westminster Foundation explains that women are often "denied the opportunity to have their voices heard, or to fulfill their potential"; this, in turn, affects the quality of "true democracy."[7] USAID explains its commitment in the following way: "in many countries, women's voices are still not as powerful as men's. . . . However, civil society offers a very powerful means of overcoming constraints and promoting women's comparable collaboration in political and economic decision making."[8] In this view, increased levels of gender equality are an integral process of democratization overall. Finally, women tend to be much more active in the NGO sphere than in the realm of institutional politics, and thus civic development is heavily organized and run by women.[9] The idea that empowering women empowers civil society has become a persuasive argument for many donors.

In this chapter and the next, I zero in on aid efforts to assist women's NGOs and untangle their effects on this one targeted aspect of civil society assistance. This chapter presents findings from quantitative survey data collected from almost two hundred women's organizations. I compare organizations that have received aid (which I refer to as "funded" organizations) with those that have not ("unfunded" organizations). Funded groups are those organizations that received monetary assistance in the form of a grant from a Western or international agency.[10] Unfunded groups did not. Unfunded groups might, however, have received financial support from solely Russian (domestic) sources, such as local businesses and local government. In comparison to Western-supported groups, their domestic base of financial support was more tenuous, even negligible, and often came in nonmonetary forms.

I compare and contrast groups using three factors: economic viability, organizational capacity, and the frequency and nature of activities that engaged the population, other groups within civil society, and the state. These are all important areas to develop for civil society to perform its internal function of social capital building and external functions of public watchdog and interest aggregator.

I found that aid was not merely a small drop in the bucket for women's groups; almost one-half (49.5 percent) of the women's groups I surveyed had received aid from a Western source.[11] In fact, this number is quite high in comparison with support to the third sector overall. Although the nature and frequency of aid varied tremendously from group to group, nonetheless, this figure was astounding. Imagine if one-half of all the women's groups in the United States received aid from an outside country—doubtless the women's movement would look profoundly different given this external influence. If this money is changing the landscape of women's activism, then it is crucial we understand how this shapes women's activism, as well as the NGO sector as a whole.

I also found that donors' impact primarily was in improving groups' capacities and short-term financial viability. In other words, funding was instrumental in providing the physical and human capital necessary for civil society. Due to the scarcity of domestic sources of income, this produced substantial differences between organizations with and without access to Western funds. Also, funding facilitated increased networking between women' s groups and with other NGOs; however, it had little impact in affecting how groups interacted with their populations and with the state. Furthermore, aid went predominantly to a nonrepresentative segment of women's groups.

In this chapter, I first present a snapshot of women's activism. Next, I discuss the results of my survey research, drawing on the quantitative tallies as well as the commentary and letters that accompanied the survey answers. Focusing on three aspects of women's groups—viability, capacity, and governance—I trace the emerging divide between women's groups. I conclude with a discussion of the significance of my findings.

WOMEN'S GROUPS AS PART OF THE NGO SECTOR

There are many excellent books that deal solely with the experiences of Soviet women[12] or with the emergence of the contemporary women's movement;[13] this is not one of them. Nevertheless, it is important to understand how women's organizations fit into the overall emergence of civil society in the post-Soviet era. The women's movement, like many other groups in the NGO sector, is a conglomeration of old and new; the movement is a mixture of leaders groomed in Soviet styles of activism and independent groups that formed in the 1990s. As late as 1985, there was only one official women's organization in an empire spanning eleven time zones and encompassing a land mass two and half times the size of the continental United States—the Soviet Women's Committee, which in turn was bolstered by local women's councils, or *zhensovety*. Women's interests were theoretically represented in a variety of committees within the state structure at the local, regional, and national levels as well as within the workplace. Their networks were substantial; in 1989, this monolithic structure encompassed about 230,000 *zhensovety*, representing over 2 million members.[14] However, despite their large numbers, the Soviet Women's Committee and networks of *zhensovety* were notable more for their rhetorical flourishes than their actual substantive activities; as was the case for many Soviet-sanctioned organizations, women's interests and issues were located within parameters defined by the Soviet state.

Covert groups not sanctioned by the state were limited to a small collection of self-proclaimed feminists who met in secret in Leningrad in fall 1979, as well as some consciousness-raising groups in the cities of Moscow and Petersburg. The most well-known result of these efforts was the publication of ten samizdat copies of "Woman and Russia: Almanach." The journal discussed such taboo topics as the conditions of working women, women's complaints about everyday life, discussions of women, birth, and the family, and even an article on drug addicts and women in prison. The results of this endeavor were quickly suppressed; after months of interrogation and intimidation by the KGB, four of the ringleaders were finally sent into exile.[15] Other small groups, such as "Preobrazheniye," the League for Emancipation of Social Stereotypes (LOTUS), and the Free Association of Feminist Organization (SAFO) avoided outright state harassment and were also active in the late 1980s, primarily as discussion groups made up of a few friends and colleagues.[16]

The experiences of independent women's groups mirrored the activities of the burgeoning realm of informals in the initial years of reform. They received a substantial boost in the wake of Gorbachev's reforms in the late 1980s as well as from initial legislation clearing an autonomous space for independent organizations in 1990. In the initial years of reform, groups formed slowly. Between 1985, when Gorbachev rose to power, and 1990, the year of legalization, organizational dynamism peaked in 1988 when eight organizations, or 4 percent of respondents, emerged from the upsurge of grassroots activity. The year 1990 was significant for women's organizations; in the previous year, six organizations had formed, but the following year this number jumped to twenty-eight, representing over 15 percent of respondents. Organizations continued to emerge at a slower, but steady clip in the following three years, followed by a wave of increased organization in 1994 and 1995, when twenty-six and thirty new organizations mushroomed out of the civic landscape. One potential explanation is that this pattern is a reaction to legislation passed in 1990, 1993, and 1995, giving NGOs legal status. Another is that increased funding opportunities from abroad provided the stimulus for organization.

The first large-scale attempt at legally organizing women's efforts outside of the Soviet Women's Committees culminated in two crucial conferences in the early 1990s. The First Independent Women's Forum, held in 1991, was the first such conference in Russia since 1908. One hundred seventy-two women from forty-eight organizations and twenty-five cities gathered under the banner "Democracy without Women Is No Democracy." Despite KGB attempts to disrupt the conference with charges of lesbianism, the conference managed to bring together a large association of women activists across all spheres and social orientations. The Second Independent Women's Forum, "Problems and Strategies," was held in 1992 and brought together women from all over the Newly Independent States as well as from Western countries such as Finland, Germany, Great Britain, and the United States. Although some of the groups represented took their inspiration from Western-style feminism, a glance at the program also reveals that conference participants were varied, united more in their biological gender than a particular ideological point of view. Some of the groups, such as the Association of Farmers of Russia, District Women's Councils, or Union of Women of Russia, were networks established during Soviet days, whereas others, such the Center for Gender Studies, were relatively new, westernized, and increasingly connected with colleagues in the West. The conferences were significant in that they signaled the emergence of a small fledgling women's movement, diverse, eclectic, and geographically scattered.[17] They were also significant in that the second conference attracted some early seeds of financial support from the West.[18]

In the ensuing years, alternative organizations to those defined by the Soviet era mushroomed; however, as with other NGO sectors, it would be a mistake to designate all of this organization as entirely new. Soviet-era women's organizations still formed a substantial bulk of women's organizations in Russia and maintained an extensive network of contacts that carried over from Soviet days. Thirty-seven percent of the survey respondents stated that they were the product of an older organization, suggesting that they could have reorganized after the fall of communism, turning old *zhensovety* into viable independent women's organizations. Stimula, in Dubna (a small town outside of Moscow), was once the Women's Council of the United Institute of Nuclear Research. The Independent Women's Democratic Initiative (NeZHDI), an independent organization in Voronezh, also used to be the Women's Council of that town, as did the Women of the Don, in Novocherkassk. In addition, many activists learned their organizational skills as participants within this Soviet system and used their skills in meeting the avalanche of problems that faced not only women but also the Russian population as a whole during the ensuing years of political, economic, and social transition.

To speak of a "women's movement" in Russia is to refer to a very large, diverse array of organizations that are led by women and that in some way address the challenges that women face in an era in which their economic and political positions are rapidly readjusting, often, initially, in a downward spiral. In the realm of economics, women were a higher proportion of the unemployed. Particularly in the initial years of economic dislocation and privatization, women over the age of forty-five, women with small children, and women of childbearing age who did not have children were at greatest risk for unemployment.[19] In the political sphere, women's quotas in representative bodies were abolished and women's representation subsequently plummeted in the following elections, from a Soviet high of 33 percent to 10.2 percent in 1997 and 7.7 percent in 1999.[20] Although this setback was offset by the emergence of a political party, Women of Russia, which managed to clear the 5 percent electoral hurdle in the 1995 elections, as with many parties during the 1990s, it ultimately fragmented and lost its political clout in ensuing elections. Socially, services that impact women, such as preschool, day care, and health care, shriveled in the face of state penury and spiraling costs.

Women responded to these challenges in a variety of ways, and an aerial view of women's organizations reveals a thematic division of labor among five types of organizations: (1) charitable and self-help groups that deal with the ramifications of economic dislocation; (2) professional associations, which often help women navigate the new economy; (3) human rights organizations, such as the network of groups known as Committee of Soldiers' Mothers; (4) an emerging network of crisis centers; and (5) a small contingency that identifies with a Western-style feminist movement. Thus, when I refer to the "women's movement," I am referring to an array of organizations grouped under a large tent. Often, women's groups advocate not only women's issues but also issues that are perceived to be important to women, as well as providing services to the population at large. The sections that follow flesh out this brief sketch and present the varied voices of activism within this very broad definition of women's activism.

Charitable, Self-Help, and Professional Groups

Reflecting broader NGO trends, the bulk of women's groups had a pragmatic objective—to survive and to step in and provide services that the state could no longer secure for its population in this period of severe dislocation. Although women's groups spanned a wide array of issues, it is estimated that two-thirds of women's groups were involved in issues of "social rights."[21] Comments drawn from my surveys reflect this; groups related their experiences, which revealed feelings of desperation, dedication, and concern for their fellow citizens, many of whom are reeling from the previous decade of upheaval. Often, activists portrayed themselves as valiantly trying to apply a metaphorical band-aid to a serious wound. More severe medicine was needed, yet their efforts were the only available solutions to address the problem. As with other segments of the NGO sector, although legislation opened up opportunities for women's mobilization, this was also hastened by the worsening political, social, and economic conditions brought on by the transition.

Women's groups organized to provide care for women whose economic position had become increasingly vulnerable in the face of cutbacks, both professionally and in terms of social services. For example, groups such as Woman and Family attempted to "raise the level of self-sufficiency of women" in response to state cutbacks of funding for maternity wards and clinics.[22] Another group counted as their members women "whose welfare has significantly worsened" regardless of profession.[23] One woman who protected the interests of pensioners noted that "in Tver *oblast'*, 26.9 percent of the population are pensioners, and in those numbers the predominate majority are women."[24] A woman from the Penza region wrote, "Our women are most beautiful, smart, independent. That's why it's hard for them to combat adversities that have been arising since job cuts, or since other issues have arisen. We are trying to help them survive in life that has become so hard."[25]

Finding solutions to ameliorate these seemingly insurmountable problems could be difficult, particularly with limited resources. Help ranged from emotional support to charitable donations. An activist from a regional Women's Council wrote, "We are just helping women to survive in our hard times."[26] Despite a lack of financial resources, members served as moral and emotional support for one another in meetings and get-togethers. Employment retraining was a common focus; another organization, Karat-4, was involved in education of unemployed women, with further employment support, mostly for knitters.[27] One group, when writing of their purpose, simply put, "adaptation to the new economic conditions."[28] Women activists repeatedly referred back to the economic dislocation of the previous ten years; often, they viewed their mission as one of support in overcoming the hurdles of looming unemployment and occupational irrelevancy.

Thus, professional organizations, such as those that unite women from common professions, such as law, business, journalism, and so forth, often served as vehicles to improve the economic situation of women in the 1990s. Often, these groups provided support to one another or provided training for their members in the hopes of improving their career chances for the future. Most frequently, organizations of this type were those that were designed to bring together businesswomen. These groups were often active in providing workshops, seminars, and support to women trying to establish a toehold in the new economy. Another active branch consisted of groups that brought together women involved in the sciences. For example, a regional chapter of the Association of Women in Science and Education provided professional support for women trying to navigate their changing and often declining position in their professions. The group Aviatrissa is a Club for Women Aviators that pushed for equal rights for women applying to aviation colleges.[29] Often, many of the networks were old Soviet-era organizations that continued to revamp themselves to keep up with the changing economic and political context.

Organizations also mobilized in response to rapidly disappearing and nonexistent social services. For example, the group Sudarenya provided free consulting and attorney services for low-income citizens.[30] This trend is also visible from perusing the list of groups that responded to my survey; it is populated with associations of single mothers, mothers of large families, disabled women, and mothers of disabled children.

Often, women's groups mobilized over the decline in social services on behalf of the population at large by drawing on their roles as mothers and caretakers. Commenting on women's activism, one respondent wrote: "You are struck by the steadfastness and optimism of our women of various ages and nationalities, ready to unselfishly help one another, taking on their shoulders worries about friends, aged parents, and often unemployed men."[31] Another woman wrote:

> I am the mother of five children. For eight years I have raised them alone. . . . once, sitting in the kitchen with my friends, we talked [about] a lot of our problems. The children are growing up and need not only clothes and shoes; we need to think about what awaits them tomorrow. They are closing up businesses where the main work force is women. A family without a father and an unemployed mother is a disaster. Many men cannot deal with this and the children end up alone. Orphanages and children's homes are growing like mushrooms. We decided to found a new organization based on our beliefs, where the primary tasks and goals are the defense of children and under protected families. . . . we were not alone.[32]

The founder of the organization Grandma's Care Association echoed these motivations in her own story. She wrote, "I founded this organization in summer, while having vacation with my grandson. We started with a real project—a school for grandchildren, which functioned . . . for 2.5 months and will be open again next summer. It is important—and at the same time possible—to bring up children in the spirit of nonviolence, secure for themselves and others."[33]

Women's groups were active on a wide array of social issues, and the themes that resonated for them, judging from their own comments, were ones that impact women but are not solely focused around women, although they all draw strongly on their identity as women to explain the reasons behind that activism.

Human Rights and Crisis Centers

The network of groups that make up the Committees of Soldiers' Mothers drew most explicitly on this symbol of women to address larger societal issues, particularly human rights issues. The Mothers, as they are known throughout Russia, were involved in the struggle to reform (or potentially end) the practice of military conscription, as well as to bring an end to the continuing war in Chechnya. Thus, wrote one group, "Our women's organization is concerned especially with men's problems which worry women/mothers. . . . the basis of our work has lain in the egotistical mother instinct—the protection of our sons."[34] Another activist had originally organized on behalf of women, but broadened her mandate upon witnessing the horrors of war. She wrote:

I founded this organization with the goal of helping women who have fallen on hard times. . . . these are the goals and tasks I set forth when I created this organization, but everything has turned out the opposite. On May 16th, 1992, the organization was founded and on the 14th of August the Georgia-Abkhazia war started. Women of Chechnya, Kabarda, and Cherkassia decided to go by bus to Abkhazia to the city of Gudauta, and I, as a public-spirited woman, went with them and saw the horrors of war and the suffering of simple, normal people. Since then . . . I travel back and forth bringing humanitarian aid.[35]

All of this activism over human rights arose, not out of an esoteric concern for the condition of humanity, but as a direct reaction to the chaotic events encompassing everyday, average citizens. A group from the Committee of Soldiers' Mothers movement in the regions explained, "Every month there are twenty to thirty coffins brought to the city and the region." As a result, her organization had formed to "stop the conveyor of youth deaths in the army," by focusing on protection for soldiers who had left their army units, as well as draftees.[36] Another Soldiers' Mothers Committee member explained her activism: "Our Soldiers' Mothers Committee was created spontaneously, when our sons were sent to the battlegrounds of Chechnya."[37]

A further area of activism, which became increasingly perceived as a human rights issue by donors as well as by some domestic organizations, was violence against women and violence in the family. Women organized a widening network of crisis centers, which worked on a variety of family issues, from sexual assault to domestic violence to familial neglect. One crisis center formed in Petersburg because "There is the biggest number of communal flats in St. Petersburg, where several families live in limited space. Single women living in such apartments turn out to be the least protected."[38] On the initiative of the Russian Association No to Violence, crisis centers organized into a network that linked them across Russia. Support from various foundations enabled them to meet periodically to exchange experiences and share lessons learned. Since 1998, USAID made violence against women, as well as trafficking in women, into a funding priority.

Feminist and Gender Research Organizations

Finally, there was a small collection of explicitly feminist groups. This was truly a small collection; a directory of 447 women's organization in Russia lists thirteen groups that described themselves as having a feminist orientation.[39] Primarily located in larger metropolitan areas, such as Moscow or St. Petersburg, these organizations often existed in the form of quasi-research institutes rather than as constituent-based groups (the concept of constituent-based groups, in general, does not really exist in Russia). Because of the lack of broad grassroots support, these groups were particularly dependent on Western donors to support their work. Although feminism and feminist thought had a venerable tradition in Russia, the task of promoting greater opportunities and better outcomes for women in a climate of overall economic and political instability for much of the population was extremely difficult. In addition, activists were unable to formulate a homegrown theory of gender, a conundrum made more severe by the problem that Soviet views lost credibility but new models did not develop.[40] Similar to other social movements, this wing of the women's movement subsisted almost entirely on the support of the West, in the hopes that external support would eventually translate into internal acceptance.

THE IMPACT OF WESTERN ASSISTANCE

Viability

As in the larger NGO community, economic conditions were, paradoxically, both the facilitator of and the impediment to activism among women's groups. The dominant mantra emerging from all the surveys, regardless of whether the groups had received Western aid, was that the economic conditions were the catalyst to organize and the reason why that activism remained sporadic in nature. This struggle to combat the losses incurred by economic dislocation was complicated by organizations' constant search for resources.

Overall, all groups relied on a diverse array of resources to keep their organizations running. The number one source of support for women's groups was volunteer labor; 62 percent of groups relied on this to survive. In terms of financial resources, sources from abroad played the largest role in supporting organizations; 36 percent of groups had received grants from foreign foundation, 18 percent from foreign governments, and 17 percent from foreign NGOs. Support from businesses was also crucial; 32 percent of groups relied on donations, financial support or support in kind. Finally, various levels of government were important sources; 22 percent of groups relied on grants or subsidies from local government, and 10 percent of groups received assistance from regional administrations. For example, one group in Tatarstan was able to coax the republic government into granting it 7,000 rubles for the publication of its journal.[41]

Sources of support, such as membership fees, which have become mainstays for NGOs in the West, were neither a reliable nor a substantial source of domestic support. Although almost one-fifth of both funded and unfunded groups relied on membership fees, these were often more symbolic rather than real; they were a substantial source of income for only 12 groups out of 186 (7 percent). Explained one group who relied mainly on Western aid, "fees are insignificant because of the level of life here in Russia."[42] Several other groups, particularly branches of Soldiers' Mothers Committees charged fees, but stipulated that payment was voluntary.[43] Given that domestic sources of money were few and far between, groups had to be creative in their strategies to stay alive. In fact, one group admitted to a novel fund-raising technique in which, as the leader bluntly wrote, "I solicit wealthy people and organizations."[44] Although the numbers indicate that organizations relied on a varied supply of resources, the comments indicate that these sources, although critical, were nonetheless minimal.

As a result, it is not surprising that, without the assistance of foreign aid, over one-half (52 percent) of unfunded groups had no budget and more than one-fourth of unfunded groups reported that their budget was currently smaller than 3–5 years previously. One leader noted that things were fine with her group, except for "one hard problem—survival," a sentiment echoed by many other leaders throughout the survey.[45] One woman wrote from the town of Kamyshin, "You cannot imagine how hard it is to work far from districts and headquarters, and here are so many problems we never imagined, so much work. . . . except for a miserly room and a telephone, we have nothing. . . . we have our own [bank] account, but all the enterprises of our city are standing still. . . . people are surviving thanks to their *dachas*."[46] An activist from Mezhdurechinsk, the site of miners' strikes in the Gorbachev era, wrote, "Only the chairperson works now because it is not possible for members of the committee to work unpaid. There is no money to buy paper or envelopes. . . . I am refused office space, and communicate with my home phone. I have no resources in general."[47] Another unfunded group described their situation: "We do not even have a typewriter. . . . we approach the *oblast'* administration and they say there is no money. We approach other organizations to print and do Xerox copies. Two years ago we received two thousand envelopes from the first deputy of the federal postal administration from the city of Voronezh."[48]

These comments portray a realm in which activists are able to eke out an existence through their own enterprising creativity, but in which many of these sources of support are barely enough to keep these organizations operative. Domestically, sources of support tended to be in nonmonetary forms. Groups often relied on local administrations for reduced rent, phones, or office space; businesses often gave donations, such as office supplies; and individuals often provided free labor. This was particularly true for unfunded organizations. Although they might sometimes receive small amounts of money here and there from local administrations or businesses, many survived on the work of a few dedicated members or worked on the leader's personal savings.[49] It was also common for administrations to give no support, and leaders continued to struggle on despite the nearly continuous hurdles in their daily existence. As one woman active in a human rights organization in the Kostroma region explained, "Administration of the city . . . does not cover any of our expenses, such as travel expenses, per diem, phone bills, cost of envelopes, post cards, etc. We cover everything ourselves, and it has now become not feasible. We have been working at my personal apartment since 1989, voluntarily; collecting our own money. . . . I am asking for your help, if possible. . . ."[50] Another leader noted that her organization operated by means of "pure enthusiasm," given the lack of sources of financial support.[51] Comments revealed moods that were at times resigned, and sometimes desperate, exasperated, and angry. The commitment to organize, however, despite all the obstacles, was clear.

Thus, getting a grant from the West was the event that brought the word "budget" into many groups' consciousness. Grants did not ensure a lifetime of stability; they could amount to anything for example, from $400 for a very small, one-time event to $400,000 for a multiyear project. Donor support did not necessarily entail a steady income for the foreseeable future; one group that had received Western assistance wrote, "we do not have a permanent budget, periodically the administration supports us."[52] Nevertheless, over one-third of funded groups (36 percent) reported that their budgets had grown over the previous five years, no easy feat in the midst of Russia's current economic woes.

Groups that received grants and assistance from abroad were slightly more successful at fund-raising and finding support at the domestic level. Funded groups were sometimes able to coax support out of the federal government. Of the four groups that had received funding from the Russian government, all four had also received Western assistance; none of the unfunded groups received funding from the Russian government. Women's groups that had received Western funding also were able to garner grants and support from other Russian NGOs at a much higher rate than unfunded groups.

Alternatively, we could argue, in looking at the data, that funding does not make a difference in groups' abilities to diversify their domestic sources of support. Although funded groups outpaced unfunded groups in every option offered in the survey, often this edge was too small to be considered statistically significant (see table 4.1). Regardless of how we

Table 4.1 Sources of Support[a]

Sources of support	Unfunded groups (%)	Funded groups (%)
Funding from local branches of organization	3.2	3.3
Grants and subsidies from Russian government***	0.0	4.3
Funding from an international chapter*	0.0	5.4
Support from foreign business*	0.0	7.6
Grants and subsidies from *oblast* government	8.5	12.0
Fees for services	13.8	17.4
Membership fees	18.1	20.7
Grants and subsidies from local administration	21.3	22.8
Grants and support from other Russian NGOs*	12.8	23.9
Grants and support from foreign NGOs***	0.0	31.5
Support from Russian business	29.8	33.7
Grants from foreign governments***	0.0	37.0
Volunteer labor	60.6	63.0
Grants from foreign foundations***	0.0	68.5
Other	26.6	31.5

[a] Difference of means test: * denotes significance at .05; *** denotes significance at .001.

interpret this divide between organizations, overall the survey results depict a realm of civic activity that, left to its own devices at the domestic level, was struggling. Given this lack of consistent domestic support, external aid was often the largest and most reliable source of monetary support for groups lucky enough to receive a grant. Conversely, groups that did not receive a grant from the West were unable to match the funded groups' financial resources by relying on domestic support alone. Yet they were managing to find creative ways to survive.

When asked to list their three most important sources (not ranked) of support in 1997, women's groups that had received aid were more likely to be able to name three. Not surprisingly, the Western variants of aid were checked off as the most important sources. As one group pointed out, "There is no other source of finances except for grants."[53] For unfunded women's groups, the array of resources was less diverse as well as less commonly cited; only five out of ninety-four unfunded groups listed a third source (twenty-five out of ninety-two for funded groups). The most important resources for them were nonmonetary: volunteer labor, followed by support from the local administration. The fact that many groups, funded and unfunded, along both spectrums were hard pressed to name three sources of funding indicates that women's groups, in general, experienced difficulty in finding a wide foundation of support. Given the lack of financial sources of support at the domestic level, this created a serious financial obstacle for unfunded groups.

For most groups, this search for support was a constant occupation. For funded groups, the temporary security provided by a grant allowed them to focus on other activities related to their organization; 22 percent of funded respondents spent approximately one-tenth, 33 percent spent one-quarter, and another 25 percent spent one-half of their time in the search for funds. In contrast, unfunded groups tended to spend either little or no time (57 percent) or all their time (22 percent) in the search for resources. A recurring theme was that most organizations lived on the brink of collapse; grants from abroad provided a temporary lifeboat of security.

The task of searching for funds was a subject of some controversy among the women's groups. This was more pronounced among unfunded women's groups; twenty-one out of ninety-four (22 percent) unfunded groups did not look for financial support at all. In fact, several respondents wrote angry responses that they did not look for funding or wrote a decisive "NO!!" in the margins of the survey. For a separate question, which asked groups to assess how frequently they engaged in a variety of activities, when the search for survival was framed as "fund-raising," the numbers were even higher; 49 percent of unfunded groups asserted that they did not engage in that activity, and another 31 percent conceded that, while they engaged in such an activity, they did not do so very often.[54] Fund-raising was a relatively new concept, introduced mainly by Western donors, and was still in the process of becoming internalized by the civic community.

Many unfunded groups did not want to spend their time in the lengthy process of tracking down funds, whether from domestic or foreign sources. Several activists felt that the search for funds was a time-consuming as well as futile endeavor. Explained the head of the group Mother and Child, "I don't have the opportunity to search for sources of financing; for this, one also needs time, and I and all of my women are preoccupied with their own jobs."[55] One woman from Maikop (southern Russia) wrote, "The organization survives primarily on my own enthusiasm. . . . Contributions take so much time and energy, plus there is the humiliation of meeting with young rich people."[56] The embarrassment factor was also listed by a Committee of Soldiers' Mothers activist, who commented on the "unpleasantness" of searching for funds.[57] Alternatively, the group Chernobyl Widows bleakly pointed out, "There are no funding sources."[58]

Most unfunded groups, despite the lack of domestic support, still remained wary of searching for international aid; 61 percent of unfunded groups did not even look for grants, while an additional 32 percent reported that they did not apply "very often." Thus, a conscious decision has been made to avoid or simply not engage in the grant search.

There are various reasons why groups decided to limit or curtail their search for support abroad. Some groups would like to apply for Western assistance but did not know where to begin. As one activist explained, "we do not write grant applications—we do not even know the addresses and conditions of application, although we very much need information and advice."[59] Other unfunded groups had previously tried to look for Western funding but dropped the search because it was not worth their effort. Another activist wrote, "three times we have applied for a grant and for some reasons our ideas are not considered worth supporting; we no longer wish to apply for grants or have the means to."[60] Other respondents wrote, "We do not do grants,"[61] and "we do not even try to look—it is useless."[62] Last, another group leader explained, "we do not turn to any grant giving organizations, because the bookkeeping and taxes are so great that it does not justify spending the effort."[63] For some groups, bypassing Western forms of support was a conscious decision, forged from a lack of connections, a lack of success, and a lack of interest.

Many other groups felt that foreign organizations were the only source of reliable support. As one activist explained, "we have exhausted all of our resources here in Russia." This support was not just financial; moral support often kept organizations such as this one active, despite the presence of an indifferent or hostile government. Thus, she explained, "We need to build bridges on the international level, otherwise we will never build a government based on rights."[64] Other groups avoided financial dependence on domestic political structures out of fear of losing organization independence. One unfunded group, searching for foreign funding, discussed the dangers of relying on domestic sources of support: "the question of getting grants for women's organizations in the provinces is very important. We consciously do not seek resources from those in the power structure—we don't want to be dependent on them."[65]

Western donors were for some an elusive prize, or, alternately, a hindrance to their activities. For others, they were a vital lifeline, a respite from constant economic uncertainty, or a way to bypass an overbearing or inattentive regional administration.

PROVIDING CAPACITY

External aid's main impact was in providing the physical and human capital necessary for civic development. Grants were crucial in supporting the day-to-day activities of groups; they were often used for maintaining an office, complete with equipment, staff, and "things" related to running the workplace. The most common purchase tended to be office equipment (64 percent), mainly computers, faxes, and sometimes even Xerox machines. Aid was also frequently used for the organization of conferences (63 percent), often for other NGOs or for the local population, on a particular topic, such as networking, learning to work with local administration, or strategizing on particular women's issues. Salaries (44 percent), travel abroad for conferences (30 percent), and newsletters (24 percent) were also popular items. Conversely, grants were rarely used for explicitly political actions, such as protests or for information about upcoming legislation. Part of this is due to a variety of U.S. laws and policies that forbid the use of funds for overtly political purposes. Even without this, women's groups overall tended to be wary of noninstitutionalized displays of political expressions.

Given that funding was structured such that the money supported tangibles such as office equipment, salaried positions, and conferences, it is not surprising that a large divide separated funded from unfunded groups in terms of organizational infrastructure (see Table 4.2). Although all organizations, funded and unfunded, had a telephone contact address,[66] office space was facilitated by the presence of a foreign grant.[67] In contrast, unfunded women's groups often used a member's apartment as a base for activities or snatched meetings wherever they could find the time and the space. Office equipment, such as computers, email accounts, and faxes were also common possessions of funded groups, whereas unfunded groups were unable to muster the domestic support to purchase these items. This, in turn, affected groups' access to information; unfunded groups relied on the traditional forms of mail delivery, telephone, and word of mouth for news of NGO activities, and this could create difficulties. As one group working with women with disabilities explained, "We need contacts, information. . . . I cannot fight my way to women's conferences where these issues are discussed."[68]

Table 4.2 Organizational Infrastructure[a]

Organizational infrastructure	Unfunded groups (%)	Funded groups (%)
Office space	55.3	65.2
Computer***	25.6	82.6
Fax***	20.2	57.6
Email***	11.7	51.1
Web page*	5.3	14.1

[a] Difference of means test: * denotes significance at .05; *** denotes significance at .001.

Table 4.3 Human Capital[a]

Office staff	Unfunded groups (%)	Funded groups (%)
Paid employees***	20.2	43.5
Paid full-time staff***	17.0	43.5
Paid part-time staff*	9.6	30.4
Volunteers***	50.0	72.8

[a] Difference of means test: * denotes significance at .05; *** denotes significance at .001.

Aid also facilitated the acquisition of human capital. Not surprisingly, funded groups were also more likely to have paid employees; although sources of domestic support might facilitate the acquisition of an office, furniture, or supplies, this rarely included support for any staff (see table 4.3). Thus, for funded groups, grants ensured that an organization could engage in activities on a relatively regular basis. Judging from survey comments, for unfunded groups work often depended on the enthusiasm and level of resources of the leader. Work for the organization happened at the tail end of long workdays or during precious free time. One woman who struggled to find consistent levels of funding wrote, "[w]e are not rich people; we pursue our work in our free time, on weekends, and holidays in trying to help one another."[69] In contrast, support from a grant could ensure a stable paycheck, which at least freed up time for harried activists and potentially facilitated the emergence of a cadre of professional NGO careerists.[70]

Given that relatively few unfunded groups could afford paid employees, it was surprising that the survey shows that more funded groups relied on volunteers than did unfunded groups. Given that most unfunded group activists were not paid for their services, their work was, by nature, volunteer. No clear-cut reasons for this fact emerged from the survey; however, judging from comments, leaders of unfunded groups did not perceive their labor to be "volunteer," which is a concept stressed by donors. Rather, many leaders of unfunded organizations wrote with a somewhat missionary zeal about their work, couching their activism as a "necessity" or moral obligation rather than a choice. Thus, one woman noted that her life was hard, but to do nothing "was criminal."[71] Another leader of an unfunded group commented that "in the organization, I work unpaid, because in helping others, one helps oneself."[72] Someone else explained that in her group there was no such thing as a "separate" volunteer; rather, all members were by nature volunteers. Perhaps funded groups began to more clearly delineate between members and volunteers;

for unfunded groups, the distinction remained unmade. Organizers, members, clients, and volunteers were all different names for the same thing—individuals coming together collectively to try and improve their lot in life.

GOVERNANCE ACTIVITIES

Next, I surveyed groups' activities. Do groups that have received funding in turn engage in different activities and more frequently than groups without access to Western assistance? I broke down a long list of activities into three categories: activities that involved networking with other aspects of civil society, such as other women's groups, other NGOs, and the media; activities that involved reaching out to or networking with the public at large; and, activities that involved interacting with various levels of government power. I looked at these three types of interaction because developing ties within and among all these groupings are important governance functions that groups need to develop under the rubric of civil society and democracy. Did funding make a difference in terms of the nature and frequency of groups' interactions with other segments of civil society, the population at large, and the state? On the surface, my survey results indicate that, yes, funding does make a difference. Across the board, funded groups engaged in more activities and with greater frequency than did unfunded groups. In no activity did unfunded groups outpace donor-supported organizations. This dichotomy was particularly visible with regard to activities that involved networking with other groups within civil society. Funding's impact was least visible in how groups interacted with the state.

Money is once again at the root, in part, in explaining the nature and frequency of group activities. Often in commenting on their activities, unfunded groups attributed their low level of activities to the availability of resources. A group from Ust'-Ilimsk wrote, "we sit idle due to lack of money."[73] A group that wanted to start a crisis center for women wrote, "We need a crisis center for women, but it is impossible to finance."[74] Yet another explained, "In these hard times in Russia . . . many women's organizations in Russia do not have the means to exist, to do things, more interesting activities. In 1996, our organization was invited to the U.S. to a women's congress in Washington D.C., but we couldn't find sponsors."[75] Another activist glumly wrote, "The low effectiveness of our activities is due to a lack of money, even small amounts."[76] Adding more fuel to the fire, one woman wrote, "Many of our actions do not require material expenses, but the level of work and the effect it would have had would have been many times higher if we could have gotten sponsors. . . . If we had had certain material resources, we could have significantly widened the circle of our activities and given more attention to the solution of the problem of troops and given help to invalids."[77] Unfunded groups were dedicated to their cause and were doing what they could, but, in their eyes, their efforts could have reaped greater results if only they had had just a little bit more financial stability.

Interacting with Civil Society

Despite this pessimism among unfunded groups about the nature of activities, many organizations were communicating, networking, and developing ties with one another. I chose to focus on networking because of the importance ascribed to a dense structure of horizontal networks in cementing democratic impulses in countries.[78] Of the three subsets of activities, networking activities with other actors within civil society were the most frequently cited (see table 4.4). Two-thirds of all women's groups belonged to a coalition or network of nonprofit organizations. Of those groups who belonged to a network, most used it to relay information about seminars (86 percent) or to pass along articles, journals, or newsletters (76 percent). Thus, although there was a lot of exchange, it tended to be in the form of information rather than face-to-face interaction.[79]

Working with other organizations, even other women's organizations, is not without some controversy, however. Some groups were wary of

Table 4.4 Establishing Civil Society Networks[a]

Activities with one another	Does not engage in such activities (%)		Not very often (%)		Often (%)		Very often (%)	
	U	F	U	F	U	F	U	F
Contact with other women's groups***	9.6	2.2	19.1	10.9	40.4	30.4	30.9	56.5
Contact with media	5.3	4.3	16.0	15.2	48.9	39.1	29.8	41.3
Organizing conferences for specialists***	30.9	10.9	41.5	25.0	19.1	33.7	8.5	30.4
Contacts with other NGOs***	16.0	5.4	23.4	16.3	41.5	52.2	19.1	26.1
Publishing material***	70.2	43.5	17.0	26.1	8.5	16.3	4.3	14.1
Conducting research*	41.5	23.9	25.5	29.3	23.4	34.8	9.6	12.0

U, unfunded; F, funded. [a] Difference of means test: * denotes significance at .05; ** denotes significance at .01; *** denotes significance at .001.

working with other women's groups. One local women's council member bluntly stated, "I would like there to be one woman's organization in Russia. The Russian Women's Union would have unified goals and tasks in addressing women's issues."[80] Another group, from the Republic of Buryatia, said it did not work with any women's groups in Russia, stating that it considered women's groups in Russia "too politicized."[81] Legacies of Soviet habits of interaction, as well as discomfort with new avenues of activities, shaped how organizations interacted.

In viewing the six activities I categorize as civic networking tasks, funded groups were significantly more active with regard to activities such as contacting other women's groups and other NGOs, organizing conferences for fellow activists, publishing material, and conducting research. I categorized publishing and research as civic networking activities because after a year of visiting NGO offices, I noticed that NGOs tended to send their newsletters and publications to other NGOs rather than to members of the general public. Activities such as conferences, which often bring together NGOs from the region, publications, such as newsletters, and research are popular grant activities, so it is not surprising that funded groups engaged in them more often. What is significant about table 4.4 is that it indicates that unfunded groups were unable to find ways to compensate for their lack of grants. In the absence of a grant, organizing a conference or writing a newsletter, an article, or even a flyer became much more difficult. Significantly, for activities that did not require financial resources—such as developing contacts with the media—the differences are not as severe.

The survey also contained questions about the changing dynamics of the groups' interactions with other civic agents. Did they feel that their contacts had increased, stayed the same, or decreased? The interpretation of the response that a group had had, for example, only sporadic interaction with the media could change if it represented an increase from previous levels of interaction. Overall, groups rarely felt that their contacts with various elements of civil society had decreased; the majority of groups estimated that the level of interaction had remained the same, or increased (see table 4.5). When estimating the dynamics of their contacts with other groups in society, women's groups felt that they had increased contact most with other women's groups (60 percent) and other NGOs (52 percent) and that they had also made strides in working with various levels of the media.

However, once again, funded groups were much more positive in evaluating the range of their interactions with various groups. Whether evaluating the range of interaction with other women's groups, other NGOs, or with various branches of the mass media, a much higher per-

Table 4.5 Dynamics of Networking with Civil Society[a]

Organizations	Decreased (%)		Stayed the same (%)		Increased (%)	
	Unfunded	Funded	Unfunded	Funded	Unfunded	Funded
Other women's groups	1.1	3.3	22.3	14.1	47.9	71.7
Other NGOs	2.1	2.2	22.3	20.7	40.4	63.0
Local news	4.3	5.4	31.9	27.2	29.8	44.6
Local TV	12.8	8.7	28.7	29.3	25.5	40.2
Local radio	8.5	9.8	30.9	34.8	34.0	35.9
National TV**	3.2	5.4	12.8	27.2	2.1	12.0
National papers**	4.3	6.5	16.0	29.3	4.3	12.0

[a] Difference of means test: ** denotes significance at .01.

centage of funded groups responded that they had increased levels of contact. This increased access resulted in potential increased national exposure. Groups that had received increased coverage from national TV or national newspapers had received Western support; whereas only 2 percent of unfunded organizations had received more airtime and attention on national TV, 12 percent of funded groups had received similar coverage. Although grant money could not buy media coverage, it facilitated the increased visibility of a handful of organizations at the national level.

Interacting with the Population

The survey also evaluated the nature and scope of activities with the population at large. Given that civil society and NGOs are grassroots by nature, how often and in what manner did groups interact with the public? Once again, funded groups reported that they performed all of these activities more frequently than their fellow, unaided organizations (see table 4.6). Funded groups significantly outpaced unfunded groups in the areas of mobilizing public opinion, organizing conferences, and publishing material and research. Thus, similar to civil society networking activities, the majority of these activities involved information distribution rather than other forms of contact and sharing of experiences such as listening to a constituency. Also, because many of these activities are popular grant projects, it is not surprising that funded groups were able to engage in these activities more frequently. When left to their own devices, without Western assistance, organizations are either unable or uninterested in performing this type of activity on their own.

Interestingly, the activities in which there were not significant differences between types of organizations were these that cannot necessarily

Table 4.6 Establishing Networks with the Population[a]

Activities	Does not engage in such activities (%)		Not very often (%)		Often (%)		Very often (%)	
	U	F	U	F	U	F	U	F
Mobilizing public opinion*	22.3	10.9	18.1	14.1	36.2	33.7	23.4	41.3
Organizing conferences for specialists***	30.9	10.9	41.5	25.0	19.1	33.7	8.5	30.4
Organizing conferences for citizens***	25.5	8.7	38.3	20.7	23.4	43.5	12.8	27.2
Building the identity of members	23.4	19.6	10.6	12.0	41.5	42.4	24.5	26.1
Publishing material***	70.2	43.5	17.0	26.1	8.5	16.3	4.3	14.1
Boosting membership	36.2	23.9	22.3	28.3	29.8	33.7	11.7	14.1
Conducting research*	41.5	23.9	25.5	29.3	23.4	34.8	9.6	12.0
Fund-raising*	48.9	34.8	30.9	29.3	14.9	26.1	5.3	9.8

[a] U, unfunded; F, funded. Difference of means test: * denotes significance at .05; *** denotes significance at .001.

be facilitated through increased levels of funding, such as building the identity of members. Although funded women's groups doubtless had the resources to engage in more activities, they spent their resources disseminating information outward, to other civic groups.

In contrast, unfunded groups described their activities as focusing inward, providing a range of support and services to members within the group, which included everything from providing a shoulder to lean on to finding alternative housing. One unfunded group described its diverse and eclectic activities in the following way: "We organize free clubs for them: health, soldier's mothers, veteran, etc. We consult women in their personal issues, provide advice, conversation, help. We managed to help a woman with many children who was under a threat of being evicted from her place. . . . We bought her a house, with the help from administration."[82] A Women's Council in the regions, in addition to its work with women, noted, "We also provide assistance to fire victims, help low-income people—gather goods, books, and other things for them."[83] Another unfunded group that was part of the Committee of Soldiers' Mothers network submitted a long list of activities that defied categorization but nonetheless added up to an impressive array of services: "our committee deals with the issues of the search for missing and captive soldiers, cessation of criminal prosecution for the relations breaking army regulations, surgeries for those wounded, payment of the daily allowance during actions on Chechen territory. We also make requests to military units, offices of public prosecutors, hospitals, in search and forwarding of documents, certificates, medical certificates, decoration lists; help in registration for disability cases."[84]

These narratives contrast significantly with funded groups' accounts and reports of organizing conferences and publishing newsletters. Whereas funded groups seemed to spend much more time engaged in specialized activities that were related to information dissemination, unfunded groups tended to involve themselves in what have traditionally been considered charitable activities, as well as a wide range of services to a select number of acquaintances.

Boosting membership was also an activity that showed relative parity between funded and unfunded groups; neither group of organizations was much interested in expanding the size of their organizations. Funded groups remained as small as those that were struggling to provide support using solely domestic source (see table 4.7). Although many groups reported a membership of more than fifty, during my year of research I rarely personally observed an organization with that many members. Rather, most seemed to have a core cadre of fewer than ten participants. Particularly for unfunded groups, the written comments displayed a strong commitment to providing support, emotional and financial, for existing members rather than searching for new ones.

Interacting with the State

One of civic groups' primary functions within democratic states is developing avenues of communication with the state, whether through conflictual or consensual means. Overall, all the women's groups were wary of interacting with the state and were also hesitant to engage in overtly political activities. Of all the activities listed on the survey, those that I categorize as state networking activities were the least popular,

Table 4.7 Membership

Membership size	Unfunded groups (%)	Funded groups (%)
<10	8.5	10.9
10–19	18.1	18.5
20–29	8.5	12.0
30–39	6.4	8.7
40–49	7.4	4.3
>50	44.7	44.6
Not available; no membership (organization in name only)	6.4	1.1

straggling far behind civic networking and citizen networking tasks. The activity "organizing demonstrations" was the most unpopular activity listed overall; only approximately 2 percent of organizations admitted to such a tactic "very often" (see table 4.8). In all forms of contact, both funded and unfunded groups, if they were going to try to establish contact with the state, preferred to do so at the local level and by developing a relationship with an individual, rather than through political parties, which many groups viewed as ineffective, given the fact that parties rarely made it from one electoral cycle to the next.

Interestingly, activities that in some way engaged the state were the one area where funded groups did not significantly outpace unfunded groups; Grants did not affect the nature or frequency of activities that engage the state. In addition, if we collapse the four frequency rankings into two (combining "very often" with "often", and "not very often" with "not at all"), the differences disappear almost entirely. One of the few exceptions, and the only activity in which unfunded groups outpaced funded groups, is working to elect individuals; 29 percent of unfunded groups did this

Table 4.8 Establishing Networks with the State[a]

Activities	Does not engage in such activities (%)		Not very often (%)		Often (%)		Very often (%)	
	U	F	U	F	U	F	U	F
Use of courts/judicial system	54.3	52.2	25.5	27.2	13.8	3.3	6.4	17.4
Contacts with civil servants	35.1	28.3	29.8	32.6	26.6	28.3	8.5	10.9
Contacts with members of the Duma	33.0	17.4	34.0	45.7	23.4	29.3	9.6	7.6
Working to elect individuals	52.1	47.8	19.1	29.3	23.4	16.3	5.3	6.5
Contacts with leaders of political parties	45.7	43.5	31.9	35.9	16.0	15.2	6.4	5.4
Participation in government commissions, advisory councils	63.8	50.0	19.1	29.3	13.8	15.2	3.2	5.4
Working for needed legislation	44.7	29.3	30.9	45.7	19.1	19.6	5.3	5.4
Organizing demonstrations	72.3	63.0	24.5	28.3	2.1	5.4	1.1	3.3

[a] U, unfunded; F, funded.

"often" or "very often," but only 23 percent of funded groups responded with this degree of frequency.

The comments from unfunded women's groups accompanying the surveys offered some commentary. A regional Club of Businesswomen commented, "This year in the elections, the Mayor ... and the *raion* Duma and our organizations worked for the promotion of women. We elected five women to the *raion* Duma from the Committee of Soldiers' Mothers, a woman from the children's policlinic, someone from the local kindergarten, and a teacher. We work under the idea that there should be more women in power."[85] Another woman wrote of the Soviet-era groups in her region, "Only owing to the activity of these women was a communist governor elected. These women acted not out of fear but out of conscience! Absolutely without compensation and in bitter cold, the women went around to cities and villages and campaigned for their candidate." Discussing what was important for her organization, she wrote "Access to education for women on a level equal with men was one achievement of Soviet power. There are more educated women than men in Russia—but the key positions of the power structure are all occupied by men."[86] Another activist wrote, "There are many problems, the main being that there are practically no women in government"; she went on to add, "for that reason, in the sphere of social protection, there has been virtually no improvement."[87]

Neither set of women's groups is overwhelmingly politically active. One possible explanation for unfunded women's groups activity in politics, however limited, is that they were much more dependent on local administrations for organizational basics, such as office space, telephones, and so on. Thus one group commented, "we work to maintain good contacts with the administrative organs of social protection. . . . A large amount of work for members of our clubs takes place during election campaigns."[88]

Despite the low frequency of these activities, this represented nonetheless an increase in communication from previous years (see table 4.9).

Table 4.9 Dynamics of Networking with the State

	Decreased (%)		Stayed the same (%)		Increased (%)	
State institutions	Unfunded	Funded	Unfunded	Funded	Unfunded	Funded
Local administration	7.4	10.9	23.4	13.0	42.6	53.3
Political parties	2.1	3.3	18.1	19.6	19.1	20.7
National government	2.1	2.2	20.2	14.1	5.3	18.5

High numbers of both groups reported that their contacts with local administration had increased (53 and 43 percent); this difference widened further with regard to communication with the national government. Although neither group thought that working with political parties was particularly effective, nonetheless one in five groups overall reported an increase in communication.

NOT ALL WOMEN'S ORGANIZATIONS ARE CREATED EQUAL

Funded and unfunded women's groups differed in how they organized, what they did, and with whom they worked. In turn, funding did not impact all women's groups equally.

First, groups that received aid were not a representative sample of the broader swathe of women's activism in contemporary Russia. Although women's groups represented a mix of Soviet-era and independent organizations across a wide array of social causes, groups that attracted aid tend to be younger—the majority of groups that received a grant formed in the mid- to late 1990s (see table 4.10). Whereas older groups often remained isolated from Western assistance, younger groups were much more successful, as well as willing, to attract international aid. Fully one-half of all funded groups formed after 1993; these groups received financial assistance almost from the cradle.[89]

In addition, aid went to women's groups that worked specifically on women's issues; although unfunded women's groups were also concerned about the condition and status of women, they were also more likely to identify the importance of a wider range of community issues (see tables 4.11 and 4.12).

This was reflected in the written comments of the survey respondents. Whereas funded groups wrote about very specific issues relating to the status of women—"elimination of domestic violence"[90] and "elimination of discrimination against women"[91]—unfunded groups often extended

Table 4.10 Year of Foundation

	Unfunded groups (%)	Funded groups (%)
Before 1990	19.8	3.3
1990–91	20.2	27.1
1992–93	11.7	15.2
1994–95	20.2	40.2
1996–97	22.4	14.1

Table 4.11 General Goals

"Very important" goals	Unfunded groups (%)	Funded groups (%)
Protection of children	57.4	48.9
Protection of the poor	46.8	42.4
Development of religious life	39.4	29.3
Protection of invalids	37.2	21.7
Development of cultural life	27.7	21.7
Economic development in Russia	23.4	12.0
Defense of rights of workers	22.3	12.0
Development of the political system	20.2	12.0
Defense of the environment	18.1	12.0
Defense of ethnicities within Russia	13.8	9.8

Table 4.12 Goals Specifically Related to Women

"Very important" goals	Unfunded groups (%)	Funded groups (%)
Educate the public about women's issues	62.3	72.0
Provide services to women	59.2	62.0
Change laws on women's issues	58.2	52.9
Increase women's access to political power	38.2	40.4
Increase women's access to economic power	29.2	27.7

their mandate to a broader constituency. One woman wrote: "In the remote areas around the Urals, typical responsibilities of NGOs are very broad, which is due to life conditions there." She then listed "the protection of children, especially disabled children, orphaned children, legal protection, help to women, especially the elderly, [and] help to women in crisis situations . . . " as constituencies her organization assisted.[92] Another unfunded group simply wrote, "protection of the rights of all."[93] Should Western donors support groups that represent the domestic shape of activism, or should they use their limited resources to support groups that envision substantive and often liberally progressive change? On the one hand, funding seemed to be going to groups with a much narrower and more clearly defined agenda; on the other, this agenda is not shared by the bulk of women's organizations. (I address this issue in chapter 5.)

Second, the survey did not demonstrate benefits in two areas. Although funding allowed groups to network more frequently with one another, this networking usually happened between NGOs that had already received funding rather than between funded and unfunded organizations. In the survey, when groups were asked to list other groups with whom they networked, funded groups tended to associate with other NGOs that had received grants; groups out of the purview of Western assistance tended to associate within their circles. Thus, the effects of aid were often contained within the very circles to which it was distributed; the networking was insular rather than designed for outreach. In addition, foreign aid did not encourage funded groups to radically extend their memberships. Groups remained just as small as those that were struggling to find support through solely domestic sources.

CONCLUSION: WHAT DOES THE SURVEY TELL US?

Given the results of the survey, it might seem strange that I adopt such a negative view of foreign funding in the beginning of the book. Funding made a substantial impact on organizations. Grants made a big difference in ensuring at least short-term financial security. Funded groups far outpaced unfunded groups in terms of having reliable and consistent office space, equipment, and staff, all helpful in launching projects, disseminating information, and facilitating day-to-day activities of running organizations. Funded groups were not facing a daily struggle for survival, and this sense of security may facilitate longer-term viability. Groups that received funding were more active; they did more things because they had a greater income at their disposal. In addition, groups that received funding engaged in activities with greater frequency and regularity than groups without financial resources from the West. Activities are important because in order for a civil society to be effective, it must "do something"; groups cannot have an impact unless they distribute information, have meetings, or provide services.

The survey results tell us a lot about women's activism, but only in broad strokes. For example, the survey tells us that money obviously matters. It captures a rough, perhaps somewhat unfocussed picture and tells us where to look further, dig deeper, and check assumptions. From the survey, I had a sense of quantity of interactions and activities, but not quality. I knew which groups had computers, faxes, and offices, but I had no idea how this affected the quality of their work. Did more office equipment translate into a greater impact? In addition, I could determine how often groups interacted with other groups, but I had no idea of the nature of those interactions. I could catalog groups' activities and their nature and frequency, but I had no idea whether these projects were effective or met an existing community need. What were their activities and accomplishments achieving? I could not tell the dilettante opportunist from the impassioned civic practitioner. The check in the box remained exactly that—a pencil mark on a piece of paper, providing a few clues from which to proceed.

In other words, I still did not know to what degree the representation of the groups on paper reflected the reality of these organizations in practice, and I had no way to immediately check the veracity of the findings. Groups would understandably want to present themselves at their best. Perhaps an activity that a group engaged in once or twice became "often" in the survey or actuality was replaced with rosy memories of past deeds. Funded groups in particular had a motivation to exhibit their success; to indicate otherwise could potentially lead to uncomfortable scenarios and possibly a loss of funding.

Initial quantitative findings need to be compared with observations in the field. Do results on paper match the realities of daily life? As a result, I emphasize that survey research can tell us some things, but not others. Thus, I rely on my interviews and my experiences out in the field to double check and flesh out the trends my survey indicates. Chapter 5 is a case study of Ford Foundation's work with women's organizations. It allows me to delve into the very questions that the survey cannot answer.

CHAPTER FIVE

Women's Organizations and the Ford Foundation

T he survey results discussed in chapter 4 show that donor support did matter tremendously. It ensured at least temporary survival in a context that was otherwise defined by extreme economic uncertainty and provided the tools that organizations need to operate: office space, staff, even paper. This investment in physical and human capital, in turn, facilitated groups' activities, perhaps even increasing their confidence, assertiveness, and motivation. Yet, perhaps I was reading too much into the numbers generated from the survey. How can I be sure that the survey results accurately portrayed the situation of women's organizations across Russia? In addition, how did a group's having more and doing more translate into actual impact? The survey pointed me in particular directions, but it could not give me definitive answers.

As the surveys trickled into my mailbox, I visited offices, interviewed members of organizations, and traveled to the regions. In some ways, my observations confirmed my survey results. Grants brought innumerable benefits to organizations lucky enough to win them. My observations also, however, caused me to reassess the significance of my survey findings and look for more nuanced interpretations. This chapter provides greater detail by focusing on the Ford Foundation's work with women's organizations to determine whether a closer look at this case study reflects the overall trends indicated by the survey.

Throughout the 1990s, the Ford Foundation was a prominent supporter of NGO development in Russia. It also was one of several donor organizations that singled out gender concerns as a thematic funding focus within its efforts to foster civic development. Although it subsequently shifted priorities, between 1994 and 1999, it dispensed over $2 million in grants to strengthen and institutionalize the women's move-ment. The foundation supported women's projects that fell within five themes: (1) information, communication, and networking among women's groups; (2) development of a gender studies curriculum; (3) prevention of and protection from domestic violence; (4) provision of social support and services to other organizations and to the population; and (5) community development and self-employment.[1]

In many ways, the impact of the Ford Foundation on women's organi-zations reaffirmed the trends I had noticed in my survey. Grant making by the Ford Foundation had had a significant effect on recipient organi-zations; funding helped to strengthen and institutionalize key umbrella women's organizations, thus ensuring at least temporary survival in the harsh and often hostile economic, social, and legal climate.[2] It created a small group of professional NGO leaders who now speak a Western con-ceptual language that includes terms such as "women's rights as human rights," "civil society," "gender," and "empowerment."[3] It allowed them to organize conferences, publish journals, and complete research and improved communication and networking abilities for many organiza-tions. In sum, the Ford Foundation supported groups looked, talked, and acted differently than other organizations that were not supported by the foundation's programs.

However, the experiences of the foundation also provided an alter-native picture, supporting some of the trends observed by previous research.[4] First, my survey told me that funded groups possessed increased physical and human capital and a greater short-term economic viability and organizational capacity. The experiences of foundation-supported groups reflected this trend, but grants and resources also became centralized in the hands of an insider, Westernized clique. A civic oligarchy within women's organizations rapidly emerged, despite donor intentions to spread resources and experience to an increasing circle of organizations. Despite efforts to bring together an array of women's organizations in order to spread experiences, in reality, the benefits of aid remained firmly in the hands of funded organizations. As Rebecca Kay and Valerie Sperling have noted, funding opportunities that were available to some organizations but not others created enormous resent-ment within the women's movement.[5] This resentment was very notice-able among groups that came into contact with the Ford Foundation and did little to develop trust and reciprocity, the essence of social capital.

Second, my survey portrayed radically different pictures of the nature and scope of women's activities. The survey indicated that funded organ-izations were much busier than unfunded groups, briskly engaging in a variety of activities with one another, the population, and the state. Yet a closer look revealed that funded groups were not "more" active but perhaps were active in different ways than unfunded groups. Funded groups focused on activities that could produce results for their grant reports. Because of this, activities tended to be structured around quantifiable "events" that could produce numbers for reporting purposes. Thus, groups focused on organizing conferences, publishing newsletters, and distributing information, often to other NGOs. The Ford Foundation often became the important constituent rather than the people the organization claimed to represent. In contrast, unfunded groups were more focused on providing less quantifiable services and support to their members and the public. Activities were based around providing emotional support or direct services to small segments of the population, rather than to other NGOs, and often involved sporadic, yet much needed charitable donations. Thus, although my survey told me that funded groups were more active, my fieldwork posed the question, activism for whom? Neither set of groups were connected with large segments of the public, but the funded groups seemed more, rather than less, isolated from Russian society.[6] They often didn't represent anyone but themselves.

In sum, it was unclear whether increased financial stability, more office equipment, and frequent conferences were making a difference in groups' impact on civil society. Grantees became so focused on producing results for the foundation that they rarely stopped to consider the qualitative effects of their work. Given this lack of focus on assessing the qualitative impact of activities, it was also unclear whether the benefits that had accrued—increased short-term financial stability, organizational infrastructure, increased activities, and greater networking capacity—could be sustained if funding were to disappear, thus questioning the long-term impact of donor efforts. Would the plethora of publications, reports, newsletters, and conferences be remembered ten years later as the genesis of a stronger, more organized, more effective movement?

Ironically, the Ford Foundation's Moscow office strove "to concentrate our efforts on the creation and support of institutional structures or organizations which over time will become self supporting."[7] Yet, there was a significant disconnect between the intentions of program officers at the Moscow office and the results of their grant-making activities. Despite good intentions, the very rules and methods of aid distribution contributed to unforeseen side effects. Women's groups behavior was, in fact, quite logical; they were simply responding to the rules and incentives provided by the Ford Foundation's strategies.

This chapter discusses the intended and unintended effects of aid to women's organizations. Unfortunately, the process of building civil society in Russia is not conducive to providing fairy-tale endings—women's organizations do not ride off into the sunset, to live happily ever after. Funding is not so simple; for every step forward, funding also created a new pattern of side steps, variations, and meanderings. Many of the dynamics that created success also led to unintended consequences. In explaining the varied effects of aid, I focus on the structure within which the rules of aid are embedded at the Ford Foundation, the rules themselves, and the Russian context.

FORD FOUNDATION—MOTIVATIONS AND ACTIVITIES

The Moscow office of the Ford Foundation is one part of a much larger philanthropic empire; the locus of activity is in New York, with field offices spread throughout Africa, the Middle East, Asia, Latin America, and, as of 1996, Russia.[8] Traditionally, Ford Foundation offices abroad were located in the developing world. The presence of an office in Moscow signaled the foundation's commitment to expanding into new territory. Perhaps "misdeveloped" rather than underdeveloped, Russia represented a new direction in funding activities for the foundation, which was trying to keep up with a rapidly changing global world.

The Moscow office of the Ford Foundation exhibits many of the dichotomies of the nonprofit business in Russia; as a Western organization, it is much wealthier than the groups it has come to assist. The Moscow office makes a sweeping impression; it is located on the third floor of an imperial pink building on the edge of Pushkin Square and is adjacent to a high-end Western shopping plaza, complete with marble interiors. Like many other nonprofit organizations active in Russia, the Foundation office requires that individuals clear several hurdles before gaining access; first people must get past the downstairs security check and then clear the videocamera and speakerphone perched at the foundation doors before being buzzed into the office. Although admittance is not enormously difficult (the security guard sizes up visitors before issuing a curt nod of approval), it is not a building where an activist or average citizen may simply wander up, unimpeded, to stop by and chat about grant opportunities when the mood strikes.

Although the Moscow office did not have a specific gender portfolio, projects with a gender focus were categorized within the mandated portfolio areas of human rights, independent analysis of Russian policy, higher education, and regional civic initiatives.[9] Despite the absence of a specific portfolio, the Ford Foundation headquarters was concerned with improving the position and status of women in all societies and since 1991 integrated this concern into their grant making. As a result, as a satellite office, the Moscow office focused on women's issues partly because of the New York office's emphasis on such activities.[10] This interest in supporting women's organizations in Russia emerged soon after the breakup of the Soviet Union. In 1992, the staff of the New York office commissioned two reports to clarify the range of issues of concern to women in formerly communist countries and to identify the main individuals and organizations active on behalf of women.[11] Delivered in 1993, these reports confirmed to the Ford Foundation the importance of initiating a line of grant making to build institutional capacity within the nascent women's movements in this area. The New York office of the foundation awarded grants to two women's groups, the Information Center of the Independent Women's Forum (ICIWF), the other to the Network of East-West Women (NEWW). Both of these organizations, although struggling, were also well versed in Western gender concerns, were well connected, and were emerging as the women's organizations Westerners came to visit when in the former Soviet bloc.

The New York office followed up on these initial steps in November 1995; they sent two employees to Russia for a week to evaluate the impact of their initial work with fledgling women's groups.[12] Based on their week of interviews in Russia, the two returned with glowing reports of the women's movement, stating that "the Russian women's movement, which scarcely existed five to eight years ago, is flourishing," although they also noted that the "challenges facing Russian women are enormous." Based on their interviews, they were "convinced that there are compelling reasons to deepen our work in this area."[13] They concluded, "The current grants to build the infrastructure for the Russian women's movement have been successful and important, particularly in strengthening regional groups and the connections between them. We should continue this work."[14]

When the Moscow office of the Ford Foundation opened its doors, it inherited the women's grants made by the New York office, as well as the general commitment to gender projects. Mary McCauley, a highly respected academic in the fields of political science and Russian studies, was hired to head the Moscow staff. Two program officers, Christopher Kedzie and Ann Stuart Hill, both fluent in Russian, assisted her. Although none was a gender expert, they nonetheless were committed to the continuation of the New York grants and expanded into new avenues of activity as they became more comfortable with assessing Russian needs. They focused their efforts with women's organizations on four main activities: information, communication and networking among women's groups; development of a gender studies curriculum; prevention of domestic violence; and provision of broad-based social support.

Information, Communication, and Networking

The majority of the Ford Foundation's work with Russian women's groups concentrated on organizations that fostered the exchange of information, communication, and networking among women's groups. Over $1 million, more than half of its entire monetary commitment to women's organizations during 1994–99, was in support of this goal. This also represents the longest running branch of the Ford Foundation's work with women's groups. Three of the projects—funding for NEWW, funding for ICIWF, and funding of travel to the NGO forum in Beijing in 1995—originated from the New York office. The Moscow office continued this funding trend by extending more support to the ICIWF to establish a network of resource centers across Russia. In addition, it gave a grant to the Newly Independent States–United States (NIS-US) Women's Consortium to develop email networks among women's groups.[15] It later sponsored a women's film festival in Naberezhniye Chelny, in the Republic of Tatarstan.

The Ford Foundation focused on this area because it was responding to what it perceived to be an obvious need for ways to increase organizations' abilities to communicate and learn from one another. Group after group, when asked what they needed, replied with the request for "more information!" Most regional women's groups with whom I spoke were quick to quote me their geographical spread and location in relation to Moscow; almost all groups spoke of the isolation they felt out in the regions, with only a handful of often unconnected women's groups dispersed across the sparsely populated territory. Even in Moscow, where information was comparatively plentiful, groups still *perceived* themselves to be remarkably in the dark about important issues related to women, women's rights, and women's positions in Russian society and on the global level. Women's organizations were constantly seeking information about what other groups were doing, about what lessons they had learned, and about which strategies had been effective. In addition, groups that were implementing foundation projects maintained that increasing women's access to technology would enable groups' efforts to address and influence government policies that affected women in Russia.

Development of a Gender Studies Curriculum in Russia

The Ford Foundation also supported two projects—one with the Moscow Center for Gender Studies (MCGS) and another with the European University in St. Petersburg—to foster the development of a gender studies curriculum in Russia. The grant to MCGS supported several two-week summer school sessions on gender studies. Activists, graduate students, and professors met outside the confines, stresses, and strains of their daily lines and spent two weeks in a more leisurely environment while simultaneously listening to lectures, giving talks, and debating topics related to gender in round tables and group discussions. Because the academic community was so fragmented in Russia, the summer school was meant to provide an opportunity for people to come together for two weeks, rather than making the accustomed quick dash into Moscow for a conference or workshop. The Gender Studies Program at the European University, attempted to institutionalize a year-round academic program on gender issues by supporting two sociology professors at the European University in St. Petersburg in their efforts to build a gender studies program for Russian undergraduates. Less focused on supporting NGO development, these grants were aimed more at developing a civic culture conducive to eventually supporting women's issues.

Prevention of Domestic Violence

The campaign to support the prevention of domestic violence in Russia was a relatively new area of activity for the Ford Foundation. In response to the rise of several active and well-organized organizations that ran crisis hotlines, the foundation increased its support to this rapidly developing area of women's activism. The majority of the foundation's financial support in this area went to the organization Association No to Violence (ANNA), one of the first crisis hotlines for women in the country. Since its inception, ANNA has organized similar organizations into a Russia-wide association of crisis centers. Ford Foundation supported this network by providing financial support for several nationwide conferences. Impressed with the strides that this network of crisis centers had made, in 1999 the foundation started a small grants program to support the creation and institutionalization of a small network of crisis centers throughout Siberia.

Provision of Broad-Based Social Support

Noting that many of their early grant recipients were Moscow-based and tended to be oriented around feminist issues, the foundation has attempted to broaden its definition of women's organizations by providing funding to two umbrella organizations active in the regions. The Women's Congress of the Kola Peninsula, located in the Arctic Circle, and the Women of the Don, active in southern Russia, both provided aid and assistance to a variety of women's groups within their region. Both umbrella organizations contained member groups that tended to come from the more traditional strain of women's activism. These groups often focused on providing services to the elderly, the poor, the disabled, orphans, or military conscripts. Thus, they focused less on women than on issues that were traditionally viewed as important to women. Grants were given to both umbrella organizations in the hopes that they would strengthen regional capabilities by establishing resource centers across the region. Thus, for example, just as the Congress of Women and Women of the Don had previously benefited from ties with larger metropolitan areas in Russia and abroad, the smaller centers would, on a lesser scale, benefit from the experiences of these two regional hubs. This would help regional groups build strong networks among themselves. Also, given that these groups focused more on service provision to vulnerable segments of the population, the foundation hoped that they would develop stronger ties to the community.

In many ways, the foundation's activities reflected the prevailing trends popular with donors at the time. The focus on gender, the belief in information as a necessary component to overall NGO growth, the support of resource centers, and the focus on networking activities were all donor priorities throughout the 1990s. The attempt to move beyond Moscow and the efforts to locate groups that represented a broader tapestry of domestic activism were also priorities identified by other donors. Thus, the foundation's activities were representative of donor thinking at the time about ways to stimulate civic growth and appropriate projects that would facilitate this. Table 5.1 outlines the Ford Foundation's efforts to strengthen and institutionalize the women's movement during 1994–99.

DESIGNING AID

How did these organizations receive aid? Unlike other donor organizations, such as the OSI, the Eurasia Foundation, IREX, or ISAR, the Ford Foundation does not sponsor open grant competitions. Rather, civic groups are encouraged to submit a letter of inquiry. If interested, a program officer then contacts the applicant to discuss in greater detail the possibility of funding such a project. If the project sounds promising, the program officer asks the group to submit a formal proposal. Demand vastly overwhelms supply; for example, in 1998, McCauley estimated that the Moscow office funded 1–2 percent of all inquiries.[16] When a grant is made, the program officer in charge of the grant writes a short, usually 3- to 5-page, report to the New York office explaining the reasoning behind funding the project, providing background on the group and

Table 5.1 Ford Foundation Grant Activities, 1994–1999

Groups	Amount (dollars)	Project description
	Information, Communication, and Networking among Women's Groups	
Information Center for the Independent Women's Forum		
1994	250,000	Support for the institutionalization of the independent women's movement in Russia
1996	225,000	Support for the broadening of the influence of the Russian women's movement into regions outside of Moscow
1998	300,000	Continued support to strengthen the influence of the Russian women's movement, particularly in the regions
Moscow Center, 1994–98	525,000	
Chelyabinsk Center, 1996–98	50,000	
Dubna Center, 1998	16,000	
Irkutsk Center, 1998	17,000	
Mirny Center, 1996	20,000	
Petrozavodsk Center, 1996–98	45,000	
Pskov Center, 1996–98	45,000	
Voronezh, 1996–98	45,000	
Zhuvokski, 1998	25,000	
Network of East-West Women, 1994	200,000	Support for establishing an email network for women's organizations and individuals in eastern and central Europe and the former Soviet Union
NIS-US Consortium of Women's NGOs	75,000	Support for improving communication and information dissemination among network's of women's NGOs
Femina		
1996	16,200	Support for first interregional festival of TV programs for women
1997	1,200	Travel support for a video festival dedicated to gender-related broadcasts on television

1997	62,000	Support for the second interregional video festival dedicated to gender-related broadcasts on television; support of a sociological survey of the gender content in national programs
Winrock, International	75,000	Travel support for the Beijing Conference

Development of a Gender Studies Curriculum

Moscow Center for Gender Studies		
1996	75,000	Support for a summer school on the development of a gender curriculum in Russia
1996	2,000	Support for a meeting to develop plans for the future of a gender studies summer school
1997	200,000	Support for two gender studies summer schools
European University of St. Petersburg	83,600	Support for the further expansion of the university's gender studies program

Prevention and Protection from Domestic Violence

Irkutsk Crisis Center		
1998	35,000	Support for counseling of women and children and for a public education campaign
1999	150,000	Support for domestic crisis centers in Siberia and the Russian far east
ANNA (Association "No to Violence")		
1998	87,600	Support for a workshop and a legal counseling program
1999	200,000	Support for an association of domestic violence crisis centers in Russia to undertake networking and public education activities

Broad-Based Social Support

Women's Congress of the Kola Peninsula		
1996	62,600	Support for the development of a regional network for the women's movement in northern Russia
1997	41,500	Support for the improvement of communication and information dissemination among networks of NGOs
Women of the Don	74,000	Support for a regional network of social and legal consulting centers

their activities, and providing a summary of the estimated budget and a diversity table.

In discussing what makes a successful proposal, program officers stressed that there is "no cookbook" answer. Rather, they look for a variety of factors: Does the project fulfill a real need? Do the groups have a track record of managing successful projects? What is the vision and quality of the leadership of the group? What are the specifics of the budget request? Does the project have an "all Russia" significance, that is, a goal that is not particularistic? Does the group have alternative sources of support? Does the project fit within the mandate of the Ford Foundation?[17] One requirement is knowledge of English; proposals and final reports have to be submitted in English and Russian.[18]

The size of the Moscow office severely shaped what could get funded. One program officer left her position in mid-August 1998. As a result, two people, the foundation representative and a program officer, were responsible for overseeing all grants made in Russia. Although a Russian staff of secretaries, assistants, and accountants assisted the program officers, this proved to be a daunting task; in 1998, they were juggling the files for 130 grants.[19]

Due to this organizational structure, the Ford Foundation chose a strategy of giving out large grants to groups or projects that had an "all Russia" significance or that would "benefit positive interaction within and between the regions."[20] As Kedzie explained, "We don't have the ability to make small localized grants like [the] Eurasia [Foundation]."[21] As a result, the Moscow office tended to work with Moscow groups that in turn worked with the regions; regional groups that focused on networking activities; and regional groups that had a particularly strong program.

In terms of their philosophy of grant making, the foundation representatives viewed their grantees as partners, rather than dependent grant recipients. Contrasting their work to that of other foundations, Kedzie portrayed the foundation's relationship with their grantees as "partners in the long haul."[22] As a result, whereas other foundations might give a group a grant once and then move on, the Ford Foundation often cultivated relationships with particularly promising groups, starting them off on smaller amounts of funding and then increasing their monetary support through the years.[23] The hope was that by picking the strongest candidates and working with them over time, these organizations would then be able to take real leadership roles as they found their own organizational legs.

Program officers were aware of their influence and were wary of getting too involved in or micromanaging groups' projects. One of the difficulties in maintaining a partnership philosophy was allowing groups to implement their own projects while also injecting input as a funder. Kedzie, for example, was very conscious of allowing recipients their autonomy. In discussing his work with women's groups, he stated, "[w]e need to be careful about who is setting the agenda." He carefully continued, however, explaining that as a donor the Moscow office of the foundation also had a responsibility to support things that have "payback." Thus, he felt it was inevitable that the foundation would inject some of its own objectives. As he explained, "it's hard to take yourself out of the picture and still be responsible for what is going on."[24] Balancing these two interests was an extremely difficult task; sometimes he felt as if he were "holding his breath" in the effort to allow groups to make mistakes, while simultaneously ensuring accountability to the foundation and their requirements. Program officers wanted to allow groups the freedom to decide their own priorities, but at the same time they needed to ensure that these priorities fit within overall foundation priorities.

Despite the foundation's efforts to strengthen the women's movement, the very methods used to distribute grants, in addition to the very real economic benefits they provided to domestic activists, encouraged unintended results. The next section takes a closer look at these intended and unintended consequences. For every step forward, the dynamics of funding created a complex trail of unexpected side effects.

FUNDING CAPACITY

My survey indicated that, given the lack of domestic resources, aid made a substantial impact on groups' physical and human capital. The experiences of the foundation-supported groups reflected this. By 1998, foundation-supported women's organizations looked remarkably different from the disorganized, motley crew of activists that had made up the movement even six years previously. The Ford Foundation's main grantees, such as MCGS, ICIWF, and the NIS-US Consortium were ensconced in large offices, replete with humming computer equipment, large Xerox machines, television sets, and VCRs. For one group, the temporary stability provided by a grant ensured that they could rent out an entire house, thus giving themselves room for an NGO resource library, as well as some office space for other NGOs in the region. This provided NGOs with a formal space within which to organize; women's groups that received grants no longer had to arrange meetings in public libraries, coffee shops, and individuals' apartments in order to coordinate activities or serve clients. The computer equipment enabled funded organizations to produce journals and newsletters, and funding covered the costs of distributing them. In addition, funding provided salaries for an array of civic activists, facilitating the emergence of a cadre of professional NGO activists and careerists who were able to spend their time devoted to women's issues and representing women's concerns. Activism no longer took place at the end of the day when dedicated volunteers returned from their day jobs to run their organization out of their apartments and on their carefully saved earnings. Thus, groups' activities did not ebb and flow with the dynamics of the leaders' work schedules, family needs, or personal concerns.

Funding also guaranteed access to technology. Funding improved the networking and communication abilities of the recipient organizations. Due to the increasing numbers of women's groups with access to computers and email, groups could find out about grant competitions, conferences, and one another's work with a few clicks of the mouse. Access to email in 1994 changed many participants' lives; documents from 1994 show that participants are joyful, even ecstatic about the bridges email could cross. "I feel like part of a group, no longer isolated," commented one woman in St. Petersburg. Another activist said participation in NEWW On-Line taught her how to "clearly formulate ideas, to present a project. I feel more flexible, less afraid to try new things." The head of an organization in Naberezhniye Chelny remarked that email had allowed her "to participate actively in the Russian women's movement on a level I had never imagined possible. . . . to be in the middle of action and still live in Tatarstan has changed my whole life."[25] Clearly, email was a revolutionizing experience for many activists when they first encountered it. Particularly in the regions, many commented on how they felt connected to activities in Moscow, as well as to the rest of the world. In addition, groups in the regions commented that they felt they could participate more effectively in grant competitions, rather than having to rely on the fickle mail system to deliver information (often arriving a few days after the deadline had passed).

Networking and increasing contact with other organizations involved more than just email. There are other ways of sharing information and experiences. One of the more interesting phenomena involved in improved networking was evidenced at a Women of Russia conference held in 1998 in honor of the ninetieth anniversary of the first Women's Congress in Russia. Yekaterina Lakhova, head of the Movement of Women of Russia, was the most prominent and outspoken figure; she also oriented her dialog closest to that of the ICIWF and the NIS-US Consortium, two foundation-supported organizations with a feminist orientation. However, her network was much larger; for the November conference they brought in hundreds of women from the region from more conservative organizations, such as women's councils and rural women's groups.

Lakhova was able to take the rhetoric of the ICIWF (they also put an ICIWF pamphlet into the participants' packets) and deliver it to an entirely new audience. Thus, even though Women of Russia is not a Ford Foundation grant recipient, indirectly and perhaps inadvertently the work of Ford enabled hundreds of women to hear new ideas and get new information, women with whom the ICIWF or the NIS-US Women's Consortium do not ordinarily work.

In comparison, groups that did not benefit from the foundation's support often struggled to afford envelopes and paper to take care of daily business. Few had the time or resources to put out newsletters or journals. Many had managed to obtain office space, whether through connections with someone or through being creative with the concept of "meeting space." I met with groups in hotel lobbies, in space granted by local administrations, and in local clubs. Activism often took place at the end of a long day, after finishing another job. In contrast to funded groups' increasingly vertical, highly bureaucratized structure, which often included an accountant, the leader, a web/tech person, and sometimes a temporary driver, unfunded groups had a much more fluid organizational structure, consisting of the person who had mobilized, and been joined by other friends and acquaintances sharing common goals. Thus, organizations reliant on solely domestic sources of support physically looked much different than funded groups.

Yet, despite their lack of physical and monetary sources of support, unfunded groups were enormously resourceful in coming up with creative and alternative ways to secure space, hunt down typewriters, and find help. Some groups were able to cajole office space from local administrations; others simply used their apartments. Many activists were willing to work unpaid and pressured friends and family into doing the same. Nonetheless, it was obvious that on their own, they would never match the tools and equipment of the funded groups. Although the personal charisma and dedication of leaders could make organizations effective in ways that the latest computer could not, funding was creating a significant divide between organizations with access to the West and those without.

Facilitating Oligarchies

Despite the wish to foster greater organizational institutionalization of women's organizations, the Ford Foundation's philosophy of "building partnerships" and providing almost cradle-to-grave financial support to certain organizations also meant that a few organizations in an extremely large country were institutionalized, often at the expense of a vast number of smaller, less-well-connected, but active organizations. Thus, the Ford

Foundation solidified a portion of the women's movement and, in doing so, tended to privilege the groups that had managed to develop a relationship with the foundation early on and shut out other groups that also wanted to gain access to the foundation's resources. Leaders well connected with Westerners headed organizations such as the ICIWF, the NIS-US Women's Consortium, and the MCGS, and these connections helped cement funding relations in ways that were counterproductive to long-term movement stability.

This problem was compounded by the fact that these organizations' constituencies overlapped to such a degree that their work was somewhat repetitive, and the activists tended to move in the same small circles of fellow civic elites. Almost all members of the ICIWF also belonged to the NIS-US Women's Consortium; groups that subscribed to NEWW's list serves also belonged to either (or both) of these organizations. Although these groups all worked to advance the cause of women's groups, it is a small select group of women activists that were able to continue to benefit from early connections. The list of participants in a 1995 conference was similar to the list of groups at the foundation-funded conference celebrating the ninetieth anniversary of the first Women's Congress in Russia three years later. As another participant (and long-time activist noted) "the faces are still the same."[26] Although Ford Foundation support has been invaluable in sustaining this wing of the women's movement, nonetheless for these three grant projects alone, almost $1 million went to support groups having similar constituencies, similar goals, and similar projects. Later efforts to expand out to the regions tended to replicate this process; regionally prominent groups such as Femina, Congress of Women of the Kola Peninsula, or Women of the Don became the token organizations from outside Moscow and became active participants of the usual round of seminars, conferences, and training in Moscow. The circle rarely expanded to include different or new groups, often encompassing only a select band of activists.

In addition, networking projects that focused on setting up regional resource centers tended to have a limited impact. Despite efforts to spread knowledge and experience, money given to Moscow-based organizations to work with smaller groups rarely trickled outside of the recipient organization. Groups in the regions still subsisted mainly on whatever materials they managed to get via the mail, through personal visits to Moscow, or through conferences. Despite the desires of larger, more institutionalized organizations to help the smaller, regionally prominent groups, this help remained sporadic and many groups continued in isolation. There was still a large gap between the resources available to Moscow groups and the regional centers.

This inequality also applied to the relationships between regional NGO resource centers and their local constituent NGOs, replicating the situation between Moscow groups and the prominent regional groups. Although the grants enabled other smaller groups in the regions to acquire some training, the main beneficiaries of the grants were the regional resource centers themselves. For example, as regional networks such as the Women of the Don and the Congress of Women of the Kola Peninsula became more successful in grant writing, they also became more formalized in structure; hired on more office staff; and spent increasing amounts of time writing new grants, searching for "fundable" projects, and traveling to conferences. Smaller groups were able to benefit somewhat from watching the rise of the Women of the Don and of the congress and learning from their successes; however, the main benefit for most groups was the occasional local conference and available meeting space.

Nor did supporting email networking projects provide the magic bullet in eradicating the gap between the center and periphery. Particularly in Russia, where there were so few that had access to the Internet, email projects in some ways widened the gap between those with access to technology and those without. Groups with access to email also had access to applications more quickly, information about funding, and information about one another's projects. It was no accident that all women who received grant money to travel to Beijing also had email.[27] In addition, although women's groups with email made email bulletins available in their offices, such bulletins rarely fell into the hands of non-email users. In light of email's still small following in Russia, groups such as the St. Petersburg Center for Gender Issues reported that they consciously decided *not* to distribute their newsletter by email; rather, they relied on more traditional means of distributing their newsletter in order to reach a wider audience.[28]

In sum, the hope that funding networks would allow resources to "trickle down" to the lowest grassroots level has had mixed results. On the one hand, information and training are being slowly, if unevenly distributed across Russia. However, the financial benefits have remained firmly in control of a few, centralized groups.

Building Unsocial Capital

This situation was not ameliorated over time. The distribution of scarce resources to a few groups created enormous resentment among organizations. This was particularly true among regional groups, which were often even more resource-strapped in the absence of significant levels of donor support. Although grant reports indicated a proliferation of conferences, increased networking, and rapidly expanding levels of communication and cooperation, in truth groups, instead of building trust and reciprocity, were sowing seeds of bitterness and hoarding information. This led to a proliferation of what we could term "unsocial capital."

Groups in the regions that had already developed a relationship with the Ford Foundation, although they were anxious to spread the word about the foundation, were not inclined to spread it too broadly. On one trip, when a group not supported by the foundation was pitching a grant idea, my escort firmly interrupted the speaker's pitch to tell her that the Ford Foundation would not fund "her type of project." On another of my trips to a foundation-funded resource center, the leader of a visiting women's group waited until my host had left the room before she whipped out a copy of her own grant proposal (to be submitted to the Soros Foundation) and asked me to review it very quickly before my host returned from the bathroom, even though the center I was visiting was supposedly a resource center formed for the precise mission of helping groups such as hers. I found myself offering five minutes of advice before the proposal was whipped out of my hands and secreted back into the pocketbook from whence it had come with the whispered request to "not say anything."

In times of stiff competition for scarce resources, the groups that had received Ford Foundation support to serve as a resource center for other women's groups suddenly found themselves not sure they really wanted to increase the pool of competition. Several groups complained that upon undertaking the responsibility of "helping" other groups get grants, organizations expected them to write the other groups' grant proposals for them. One center complained bitterly that they had achieved all of their grants "through their own hard work," but that now groups were coming to them, expecting them to think up ideas that would be marketable.[29]

As a result, although the Ford Foundation prided itself on building partnerships with women's groups, it also enforced the perception that there is an "in" crowd and an "out" crowd in the women's movement and that funding was secured through establishing patrimonial ties with the donor rather than through the transparent, open mechanisms of competition. The name "Ford Foundation" certainly had a mystique. One activist who had never received funding from the foundation, but had twice submitted letters of inquiry, said that even though she had been very successful with grant writing, nonetheless, the "stamp of approval" from the Ford Foundation meant something that other grants did not impart. Part of this was due to the perceived selectiveness of the foundation; although the Ford Foundation funded many different women's initiatives, the belief was a that it had given money only to "Khotkina, Ershova, and Bashkova" (activists from MCGS, NIS-US Women's Consortium, and ICIWF). Among unfunded women's groups, this created the perception that there was some mysterious trick to forging a clientelistic relationship with one of the program officers at the Moscow office. Although funded groups view this positively as "building partnerships," nonfunded groups saw this as the older practice of cronyism, especially because the Ford Foundation gave out larger sums of money to fewer grantees.

This tension was evident early on in the foundation's activities. The consultant who had initially been sent from the New York office to scout out women's organizations in 1994 had already discussed the rising tensions over the elevation of the Independent Women's Forum to protégée status. She wrote, "In general, other women's organizations resent Forum groups because they have been more successful in raising funds from Western donors." She noted that "the independent women's movement was initially largely funded by the West," although she also commented on the presence of groups, particularly in the regions, that survived on minuscule budgets without Western support. This trend, already evident in 1995, was serious enough for her to recommend that "Because the women's movement is highly personalized and politicized, we should be particularly careful not to become too closely identified with the Information Center," its main grantee at the time. Thus, the institutionalization of a few select groups, although providing temporary stability, tended to also create an oligarchy of powerful, well-connected women's civic groups that were able to establish a record of grant success, thus bolstering their future chances to garner scarce and coveted resources from Western organizations.

FUNDING ACTIVITIES

My survey indicated that funded groups were more active in scope, range, and frequency of activities; they were much busier putting on conferences, publishing material, and doing research on their issue. In contrast, unfunded groups portrayed their situation as one hobbled by their constant search for funds. My observation of group activities, however, indicates that perhaps it was not that funded groups were more active but that they were active in different ways. Funded groups tended to work on projects providing services to other NGOs that could provide quantifiable results. Unfunded groups tended to focus on working with small segments of the population, providing support to one another, and engaging in a range of charitable activities not easily caught by the options listed in my survey. Underscoring this difference, the two sets of groups almost spoke different languages; whereas funded groups discussed civil society, gender, human rights, and NGO development, unfunded groups discussed charity, declining social services, and daily deprivation. Inadvertantly, funding helped marginalize the theoretical concepts from the real life issues that addressed them.

In many ways, Ford Foundation support allowed groups to pursue activities not open to them before. Groups were able to travel to Beijing for a UN conference. TV reporters were able to show their work relating to women's issues to their peers at a regional film festival. The ICIWF was able to set up a network of resource centers, so that women's groups in the regions could exchange information. Crisis centers were able to sponsor conferences on preventing domestic violence. Almost every group supported by the foundation published a newsletter about their activities and dutifully sent them out to their fellow NGOs. When meeting with organizations, they were able to provide me with thick packets detailing their activities: numbers of newsletters published and distributed, numbers of attendees to conferences, numbers of visitors to the organization, and numbers of articles written about organizations in the local paper. Activities were carefully tabulated, quantified, and presented in rapidly multiplying reports.

Unfunded groups were active, but in different ways. They were much less likely to produce newsletters; most did not have a computer, and they did not report their activities in carefully tabulated overviews. Conferences were not really important to them, although they often attended those put on by the local organization supported by a particular donor. Rather, many unfunded organizations were intent on serving as small-scale support groups for individuals suffering through difficult times. This included meeting for coffee to share experiences and going out on group outings or excursions.

Other unfunded groups provided a range of services to members of their organizations. For example, one unfunded group raised a little money to provide low-cost shoe repair and barbering services for mothers struggling to support their children. Another unfunded group managed to cajole the local administration into donating an old abandoned building. Members renovated it and used it as a center for their children who, because of mental or learning disabilities, were unable to attend school. Yet another unfunded organization, in the absence of government services, spent its time searching for medication and transportation for disabled children. These are not activities that can be easily checked off in a box; yet these groups were active, providing support to members, collecting small sums of money for presents for children at holiday time, and tussling with the local administration to help them provide social services.

Some of these unfunded groups, unable to find substantial monetary support from a Western donor, found alternative ways of forging partnerships with Western organizations. Some managed to establish a relationship with a group in the West that could sometimes donate a few supplies. For example, one group in southern Russia received an old car from a group of doctors in Germany, which they used to ferry children about the region from appointment to appointment. Other unfunded women's groups, particularly those that were situated closer to northern European countries such as Finland or Norway, established exchange programs with sister clubs. Not flashy or clearly connected with specific donor priorities, these exchanges allowed groups to learn about one another, build friendships, and trade experiences and skills in ways that did not involve the exchange of money. Although it is important to not overstate the possibilities of activities of this sort, these small, yet regular contacts with Western groups nonetheless helped many unfunded organizations in ways that a one-time supply of money could not.

Providing an Alternative Language

Funding provided women's groups with an alternative language and alternative forms of discourse; they talked differently than groups that had not received funding. Funding brought along with it exposure to concepts such as "women's rights as human rights," "civil society," "gender," and "empowerment."[30] This was particularly evident from the experiences of foundation grantees who had traveled to the Beijing conference for women's NGOs in 1995; the Beijing conference enabled women to talk of women's rights as human rights, thus opening up a new level of discourse. As participants explained, it gave them a new standard; they could now go to the Russian government or their local administrations and demand to know why the reality of women in Russia does not compare to international standards. Many women's group leaders returned from Beijing inspired to write their local administration, demanding that the government take women's issues seriously by establishing, for example, a regional Commission on the Status of Women.[31]

Exposure to Western ideas, such as those discussed at the Beijing conference, can help women's groups fit their agenda into a broader framework and create a common language of activism. In practice, this gave funded groups new ideas and helped them put their ideas within a broader context of NGO development, civil society, and democracy. Funded groups, overall, spoke of a Russian society that could, one day, change.

Groups that were not direct recipients of grants had a completely different discourse. Many were more concerned with articulating immediate, short-term goals and were much more likely to work as a support group for others, mainly women, suffering through Russia's economic woes. Often, in sitting down with these groups, I listened to a very articulate listing of problems, whether it was the price of medication, the status of health care, or the situation of disabled children. I also listened to a very cogent analysis of why these short-term problems were difficult to solve, due to larger political and financial factors. It was not that these groups were not interested in larger political developments; however, they were also much more pragmatic in discussing direct strategies and plans for action to get through the immediate time horizon. They were more interested in adapting to the system than changing it. Thus, they often had cultivated relations with the local administration in order to fight for immediate benefits for their members. The economic stability and exposure to Western ideas provided by grants enabled funded women's groups to speak in terms of long-term aspirations, whereas unfunded groups were more concerned about daily existence and achieving pragmatic goals.

Which of these activities are "better," more effective, or more important? Who should be funded, the visionary opportunist promising ambitious programs or the pragmatic realist ready to implement incremental plans? Should it be the liberal minded, Westernized activist talking about promoting big changes at the federal level someday? Or the potentially conservative activist working locally and not really thinking globally, but achieving real change in different and verbally less dramatic ways? Those questions are difficult to answer. As I observed funded group behavior more closely, I also noticed unforeseen side effects from what had seemed liked a rosy picture. Although funded groups had learned a new language, they were speaking it more for the donor than their own constituency. In addition, it was unclear if this language had been internalized or was used beyond grant writing. Thus, the larger impact of the grant activity was unclear. Also, despite their ability to talk about big concepts and long-range plans, funded groups were continually searching for the next fundable idea and thus were in danger of undermining their own long-term stability by shifting goals and agendas from project to project. Ironically, talk of long-term projects often demonstrated short-term visibility.

Donors: The New Constituents

After numerous discussions with funded organizations, I often came away with an impression of dichotomy. On the one hand, these groups were undeniably active. They were busy talking about civil society, organizing conferences, attending round tables, and collecting articles for the latest newsletter. They knew the language that Westerners wanted to hear: civil society, gender empowerment, advocacy. Although many also believed in these words, the comments were geared for an audience other than their domestic constituents. The organizations did not seem interested in using this language with citizens at the local level, and there were relatively few incentives to do so. Rather, the need to ensure accountability to donors encouraged groups to focus on them as the important target audience. This problem was exacerbated by the Ford Foundation's well-intentioned support of feminist groups, which already had little or no connection to domestic constituencies.

One of the issues which foreign funding introduces is that of audience. Despite the Ford Foundation's more recent attempts to broaden its outreach to include women's organizations involved in social defense issues, funding went almost exclusively to women's groups that professed a feminist orientation, thus underfunding more traditional women's groups, which had greater connections with the community.[32] A women's movement did exist in Russia, but it was a women's movement that was often more comfortable at international conferences with fellow Western activists than at home, working in the community. In discussing the women's movement in particular, one NGO activist commented on the new cult of international prestige: "They have a reputation on an international level, so they spend a lot of time going to conferences and beefing up their reputation abroad."[33]

Women's groups, such as the MCGS, which were known in academic circles in the United States, were completely unknown to the average Russian, yet their budget was exponentially larger than groups that were more conservative and worked with small segments of the population. By selecting feminist organizations over other women's organizations, donors such as the Ford Foundation assisted groups who, from the beginning, were more firmly embedded in transnational networks than domestic ones.[34] Although, from an optimistic viewpoint, this support may keep a movement alive until it is able to frame its message effectively for a domestic audience, thus far it has tended to discourage groups from finding ways to frame that message for domestic audiences—as a result, activities, goals, and missions have not been clearly articulated because there has been no compelling need to do so.

One grant evaluator and former women's group activist commented, "It has amazed me how often foundations are satisfied with the rather slim products of women's organizations. This is probably due to foundations' interest in supporting 'legitimate' women's organizations and their lack of real knowledge about the NGO activities in this part of the Third Sector."[35] Others echo the observation that these organizations had received a very substantial amount of funding but had produced relatively few results. As one program officer at the Eurasia Foundation commented, "It seems to be that they [women's groups] are not very effective in operating. . . . they received a lot of funding but they were not able to choose the right goals or the right targets. . . . it's not clear, it's not aimed at concrete purposes or concrete needs of society. They should start from concrete problems that Russian women face."[36] Analyzing this ineffectiveness, the program officer discussed why she thought feminist groups experienced such difficulties in finding a compelling message:

> I would call it a "social competitiveness." Women were more vulnerable (in comparison with men) and had too many "weak points"—children, who used to be ill; a necessity to visit school teachers, to bring children to extra-school groups, etc. So, when there was an opportunity to hold a higher position or receive a higher salary (rather rare situation, to say the truth), women knew it could be the only chance in their career and were not friendly with colleagues (women). That social relationship was automatically carried over to the new period and was even sharpened. Women are not sisters. That played a negative role in running the "women's projects."[37]

Domestic legacies such as these are exacerbated by the problem that grant recipients seemed uninterested in finding a language that both donors and local communities could understand. In visiting groups' premises, it was obvious that women's groups spent an inordinate amount of time producing material for the Ford Foundation in order to prove that they had been active with their grant money. The groups became so focused on producing "results" for the foundation that they rarely stopped to consider the qualitative impact of their work; nor were there any incentives to do so.

ACTIVITY VERSUS IMPACT

After numerous office visits, interviews, and observations, I was unclear whether increased financial stability, more office equipment, frequent conferences, and a new language were making a difference in groups' impact on civil society. Although many funded groups knew the language of civil society well, implementing that language rarely involved something beyond circulating paper and information. Although funded groups were very productive, the impact of these activities was unclear.

Certainly, newsletters, conferences, and resource centers were valuable kinds of information distribution; however, grant projects also encouraged groups to shift from using the information to simply acquiring it. In discussing projects, past and future, with grant recipients, groups often forgot why they were proposing specific projects; as they continued to seek funding, missions become secondary as groups concentrated on "producing" for donors rather than listening to Russian citizens. As a result, many women's groups that were Ford Foundation recipients were so focused on collecting more information that they rarely stopped to assess the materials they already possessed or the technological skills they had already learned.

This was particularly true of groups in Moscow, such as the ICIWF or NIS-US Women's Consortium, which often had fairly extensive libraries and access to the Internet as well as to a wide array of libraries in various foundations and other nonprofit organizations. We could almost argue that there was a surfeit of information on particularly popular themes because various women's groups had gotten grants from different funders for similar projects. The ICIWF, the NIS-US Women's Consortium, NEWW, and the East-West Innovation Fund were all women's groups based in Moscow that served similar functions as providers of information about grants, conferences, events, and other women's groups. Five separate groups in Moscow produced five glossy journals of women's issues in Russia, often overlapping in themes as well as content. Several different women's groups were working on producing databases of information about the groups in "their" network of women's groups. Databases, email bulletins, conferences, and publications on "women's rights as human rights" were all constant themes and activities. Yet it was unclear whether this information was being shared, absorbed, or digested and transformed into action or outreach to a wider community of women. Information itself had become the goal rather than a tool to accomplish other tasks.

This overfocus on activity as opposed to impact was apparent with the ICIWF, one of the foundation's earliest collaborations. In many ways, it represented an ideal NGO on paper. One of the original organizers of the Independent Women's Forum conferences of the early 1990s, the organization had expanded into an Information Center and NGO network, serving as the center and coordinator of a network of women's resource centers scattered across the country. It became a source of consistently reliable information about other women's groups through its email information bulletin and its quarterly publication. It also conducted numerous seminars for women's groups, both in Moscow and in its regional centers. It produced a lot of material, which slowly made its way through Russia's regions through the regional information centers and the ICIWF's email bulletins.

Yet, although the ICIWF produced a lot of information, problems that had plagued the organization from the start still existed five years later.

Its mission, and the actions and goals to achieve that mission, after five years of writing grants and despite the numerous leaflets, copious reports, and extensive reporting, remained poorly justified. As the grant applications and reports piled up, the ICIWF had drifted from fitting a project into an overarching mission or set of goals to writing goals to fit within a self-perceived fundable project. The grants themselves became more organized, but the justification for the programs became less and less evident.

The first grant proposal, although virtually incomprehensible, discussed the status of women in Russia. Thus, even though the ICIWF proposal itself did not make explicit connections between goals and context, the reader could infer that, due to various conditions unfavorable to women, the ICIWF was undertaking the following projects. As the organization became increasingly institutionalized, it no longer explained why it needed to implement a particular program or why getting a new computer, publishing a journal, or emailing to the regions was a useful or important activity. It had improved at quantifying its activities (so many conferences conducted, so many journals distributed), but the reason for conducting these activities remained unwritten. Establishing a center or publishing the newsletter became the new goal and accomplishment rather than a means to a larger objective, such as changing the status of women.

As a result, the lasting impact of their work was uneven. Several of the resource centers were no longer being used, were underused, or had become sources of employment for friends. One center located in the outskirts of Moscow was barely operative, and it was unclear why ICIWF had expanded there, beyond the fact that many of the women who had passed through the ICIWF were themselves from that area. The information center was located in the old library of another, separately funded and defunct, aid project—Archives. Database. Library.[38] Open sporadically and deprived of a telephone connection (and hence an email and Internet connection—the purpose of the center), the new center consisted of a small shelf of housing-reform publications in one corner. The rest of the office was devoted to publications about women's issues—several thousand books, pamphlets, and material related to women—from the library project and was, at that time, no longer in use. The previous co-director of the ICIWF (and former director of the library project) had found a job at the Soros Foundation, and the library soon became unused, unread, and unvisited. It was a sobering testimony; information about women can only be effective if it leaves the room and is used; resource centers are effective only if they attract visitors beyond those who work there.

Other projects had limited impact because the grant recipient became so focused on getting the grant and balancing it with other projects that follow-up activity was less important. As a result, there were few results that were sustained. For example, a project to the NIS-US Women's Consortium was funded by the foundation to set up an email network; Yet the activist who wrote the project did not even know how to use email.[39] In addition, women's groups that were included in the network were given training on how to use email, but then were left on their own to do with it what they chose. Part of this was due to the philosophy of the project director[40]—respecting their autonomy, she wanted the groups to do what they wanted with their accounts. As one interviewee commented, however, in the absence of a common list-serve, "Only I know what is in my email; my information is only useful if I share it through a network."[41] As a result, although thirty-five new groups were introduced to email, many of them used it only for personal email. Although these groups could still be creating strong networks among themselves, the grant might have been more effective if the consortium itself had taken a stronger role in motivating or providing leadership to those receiving e-mail. Mirroring the experiences of many funded organizations, the modem project was but one of many such activities in which the goals of the project became lost in the scramble to complete other grant projects.

Mission Drift

This scramble for grants was complicated by the fact that donors themselves, in trying to be responsive to Russian needs, often keep changing funding priorities. Thus, donors tended to move in what, from the outside, seemed like fads. Russian NGOs then learned the language of the latest project in order to follow the supply of donor dollars. In the long-term, this often destabilized organizations, as they shifted priorities to meet donor supply.

This phenomenon was evident in the Ford Foundation's work. Although the mail was consistently unreliable in Russia and phone connections remained fickle, nonetheless news traveled fast in Russia. Groups from Moscow suddenly wanted to do outreach and work with the regions, and all the regions wanted to form their own networks, complete with separate computers and email accounts for each organization. Although all of these projects were admirable, perhaps needed, it is nonetheless unclear who really wanted the network. Was the project created by the self-identified, potential future regional resource center? Was it created by the donor, who was now impressed with the accomplishments of another resource center he or she had heard about? Was it created by the successful NGO, located in Moscow, in search of new projects? Or was it created by the many small regional groups, currently poorly linked with one another and desperate for greater contact? From observations of foundation-supported network projects, although prominent local women's groups often argued for networks of women's groups, it was not clear that the unfunded women's groups felt equally passionate about establishing a network simply because these groups all happened to be "women's groups." Establishing a network can build bridges, but funded women's groups were beginning to see the marketability of networks and regional work while losing sight of the justification for these activities. This creates technically competent, formatted applications with all the appropriate headings, deemed necessary for funding success, yet the impact of such projects can be negligable. Thus, women's groups often created new projects or developed ideas because they thought it was what the Ford Foundation wanted to hear.

Following funding fads can do more than create "empty words"; it can also destabilize groups' long-term stability. Gabrielle Fitchett, the head of the Russian Women, Law and Development project, lamented the strains that the funding hunt put on groups. Although the mission of her work was to support domestic violence projects, the funding battles were causing groups to chase projects that were not really included in the original mission statement. Discussing the experiences of a crisis center, she shook her head and said, "Now they are applying for a grant to work with the elderly. This is just not their mandate."[42]

The new fads in funding in 1998 included domestic violence and trafficking initiatives. Other donors in addition to the Ford Foundation were moving in to substantially support and initiate organizations that work on these issues: the U.S. State Department projects funded combating domestic violence and the OSI and IREX sponsored projects combating the trafficking of women. One civic trainer commented, "The other thing that I am seeing is this new fashion of domestic violence and trafficking of women. Now, this is great but, again, you can't skip over the basics. The best way to combat trafficking of women is to provide equal opportunity for jobs here. I mean, most women are not going to be wild about going off to be an exotic dancer if they can make a decent living here and be with their family."[43] Despite the importance of the issue, its faddishness may now undermine its chances of becoming a sustainable movement.

What Makes an Effective Project? The Crisis Centers

This chapter parallels chapter 4 in discussing how aid impacted how groups organized, formed goals, and implemented those goals. Funded groups looked, organized and acted differently than groups not supported by the foundation. Aid facilitated positive accomplishments, but also masked deeper problems that could undermine long-term stability. In addition, Ford Foundation efforts had varying impacts; some projects were more effective than others in terms of ensuring long-term viability, strengthening ties with local communities, other groups, and the state. Of the varying projects, the support for crisis centers was most effective in that centers established other sources of support, developed a cadre of dedicated volunteers, and were slowly implementing mechanisms for affecting public policy. Many successes were due, however, to the presence of charismatic leadership, the quality and/or presence of volunteers, and the degree to which the issue was translated into a language that worked within the fabric of the local society. Thus, any attempt to simply replicate projects that address domestic violence on the crisis-center model without considering the specific factors that ensured the previous success will result in mixed results at best.

One of the most striking aspects of the crisis center movement was that, similar to the Committee of Soldiers' Mothers, it built on the dedication and hard work of volunteers. These volunteers repeatedly stressed their sense of immediate gratification from their labors; they felt useful and personally involved in a way that they had not felt with other endeavors. "Every time I pick up the phone and talk to a victim, I know I have accomplished something," explained one volunteer.[44] Others said they felt a personal responsibility in carrying out their work; many felt they had developed a personal stake in the issue of domestic violence. Russian society was still unwilling to talk about domestic violence, but volunteers were been able to turn this to their advantage; it intensified the bonds of loyalty and trust between hotline workers. In Pskov, as of 1999, not a single hotline worker had left the line since the hotline started in 1997; although a small group, the loyalty and dedication was intense. In addition, crisis center work attracted volunteers of all ages. Unlike the feminist movement, which was dominated by women in their forties and fifties, the crisis center movement attracted younger activists, which will hopefully prolong the movement into the future.

Crisis centers also, more than other areas of women's activism, were able to develop relations with sister organizations in Western Europe and in the United States. Thus groups were able to benefit not only from grant money, but also from the experience of going to other organizations, observing how they worked, and learning from their mistakes or successes. These partnerships had extended for several years so that groups were able to develop relationships with other activists in different settings, rather than trying to learn everything in three-day seminars. The West's interest in domestic violence as an issue lessened the stresses of continuing funding needs; crisis centers might have greater luck receiving small grants, donated office equipment, and phone lines, if not from Russian donors, then from foreign businesses active in Russia. This supplied them with a more varied palette of external support than a one-time grant for a newsletter or conference.

Some crisis centers were also successful in adapting to local community needs. For example, activists in regional cities developed crisis centers that served women and children. Some did not use the term "domestic violence," a word combination that did not yet have cultural resonance in many areas, but talked about violence in the family in general, which garnered more sympathy and support from small segments of the public. The few groups that tried to directly implement Western-style projects, such as "safe houses," had less success; most Russians were not familiar with the concept and were wary of the usefulness of such a project.

Unfortunately, the danger was already evident in 1998 that domestic violence would become the popular funding flavor of the year, as donors sought to replicate the crisis center success by assuming this issue would translate immediately across different environments. The Ford Foundation was also expanding its own activities on domestic violence as a result of their satisfaction with previous projects. Instead of funding the existing networks, however, they were funding the creation of ten new groups to establish hotlines. This move is dangerous; whereas past funding rewarded networks already in place, the new funding instead supplied projects to groups that had yet to form. This could lead the crisis centers to repeat many of the problems evidenced by other funded projects, as discussed in this chapter. Supplying a new project blindly will create very different results than supporting a project that has already been demonstrated to be successful in a particular context.

CONCLUSION

Women's groups were targeted in the 1990s as an integral component of civil society. Donors focused on feminist organizations, crisis centers, social service providers, and resource centers as ways to facilitate deeper civic development among women's groups. This aid encouraged recipient groups to organize, talk, and act differently than groups that did not receive outside financial assistance. Yet in assessing the impact of the Ford Foundation's work with women's groups, I found a complex picture. On the one hand, most projects were "successful," if success was defined as "the group accomplished what it set out to do within its original grant proposal." That is, most groups wrote proposals for projects to fund salaries, put on a conference, publish a newsletter, set up a network, or establish a center. For the most part, the grantees did these things, some with more skill and interest than others. In this sense, donor efforts have also been "successful": projects were implemented, women's groups were sustained, activists were trained, newsletters were published, and funding created products that, in one way or another, have passed through the lives of hundreds of women activists.

However, there is also the issue of impact. What lasting legacy will funding leave, particularly if donors pull out suddenly? What will be left? That question produces more ambiguous answers. Funding did not really "trickle down" to organizations that were not the direct recipients of aid, and the groups that received the grants remained the primary beneficiaries. This centralization helped produce "unsocial capital" as groups fought over funding. In addition, funded groups, although seemingly more productive, often had little interest in assessing the qualitative effects of their work. This raises the question of the sustainability of these organizations—what their long-term chances are for survival.

To what degree do women's NGOs serve as an accurate measure of the NGO community at large? Although I did not send out surveys to other NGO sectors, in my interviews with other organizations and with donor agencies many of the problems that plagued women's groups in Russia were revealed as typical of NGO development as a whole in Russia. The dependence of the emerging third sector on grants from Western sources was a common phenomenon, as were poorly defined mission statements, small constituencies, and increased factionalization of organizations. I found, however, that the intended and unintended consequences of aid to women's organizations were particularly concentrated, although this was a difference of degree not nature. In other words, women's NGOs did not respond fundamentally differently to the incentive structure of aid, but they were more strongly affected by it. Chapter 6 discusses the trends developing in the entire NGO sector and discusses why this matters for long-term civic development.

CHAPTER SIX

The Paradox of Externally
Promoting Civil Society

The support of civil society initiatives represents a new direction in democracy promotion programs. Civil society has traditionally been viewed as a product of the interests, dynamics, and cultural norms of a country's population. Although activists, movements, and money crossed traditional nation-state boundaries in the past, the external promotion of civil society, which rose to prominence in the 1990s, represented a much more systematic and self-conscious attempt to foster the development of civic institutions. In addition, this focus on grassroots, rather than state elite institutions, represented a shift in thinking on how to promote the larger processes of political, economic, and social development. In fostering this development in Russia, donors had to stretch limited funds to encourage civic norms, attitudes, and habits in a country nearly twice the size of the United States, with nearly 145 million citizens, spread across eighty-nine various territorial units. Given these constraints, many donors focused on a select group of NGOs, in particular those that might advocate for more far-reaching trends in Russia's ongoing civic and political evolution.

What can we say after just over a decade of civic growth in Russia, and after nearly a decade of efforts to promote such growth from abroad? In September 2002, I returned to Russia to see what had changed and what had endured since my last research visit. In twelve weeks, I visited five regions, moving from central and then southern Russia to the Urals, Siberia, and finally the Far East. I spoke with nearly one hundred activists and program officers scattered across Russia, working on a range of issues from the protection of human rights to raising breast cancer awareness to promoting traditional hobbies.

When I arrived in Moscow, I discovered many things had changed. Many of the program officers I interviewed in 1998 had moved on and been replaced by people with different perspectives, implementing new programs. Some donors, such as the Ford Foundation, the MacArthur Foundation, and USAID, were revising strategies, phasing out old programs and bringing in new approaches. The Eurasia Foundation and OSI were negotiating to merge and form a new foundation. New players in NGO development in Russia, such as the World Bank and the Bradley Foundation, had started funding projects. Russia Donors' Forum, a coalition of private and public grant makers from Russia and abroad, had grown rapidly since 1998, which allowed donors to better coordinate activities, exchange information, and trade experiences. Some of the old buzz words were out; "fundraising," "social marketing," and "networking projects" had faded and been replaced by "coalition building," "advocacy campaigns," and "anti-corruption projects," which emphasized the NGOs' evolving relationship with state power. Donors prioritized further regional NGO development and were working to broaden their support for wider slices of NGO activity, such as those organizations involved in issues of social support.

Donors were cautiously excited about a variety of developments in the NGO sector. Many program officers now discussed sources of domestic financial support for the sector, such as the emerging trends of corporate philanthropy and community foundations. NGOs were reportedly making inroads with political elites at the federal, regional, and local level, particularly in the Volga region, where various local and regional administrations had actively courted and financially supported NGO involvement in social service provision. The 2001 Civic Forum was potentially encouraging; the federal government was urging various levels of the government to acknowledge and work with NGOs. Other developments, such as tax legislation, or the failure in the Duma of an alternative military service bill championed by human rights groups, were disappointing, but change was on the horizon.

I left Moscow and headed for the regions, wondering how many of these developments had trickled down to Russia's regional capitals. It turned out that regional NGO development, and aid's effectiveness in fostering this process, varied tremendously. Some regional communities had benefited significantly from the dedication and work of NGOs; in Novosibirsk, the Siberian Civic Initiatives Support Center, with the assistance of consistent and substantial donor support, launched a series of innovative and far-reaching programs across a region larger than the continental United States. Other regions, such as southern Russia, had also received substantial support, but had struggled to have significant impact on regional NGO development. In areas of the Russian Far East, the influence of foreign aid was barely visible, even though some significant donor-funded projects had been invested in the region. Groups were referred to as "informals," and many were still small-scale, grassroots initiatives, dependent on the time and energy of the leader for operation. My follow-up research in Russia revealed that aid dollars could make a difference, but that financial investment alone did not always reap consistent or even minimal results. As I moved from city to city, it became increasingly apparent how thinly foreign aid was spread across a massive geographical space, and robust NGO development, let alone the growth of civil society, despite all the optimism in Moscow, was still a distant goal. There were many domestic legacies, roadblocks, and impediments that made civic development, even in areas targeted by donors, a long, difficult, and uneven process.

After ten years of this momentous civic development project, the NGO community did look substantially different from the early 1990s, when many groups had never encountered the words "nongovernmental organization." My 2002 trip reinforced my earlier findings that aid had been crucial for NGO development. A relatively small amount of money could go far to keep a struggling organization going; in a domestic environment that provided few monetary resources, outside assistance kept many organizations afloat. Foreign aid improved NGO capacity through its efforts to build infrastructure and provide training. It significantly increased the information and knowledge available to NGOs regarding such important topics as government legislation, sources of financing, and the activities of their counterparts throughout Russia. Donor support helped many groups initiate and sustain dialogue with various political elites, to think about and propose legislation, and to impact the political process. When many Russians were occupied with materialist concerns of day-to-day survival, donor organizations often provided the moral and monetary support for civic activists to learn and speak the language of "civil society." One Russian NGO activist who had not received foreign assistance commented, "It is hard to think about civil society when you are poor and have no job."[1] Foreign aid, by supplying support for physical and human capital, allowed groups the space to discuss the larger picture and meaning of civic development.

In particular, aid facilitated the continued survival of Western-style social movements that could not find enough domestic support to exist on their own. Donor support funded the Memorial Center of the History of Political Repression to raise "awareness about the importance of human rights and democracy in Russia."[2] Another organization provided money to raise public awareness and educate law enforcement officials about the trafficking of women.[3] A further project provided professional-level training for environmental NGOs to introduce ecologists to professional film-production techniques and to explore tactics for raising environmental awareness through documentary film and television.[4] Such projects, which attempt to emulate Western values, styles, and tactics of grassroots activism, would have never gotten off the ground without crucial Western aid. They probably could not survive in the absence of this aid, given the lack of domestic support for these issues. Donor assistance can potentially keep these Western ideals alive until domestic support develops.

Yet, despite this impact, many of the problems that I had noted in 1998–99 still remained, and perhaps hardened into clearer trends. Aid could only trickle down so far from recipient organizations, and there was a vast divide between organizations that had received external support and those that struggled on domestic funding sources alone. Many donor-supported organizations had impressive offices, produced a large collection of NGO publications, and could speak the right language of advocacy, civil society, and democracy. Some of them, such as the Siberian Center, were operating at full capacity and were working on timely, interesting projects that provided valuable services to their clientele. But for the majority of funded organizations, the offices remained unvisited and the publications usually sat on a shelf with a multitude of other brochures, newsletters, bulletins, guides, and directories that had been published and distributed only to the same circle of NGOs. Rather than actually engaging the population, administrators, or legislators in a dialogue, NGOs often organized a conference around a topic for other NGOs and published a pamphlet about it.

In addition, despite all the talk in Moscow about the importance of the regions and funding social service organizations, thousands of groups were continuing their work untouched by foreign aid. A "trickle-down" civic approach was problematic; it placed enormous faith in the abilities of a few centralized NGOs to disperse skills, lessons, and eventually money to other NGOs. In practice, the performance of these civic hub organizations was uneven, often depending on the energy, compassion, dedication, and professionalism of a center's staff. A good center could spark grassroots activism; a bad one kept organizations isolated from one another and minimized their potential impact. In addition, funding continued to be dominated by democracy-related themes that sounded good on paper but often targeted only a narrow slice of organizations. In looking at a wide range of funded and unfunded groups, it was unclear to me why one unfunded group's ability to attract 2,000 people off the streets to a health screening clinic sponsored by the local administration was not, in donors' eyes, building civil society, but yet another cookie cutter round table for a smattering of NGO leaders on "working with local government" was. Despite the rhetoric of support for regional development, donors still tended to perceive many service provision organizations as temporary social Band-Aids while a select group of Westernized NGOs were seen as fundable catalysts of change.

In sum, increased infrastructure does not guarantee heightened impact, information is useful only when it is put to use, activities are consequential only when they are effective, and Western language in Russia is meaningful only when understood and spoken by the domestic population. Providing tools to groups does not mean that they use them in useful or expected ways. Furthermore, groups capable of speaking the Western language of activism are not the only ones capable of stimulating greater civic development.

As James Richter has noted, providing the tools to encourage NGO development is not the same as developing civil society.[5] These are two separate tasks, which only sometimes mutually reinforce one another. In the case of Russia, donors often conflated the two, and, in practice, funding the first task (NGO development) can inadvertently discourage groups from furthering the second (civil society development). Ironically, the methods that donors used to successfully expand NGO capacity also sometimes discouraged funded NGOs from *functioning* as a civil society. Furthermore, these unintended consequences cannot all be fobbed off as Russian civic "deficiencies"; they are also a result of largely avoidable mistakes in the foreign aid process.

The design of aid, the interests of donors and Russian activists, and the domestic conditions combined to create three large problems for civic development. By nature, donor programs to foster civic development were, as Marina Ottaway has characterized it, supply driven. Despite donor efforts to meet Russian needs, donors still defined the programs and Russian organizations responded to the parameters set by these programs. This substantially altered the incentives for grassroots mobilization, turning it from a diffuse, bottom-up process of organization that responded to constituent demands to a centralized, top-down process of organization that responded to donor supply. The result was what I term "principled clientelism"; despite funders' self-proclaimed moral intentions, the outcome was the development of unequal vertical relationships between domestic groups and foreign donors, often at the expense of horizontal relationships among domestic groups, or between groups and their domestic constituencies. Instead, donors took on roles that traditionally had been taken on by domestic actors. This facilitated the emergence of a "guardian" civil society that advocated on the behalf of largely disconnected and silent citizens, who were rarely consulted, often ignored, and underutilized as a source of support and legitimacy for the NGO community. To some extent, donors and grantees unconsciously colluded in the creation of a "virtual" civil society. Each portrayed to the other a picture of Russian civic development that was healthier and more robust than it really was.

Aid did not create these effects all on its own; many of these habits merely reinforced older patterns of organization and interaction. Even in an ideal environment, aid can only accomplish so much in ten years; in the Russian context, money, enthusiasm, and work could not single-handedly overcome institutional legacies embedded in a complex history. Yet aid tended to exacerbate, rather than ameliorate, these conditions. External aid influences group priorities, activities, and ideas in the East, the South, and the West. However, in a country such as Russia, historical legacies, domestic economic scarcity, and poorly functioning political institutions ensured that the promise of aid significantly impacted how recipient NGOs organized. Given that this aid came at the developmental, rather than the maturation, stage of Russia's civic community, the patterns that were launched in these initial years will substantially shape Russia's nonprofit sector into the future. Subsequent attempts to change policy to correct for some of these unintended consequences will be slow to take effect.

In this concluding chapter, I broaden my focus from women's groups to the NGO community at large. I discuss the larger unintended consequences of foreign aid: supply-driven civic development, principled clientelism, and the guardian civil society. I argue that despite these problems funding to support NGO development is worthwhile. But policies should be reformed to correct some incentive structures that encourage relevant actors to defect from performing their civic functions. Finally, I suggest ways in which foreign aid can be reconstructed to facilitate greater civic development.

A SUPPLY-DRIVEN CIVIC DEVELOPMENT

If donors want to support the development of a civil society in a country where domestic impulses for such a development are lacking or weak, how should they go about it? Whom should they target? What strategies should they use? Which projects should they support? How should progress in or impact of these efforts be measured? With limited funds to address a seemingly unending laundry list of social, economic, and political problems, donors had to make difficult investment choices.

Particularly in the initial years of funding efforts, many donors were entering new theoretical as well as geographical terrain, and were on as steep a learning curve at times as their Russian grantees. Supporting civil society sounded intuitively appealing; helping to construct it was a much more complex endeavor.

Many donors chose to focus on NGOs rather than on the population as the engine of civic development. As one development specialist explained, it would be physically impossible for donors to develop aid projects that would involve the entire population.[6] Even focusing on NGOs as a whole was problematic; how could donors interact with even a significant percentage of the over 450,000 NGOs in Russia? Many donors narrowed their thematic focus even further by concentrating on NGOs that were perceived to contribute directly to greater democratic political reform. Donors implemented programs that supported organizations focused on human rights, environmental, or gender concerns; the groups that most explicitly tied their rhetoric into working for a more just, accountable, and progressive government. Geographically, donors tried to magnify their impact by focusing on umbrella organizations, networks, and resource centers. These types of organizations had, in theory, greater capacity to organize potential campaigns, put together coalition projects, and mentor smaller, less skilled organizations. Leading organizations could act like a "spider plant," inspiring offshoots of community activism in smaller communities across Russia.[7] Grassroots development, in this view, could be facilitated by a top-down approach—picking strong organizations in the hope that the practices, norms, and habits of these NGOs will trickle down to other less politically oriented NGOs and subsequently, to the population.

In focusing on pro-democracy programs and centralized "hub" NGOs that promote or adhere to Western liberal values, donors are taking a gamble. The gamble is that by picking a few NGO winners out of a sea of organizations—the clear majority of which do not engage in transparency campaigns, self-conscious civic advocacy, and democratization goals— external support will create the momentum to foster more substantial change. The hope is that a supply of civic development and democratization programs will foster concern for these topics and help create demand for civil society and political reform.

However, despite these hopes, I argue that supply-driven visions of NGO development can create some serious impediments for the development of civil society, because civic activists respond differently to a vision of development that is driven by donors than to one that is driven by local constituencies. Supply-driven civic development alters the who, why, and what of mobilization. In addition, it tends to further centralize resources to a select group of organizations in a sector that ironically, is supposed to counter such centralization in other political institutions.

Altering Civic Impulses

The rules governing most donors state that they cannot simply give support to charismatically-led organizations with a solution to some pressing problem. Rather, aid is carefully portioned out into predefined mandates aimed at ameliorating particular issues, which for Russia, are often related to strengthening Russia's democracy. As donors supply programs on an array of thematic emphases, recipient organizations are responding to this supply. Activists in turn make choices about whether these programmatic emphases match their own mission. Ideally, the space between these two is negligible. However, past donor emphases created conflicts for many organizations trying to decide between domestic demands and donor supply. Supplying projects on particular themes created larger long-term sustainability problems for a sector, that, when left to its own devices, looked quite different than the one donors envisioned.

Trying to bridge the gap between donor supply and domestic realities has been problematic; Russian organizations in search of funds faced the challenge of responding to donor priorities targeting civil society and democratization rather than charity and self-help. One activist commented, "It has been difficult to explain this to many organizations . . . that their orphanage projects, etc., don't fit the mandate but if they create a project that is children's rights oriented it fits."[8] Overall, many service organizations felt shut out because they could not speak the language funders wanted to hear: advocacy, civil society, and democratization. One activist in Novosibirsk explained, "The problem is that sometimes the programs (those that don't get funded) seem to the funders too medical, too cultural, too professional. Therefore, often times the money goes to those who know rhetorics [*sic*]." However, she added that it was a positive development that at least people "are beginning to speak in terms of civil society."[9] Others, because they did not know how to shape their proposal, simply did not bother to apply for a grant, defeated by their own self-perceptions of inexperience.[10] As a result, groups in search of funding had to learn how to repackage their proposals into themes that the funders (and not necessarily their supposed constituency) would find attractive and that complemented funders' overall mission.

This method of supplying civil society projects had significant consequences for recipient organizations. In the absence of a domestic clientele, well-intentioned projects that were designed to address Russian problems quickly turned into fads, leading to a surfeit of similar projects. Jon Snydal, reflecting on his work with NGOs, commented on the repet-

itiveness of "popular" funding ideas, and complained, "it's all buzzwords
. . . After a while, every project starts to look the same. People from all
over the country are giving me the same proposals, ideas, projects."
Snydal felt this was exacerbated by the enormous competition among a
myriad of NGOs for relatively small pots of funding. As he explained,
"Everyone is working in closets here, reinventing the wheel. Most NGOs
are suspicious and hoard information because they don't want to give up
their toehold on funding."[11] This method of supporting development can,
in the long run, undermine civic growth by creating organizations with
few domestic anchors.

These "buzzwords," so essential for organizational survival, often
changed from year to year as donors tried to move civic development
forward, causing groups to run from project to project in search of continued support. Social marketing projects were popular one year, networking projects the next, coalition building the following year, and so
on. Groups responded to this changing supply by reworking the logic of
their organizations, altering their missions to meet project demands.
Groups that received large amounts of money several years previously
were later looking for new funding options; projects that were once
fundable were no longer "in style." Larisa Flint, an NGO consultant,
commented, "I have seen many organizations sit down with the grant
requirements and stretch their organization's mission to fit within the
bounds of requirements for new grants available. Practically speaking, this
has been the ruin of many organizations after the second or third grant
because it doesn't allow for stable growth and fulfillment of the NGO
mission."[12] Certainly, good organizations were able to absorb changes and
grow; for many, however, projects were picked up, implemented, and then
abandoned as the group moved on to the next theme.

Supply-driven civil societies not only created a market for narrowly
defined civil society projects; they also created a market for civic activists.
On the one hand, this can help protect against "brain drain"—talented,
hard-working individuals had more incentives to stay in the nonprofit
sector because it paid relatively well. Supply-driven civil societies also,
however, tended to attract civic entrepreneurs interested in mining the
financial benefits provided by aid. The arrival of substantial sums of
money from donors coincided with many NGOs' first steps toward establishing an independent organization. But, given the large socioeconomic
differences separating Russia from the West, groups received the impression that NGOs were a quick and easy avenue for making money.
Discussing the transfer of skills from West to East, one activist noted, "the
NGO people there were introduced to this through endless highly paid
consultants from the west, not activists. So, that is the paradigm, that is

what they know of the Third Sector. They are only replicating what they saw."[13] Jenny Hodgson, of Charities Aid Foundation, felt that newly organized nonprofit organizations in Russia that received grants were receiving a false impression of life as a nonprofit organization: "Organizations here have trouble realizing that charities and nonprofits are by definition the poorest groups in society. They're the last groups in society to get the new computer. They've gotten it all backwards here. It's gotten all mixed up."[14] By using corporate Western NGOs to train Russian groups, donors in some ways encouraged the civic entrepreneur without exposing them to the broader structure that facilitates that entrepreneur.

As a result, paying for activism on select themes had an uneven impact on the recipient NGO community. Financial support of worthwhile projects did not guarantee worthwhile results. Often, projects that sounded great on paper—networking, advocacy, or anti-corruption activities—faltered when it came to implementation. Projects that promised big results, such as national level coalitions, increased contact with local administrations, or greater communication within the NGO community, often were conceptualized as yet another seminar, round table, training session, or publication for a select group of NGOs. The proposed round table, workshop, or training became the end in and of itself, rather than a means to the end that donors were hoping to see—greater advocacy levels, more access to elites, or open budget processes. As a result, many of the promised results never materialized once the project ended, for organizations had moved on to the next fundable project.

For example, one popular funding theme involved projects that fostered networks among NGOs. This arose out of donor organizations' attempts to broaden their projects to have a geographical impact beyond the larger cities, where funding had first been concentrated. A program officer at the Eurasia Foundation who had overseen networking projects commented, "Still, the real impact, especially a long-term one, was rather low. The reason, as I can take it, is in the following: those organizations didn't concern themselves about the qualitative result of their activity, and in this respect their influence . . . was passive and formal. Thus all the attempts to create any sustainable network failed."[15] The effect was that many organizations started creating networks of NGOs even when there was little or no demand within the local NGO community for them, or even any interest on the part of the implementing NGO.

More recently, in fall 2002, I sat in on a transparent budget seminar for NGOs. These types of projects were supported by donors in the hopes that NGOs would pressure local administrations into a more open budgeting process. However, the NGO leading the training had no experience in working on budget issues because their own local administration had refused to open up the process. As a result, training consisted of a few handouts on why it was important to get involved in budget oversight (according to the participating NGOs, it was so they could claim their own piece of the budgetary pie). This soon degenerated into a lengthy argument about why some NGOs in the room had received grants and others had not.[16] Thus, the round table had limited impact in terms of getting NGOs (let alone citizens) involved in a process that sounded good on paper, but was poorly matched to the reality of Russia's NGO sector. Providing funding to Russian NGOs to implement projects on budget transparency in no way ensured that organizations would ever engage in such an activity in a meaningful and productive way with local authorities, other NGOs, or the population at large.

The appearance of foreign aid can affect why NGO leaders become active, which goals are chosen, how these goals are pursued, and the outcome. When donors provide programmatic support for a wide array of projects that do not easily match the contours of existing civic activism, organizations respond with programs and activities shaped by what donors are willing to support, which may or may not reflect what the organizations are qualified to do or what the community needs. It is unclear where the causal arrows are pointing; are organizations receiving grants because they propose a solution to a real need or because the donor has decided that the need exists? Andrei Vakulenko, a former program officer at the Eurasia Foundation, commented, "Funders sometimes think they are supporting the existing movement but they're really creating the movement . . . but Western funders don't really think about what they are doing. If they receive a proposal, then they assume there is a movement. They never think strategically—it's always reactive grantmaking." In evaluating funders' past performances, he said, "funders should concentrate on NGOs that match the real problems of Russia."[17]

Which of the various parties involved in Russia's civic development should get to diagnose and prescribe the solution for Russia's "real" problems? Deciding which problems to address, how to solve them, and who should implement these solutions is an ongoing struggle. Donors walk a fine line between encouraging existing activism that has already developed in local communities and trying to foster new developments that can engender greater processes of reform. In a country with few civic traditions and trends, the themes and the organizations to which donors supply support can have a significant impact on how organizations work, in both positive and negative ways. Donors should fund human rights and gender concerns, however, the test of whether organizations can implement such projects should be judged through their abilities to interpret that concern broadly and in tune with local community needs, rather than in their abilities to speak a very narrow and specialized language.

Civic Leaders or Civic Oligarchy?

Despite these problems, some savvy, well-connected, and talented organizations learned the rules extraordinarily well. As a result, they took leadership positions within the NGO community. Yet, given the lack of domestic resources and the early stage of civic development, this also tended to polarize resources into the hands of the organizations that learned the language that donors wanted to hear, while marginalizing the rest of the sector. Many of these patterns were created in the initial years of foreign assistance, when many donors were initiating fledgling programs.

At first, in the early 1990s, this need to learn the language of donors was literal; the choice of who to financially support was often driven by the need for Russian activists to speak English. When funding initially arrived in Russia, much of foreign aid consisted of hiring U.S. consultants and trainers who spoke little or no Russian but who were responsible for setting up and implementing programs that required them to interact with Russian civic activists on a daily basis. As a result, many Russian activists who spoke English benefited enormously. Discussing the experiences of the Civic Initiatives Program (CIP), one activist noted that because none of the Americans hired to get the program started spoke Russian, this required hiring a bilingual staff. As a result, she commented, "the first requirement was not commitment to the sector but English, which is not very promising in terms of sustainability."[18] Often, the best English speakers were not always the strongest civic activists. Although Western donors began to focus on making NGO development more indigenous by hiring more Russian staff and using Russian trainers, the more obvious language requirements were replaced by subtler ones. Learning to speak the democracy language donors wanted to hear was crucial, and establishing a past record of success became important in terms of establishing one's credibility as a civic activist.

Thus, aid often generated and reinforced the inequalities already evident in the developing civic sector. Many of these patterns were set into place in the early years of foreign funding, when English speakers from the largest cities of Moscow and St. Petersburg got their feet in the door. This allowed them to establish a track record, ensuring continued funding. One activist discussed her own experiences with finding funding for her Gender Studies Center. Reflecting comments made by other activists, she felt the search for external support was primarily about connections and establishing a track record of grants in order to ensure future funding possibilities. Looking back on the first proposal that her organization wrote in English, she felt that it had been poorly conceived, although it did receive funding. She felt that this initial award was crucial in establishing a record of success, which ensured that the organization would continue to receive support. Having connections, both with the grant-making institution and with Westerners who could proofread the English, also helped.[19]

Establishing a track record often was conflated with having a qualitative impact, although the two were not necessarily synonymous. One NGO evaluator complained that many NGOs, because of their success in "getting grants," were often given more projects based "on their long record of funding rather than their history of success stories."[20] Another civic activist echoed this, stating, "I am currently very concerned about our establishing an oligarchy in the NGO sector where strong groups with grant track records are the only ones who get funding."[21] The skills needed to get grants were not necessarily the same skills needed to be a strong community activist; yet, often, success in the former was taken to imply success in the latter. The intense competition between many groups for relatively few sources of money raised the stakes considerably.

Moscow-based organizations, as the primary targets of NGO development in the early years, benefited enormously from this head start in creating relationships with donors.[22] As a result, even though donors were trying to curb support for Moscow NGOs and expand out into the regions, the advantage given to groups in the large cities allowed them to solidify their status as "leading NGOs." Frequently, when donors stressed the need to spread funding to the regions, centralized groups responded by promoting networking, coalition, or advocacy projects with regional groups to demonstrate that they were also interested in regional civic development. Tatiana Barchunova, an activist from Novosibirsk, noted, "Organizations in Moscow have access to resources, information, power institutions that makes them able to get grants which seem to be able to contribute to major changes. This is what big grantors basically want. Legislation, actions etc. Knowledge of languages makes their applications valid and consistent."[23] She explained, "Suppose I am a reader and I have two applications—one is a professionally written one from Moscow and it says they will share the funds with the regions. The other is from a small provincial town and it is badly written and self-oriented. I think that very often the priority is given to the professionally done applications. That's it. One cannot resist the temptation—to prefer someone who sounds professional."[24]

Because Westernized groups can speak the professional language, they often become the interpreters of Russia's civic development to donors who often do not have the time or the ability to track regional development. As a result, a few prominent NGOs with established relationships with donors have captured the discourse on civil society, leaving many other Russian NGOs out of any debate about the emerging shape and nature of Russia's civic activism. As donors attempt to evaluate past work and head in new directions, these few NGOs become the sounding boards for discussing current evaluations, defining new challenges, and identifying future needs of civic sector programs for all of Russia. Yet, their status as unofficial spokespeople often rests on their abilities to talk to donors rather than their close connection to grassroots developments. Nonetheless, they serve on grant selection committees, advise on program design, and help make decisions that will affect the rest of the sector.

Donors pointed out that focusing on Moscow-based organizations made good strategic sense. John Squier, program officer for Russia and Ukraine at the National Endowment for Democracy, in discussing the focus on Moscow, argued, "by giving, say, a Moscow-based coalition a few tens of thousands of dollars to carry out a nationwide campaign on transparency in regional budgets, the NED can help Russians open up their system a little bit and make it at least a bit more responsive to public demands." Discussing the need to involve Moscow, he maintained, "If you want to have an effect on a political system as centralized as Russia's you have to work with organizations in Moscow, because Moscow is where all the people who make the decisions are. It's just a fact."[25] In part, centralization of aid to the civic sector is justified because the trends in the political sector have gone that way as well.

Unfortunately for many groups out in the regions, a Moscow-directed conference has limited impact when these organizations must implement a campaign based only on a collection of publications, handouts, and round table brainstorming sessions. Alternatively, when trainers from the capital have flown to Russia's regions to conduct training for local activists, these trainers are often poorly versed on local conditions, contexts, and environments, or even on the local NGO communities themselves.

Further, in interviews with NGOs, while many felt federal legislation was certainly important, they were more concerned with the challenge of encouraging local governments, overwhelmed with changing federal and regional contexts, to implement the legislation that had already passed. The problem was not so much affecting government policies at the federal level, but encouraging elites at the regional and local levels to sort through the maze of legislative changes and set up a workable schedule of implementation. While the practice of legislation may be centralized, law implementation is not. Thus, building regional strength to apply pressure on local administrators to actually enforce legislation calls for strong regional NGO involvement, not centralized NGO influence.

Other donors prioritized funding NGOs in the regions, yet the money targeting "regional development," although welcome, barely made a dent in the expanse of Russia. Despite the rhetorical support for spreading aid, as one activist explained, "grants are like winning the lottery out here."[26] Often, focusing on regional development entailed providing substantial support to a select group of regional umbrella organizations and resource centers. These groups served, in a sense, as civic gatekeepers, monitoring the situation in the region, identifying up-and-coming organizations, and evaluating local NGO needs and problems. Some of them were able to use their donor funds to sponsor small grants competitions for local organizations, thus becoming donors themselves.

This type of top-down funding, by choosing strong domestic NGOs to mentor smaller ones, worked when the hub center itself functioned effectively. Thus, for example, with the help of external aid, a resource center in Siberia succeeded in building up an impressive network of NGO resource centers, establishing an ongoing and extensive small grants program, and developing a democratic and responsive system of internal governance over nearly a decade. However, poorly organized, ill-conceived, and badly managed resource centers often absorbed most of the financial support without having a large impact on the surrounding regions. Resource centers became increasingly popular mechanisms through which to channel support, although their performance was uneven, and continued funding seemed to be based on a reluctance to admit to poor civic investment choices rather than an acknowledgment of past impact.

In sum, donors' choice of NGOs that can deliver promising change has tended to centralize resources in the hands of a small collection of relatively Westernized, English-speaking activists. Despite efforts to spread funding across Russia, strategies have tended to institutionalize a few organizations in the capital cities, while marginalizing the rest of the sector. While this may mirror the reality of Russian politics, it has not helped decentralize a sector that theoretically is supposed to counter this trend in other areas. The civic sector was no more immune than the political or economic sector to broader trends of centralization of resources and power. To some extent, however, aid was facilitating this process.

PRINCIPLED CLIENTELISM

The dynamics of foreign assistance in building civil society introduced new players and new relationships, realigning and adjusting linkages between civic actors, the state, and the population. Not only were civic associations developing ties among fellow citizens, they were also developing relationships with foreign embassies, foreign NGOs, and transnational organizations. The entrance of foreign aid into the picture created a new set of allegiances and loyalties that crossed traditional nation-state boundaries. Foreign aid was beholden not to the government of the country that it was trying to help but to the government or office that sent the assistance. In turn, the recipients of aid had to satisfy two clients—their domestic audience as well as their donors. As groups looked outwards toward potential constituencies, many often concentrated on donors as the "voice that matters" in terms of garnering support. The result of foreign aid designed to facilitate the development of a civil society dominated by horizontal networks among civic groups has been the creation of what I term "principled clientelism"; in other words, despite funders' self-professed intentions, the result has been the establishment of unequal vertical relationships, in which donors and NGOs mutually justify each other's continued work.

Patron-client relations are based on inequality and differences in power between patron and client. The most crucial element of this inequality is the monopolization, by the patrons, of certain positions that are of crucial importance for the clients.[27] In addition to inequality and asymmetry in power, patron-client relations are also marked by seeming mutual solidarity expressed in terms of personal identity and interpersonal sentiments and obligations. The patron usually extends some type of favor, benefit, or access to a valued resource while the client returns the favor with promises of loyalty, fealty, and moral support.

At first glance, foreign aid may seem a strange candidate for the patron-client appellation—a cornerstone of aid has been that U.S. organizations and foreign missions are to some extent the equal of their Russian civic group relatives. Thus, the distribution of aid, assistance, advice, and so forth could only build stronger horizontal ties between foreign NGOs and Russian organizations, as well as among fellow Russian NGOs. Yet the presence of aid blurred that division and altered the nature of horizontal ties.

Although donors and Russian NGOs often used the rhetoric of equality, the reality was that donors possessed millions of dollars and that recipients received whatever donors decided to give them. Donors distributed cash to Russian NGOs, which then used that money for some specified purpose, spelled out in a grant proposal. In return for the money, the organization implemented their proposed project and wrote up a final report tabulating the results of using the grant money. Materially, Russian NGOs that received foreign assistance were financially dependent on their wealthier Western counterparts. Russians and Westerners found themselves separated by a historical wealth of experiences and resources.

Initially, it seems as if Western organizations received little in return; thus the "principled" nature of the relationship. The argument here is not that Russian groups that did not receive Western assistance were somehow more "pure" or altruistic. Alternatively, Russian civic activists who did receive aid from the West were not purely self-interested hacks trying to make some easy money. Nor were funders merciless bureaucrats and international carpetbaggers just trying to make a quick dollar. Rather, those involved in building the civic sector were earnestly implementing grant programs in the effort to do some good. Nonetheless, Russian NGOs that worked with foreign assistance players could give one major gift in return—a raison d'être for the funders' continued and future funding from their own funding source. Russian NGOs served a valuable role in ensuring the donors' field offices' own future survival by providing data for reports and justification for continued spending.

To some extent, donors and funded organizations were locked in a relationship in which they both tacitly cooperate to create a "virtual" civil society. In an influential article published in *Foreign Affairs*, Clifford Gaddy and Barry Ickes argued that a new market system had emerged in Russia, with its own rules and its own criteria for success and failure. They referred to it as a virtual economy because it was based on an illusion; the economy seemed much larger and productive than it really was. To some extent, aid has helped sustain a virtual civil society, portrayed as much more significant and productive than it really is. Donors and recipient NGOs to some extent kept up a pretext of carefully documenting activities, success stories, and future needs in order to justify their continued existence. It served the interests of everyone involved in the external promotion of civil society. Yet this portrayal masked real, deep problems. NGOs did not function as they should; they were targeting the wrong constituency, and overlooking a key one—the domestic population.

GUARDIAN CIVIL SOCIETIES

By inverting how and why groups organize, external assistance encouraged foreigners to take on roles that traditionally were filled by domestic actors. In turn, this discouraged Russian groups from developing the roles they themselves should have been filling. In particular, it discouraged groups from developing domestic constituencies; rather, it encouraged groups to bypass the very actors they need to engage if civil society is to encompass more than a select group of nonprofit organizations, or if aid is lessened or leaves Russia altogether.

In the short term, the danger is that foreign aid creates a civil society that is financially unsustainable after aid leaves. A more long-term problem is that it is creating a nonprofit sector that is not interested in performing its community functions because the incentives encourage groups to focus their attentions elsewhere—on their donor, the transnational network, and the international community. If donors really do want to encourage local NGOs to develop relationships with various levels of governments so that they can advocate for local constituencies, these same NGOs will need to develop local sources of citizen support to carry weight with their policy demands. NGOs in fragile democracies are often poorly connected to the state and to the public, but foreign aid does nothing to provide incentives for NGOs to overcome this weakness.

IMPLICATIONS

What do these results imply about the external promotion of civic development? Did the problems arise because the task of externally promoting civil society is inherently contradictory or because the task was not always clearly conceived? Did aid do irreparable damage to the fledgling civil society? Was it all just a waste of money? Or did the benefits outweigh the unintended consequences?

Some argue that the very forces capable of sustaining and nurturing a civil society inherently must come from within. Although democratic institutions and economic resources can be transplanted, the civic "spirit" needed to drive these institutions is more difficult to transplant.[28] Yet it seems as if democratic political institutions, economic resources, and civic impulses in fact come out of the same mixing bowl and that if we accept the feasibility of one project, then we accept the feasibility of all three. Perhaps we have less experience with fostering civic development while the external promotion of stable political and economic institutions has a longer track record; perhaps we have less longitudinal data from which to make assessments and create policy recommendations. The trick, however, is in finding ways to trigger this domestic civic "spirit" rather than reproduce it. This book argues that, to date, the methods used to trigger this spirit have not developed in expected or anticipated ways, but that the task is worthwhile.

Has foreign aid thus far created a civil society? No. It has, however, facilitated the emergence of a nonprofit sector, which is one component of the larger network of civic groups that make up civic development. These are two separate tasks—while the term "civil society" refers to the numerous forms of associational life between the state and the private realm; the NGO sector refers to a much narrower slice of activism, the "formal, functionally differentiated and frequently professional nonprofit organizations that interact with the state and market actors."[29]

Optimists could argue that aid is fostering a bifurcated civil society. Unfunded groups were more successful in providing mutual support networks to small segments of the population. They might be better equipped to perform civil society's internal functions of building norms of trust, reciprocity, and cooperation. The groups that perform these internal duties of civil society are precisely the ones that are often overlooked by funders because they are deemed too insular, too particularistic, and too self-oriented. Externally supported organizations may be able, in the future, to perform civil society's advocacy functions, albeit for a detached population. Perhaps this is creating an elaborate division of labor, in which funded groups perform some of civil society's external functions (such as advocating on citizen's demands), while leaving many of the groups that perform civil society's internal functions (facilitating trust, mutual reciprocity, and cooperation) untouched.[30]

In addition, two reasons to be optimistic emerge from the experiences of aid that targets democratization initiatives. First, aid to the civic sector did not go the same route as the aid designed for economic reform in Russia. Civil society aid was spread out to enough recipients so that, even though it encouraged them to protect their funding sources, it did not evoke the same reaction as economic reform aid did among those controlling the state. The state embezzled or misappropriated billions of dollars of economic reform loan money. In contrast, civic activists did not steal the money; the money involved simply often provided incentives for them to value their own careers and the institutionalization of their organization at the expense of building more long-term community ties. The money was merely misused, occasionally wasted, but it was not stolen. This in and of itself represents enormous progress from previous aid attempts that channeled money to the state.

Second, perhaps even building unsustainable NGOs is not a waste. When I discussed aid with an NGO practitioner who had worked extensively in Zimbabwe, she laughed at my tale of aid to civic groups in Russia. "It was the same in Zimbabwe," she replied. "The number of NGOs in Zimbabwe in the 1980s was incredibly high. We had an information booklet this thick (holding up her fingers). But then Eastern Europe collapsed, and all the aid left Africa."[31] Even though many of the NGOs dried up, she reported that when it came time for Zimbabwe to write a new constitution, the very same civic entrepreneurs who had built up often unsustainable NGOs were the ones who designed the constitution that was to govern Zimbabwe. Shrugging her shoulders, she said, "maybe we didn't build a civil society, but the people writing the constitution are the very same NGO activists who used to receive grants twenty years ago." Although in Zimbabwe's case, power remains in the hands of an aging, yet determined dictatorship, perhaps civic activists will be able to serve as a real political alternative some day in the future. Similarly, perhaps today's civic activists will be tomorrow's democratic leaders in the new Russia. Having honed their advocacy skills in donor-supported civil society projects, activists may focus their abilities and talents on building political society.

ALTERNATIVE POLICIES, ALTERNATIVE INCENTIVES

However, I believe that aid targeted to civic development can accomplish more than training advocates and preparing future political elites. Yet, we are still early in our own learning curve of implementing effective policy. We are still discussing, for the most part, whether civic aid "works," rather than asking under what conditions, in what contexts, and with which strategies it works. What has emerged is a consensus that aid can accomplish only so much, given the larger, less flexible context of historical legacies, culture, levels of economic development, current political institutions, and geopolitical location. Unfortunately, initial research indicates that, similar to the realm of economic development, aid often works best in those areas that need it least. Carothers and Ottaway stress that history and culture play a large, although not always determinate role, in influencing aid's outcome.[32] In a comparative analysis of aid strategies in the formerly communist region, Mendelson argues that the level of integration with Europe, and implicitly, the West, was the determining factor in understanding the degree to which civic aid was effective.[33] In other words, geography and state elite attitudes, rather than NGO activities, played a large role in fostering an environment conducive to Western aid strategies. As a state on the semiperiphery, Russia is better off than the central Asian republics, but behind most of the countries of Eastern Europe. Cultural and geopolitical factors are larger issues outside of donor control.

In the small arena that donors have to maneuver, it is important to do the best with limited resources. Aid, as it is currently structured, rewards Westernized groups who can speak the language donors want to hear. It encourages recipient organizations to resemble corporate entities, valuing their own survival over their original mission. It encourages groups to remain small, centralized, and hierarchical. Given the intense competition among Western development NGOs, there is little incentive for donors to admit failure, attempt radical change, or cut old programs in the search for new development approaches. Donor agencies remain wedded to projects that promise to yield impressive outcomes for small amounts of money. As a result, they have favored projects such as "train the trainers," advocacy, and coalition projects because they promise big changes while maintaining the rhetoric of grassroots power, even if the results are sometimes slim. While donors active in the field have tried adjusting funding strategies by shifting more funding to the regions and changing some funding priorities, often it can be hard to successfully lobby the home office for a major overhaul of funding strategies when previous work has ensured steady budgets and continued development work.

As I traveled around Russia in 1998 and then in 1992, I met with a range of civic groups and development practitioners. I met with organizations that had received donor support and had done interesting and innovative things with small amounts of money. I met far more that knew the right rhetoric, but didn't always connect the funded project with clear, directed, domestic-oriented actions. I met unfunded groups who had done impressive things with small amounts of money, and I wondered why they were not considered by donors to be crucial to civil society. And of course I met many groups that were small, insular, and self- oriented, and did not need (and also did not want) any external support. I spoke with donors who felt they had their fingers on the pulse of civic development in Russia as well as with program officers who were still fine tuning strategies, looking for new partners and fresh approaches. This range in attitude and activities enforced my belief that it is not aid in and of itself that is flawed but the way in which it is designed and implemented.

However, for more effective policy, donors need to redefine their vision of civil society and the appropriate policies for supporting civic growth. In their mission statements, donors all emphasize their commitment to building civil society, many using arguments straight from Tocqueville and Robert Putnam. However, there is a large disjuncture between what they are trying to accomplish and what they are actually bringing about. Have donors built a nonprofit sector? Yes. Have they kept alive a variety of movements that would not have survived otherwise? Certainly. But if donors really want to work toward their stated approach, there are several clear steps they could take.

Broadening the Definition of "Good" Civil Society

Donors, in their efforts to identify organizations that could serve as ideal incubators of more civic-minded and democratic political cultures, favored a relatively narrow slice of civic activism. Groups that claimed to engage in "building civil society" were favored; groups that were active in civil society but were unable to frame it as such were often excluded. Groups that talked about advocacy received support; those that performed it but called it something else were left out of the loop. In sum, donors need to broaden their definition of groups that contribute to civic development beyond the most obvious exemplars of "good" civil society—those organizations involved in civic development, support for human rights, gender concerns, and environmental sustainability. A civic community does exist in Russia, but it is a civic community more comfortable at international conferences with fellow Western audiences than at home working in the local community. This international civil society is developing not in conjunction with, but perhaps at the expense of, domestic civic development.

While these "good" civil society groups are important, they are not the only ones that perform important civic functions, such as building social capital and linking private demands with public forums of discourse. Organizations that work directly with the general population for immediate, tangible, and practical improvements in Russian lives have also been critical, but underappreciated players in Russia's civic realm. By providing a needed and valuable service to a grateful and often growing clientele, usually after intense interaction with local government elites, they too are able to perform crucial civic functions. Yet donors tend to overlook these organizations because they don't promise big change and high payoffs at the federal level, even if they have made impressive changes at the local level. In addition, many have already established small domestic sources of support, which means that they at least have some experience with sustaining themselves outside of donor sources of financial assistance, which will be vital if Western aid disappears.

Supporting Non-NGO Civil Society

In addition, donors have taken Tocquevillian logic too much to heart. In a famous, oft-quoted passage, de Tocqueville observes that "Americans of all ages, all stations in life, and all types of dispositions are forever forming associations."[34] Donors, in justifying their programs, have echoed this stress on the important role of voluntary organizations in subsequently affecting the quality of democracy. Yet, when Tocqueville was writing, he was not thinking of the complex maze of 501(c)(3) organizations that now qualify as nonprofit organizations in the United States. NGOs are only one marker of civil society and occupy one slice of activity; NGOs are not synonymous with civil society. Yet donors have chosen to focus, however understandably, on NGOs as the primary vehicles of greater economic, social, and political benefits. Before a democratizing country can have vibrant, flourishing organizations, it needs citizens interested in joining or interacting with such organizations, either as full-fledged members, or as concerned citizens willing and able to turn out for an issue that is compelling to them. By focusing so intently on NGOs, donors may miss the larger important spirit of voluntarism that underlies these more formalized attempts at organization. Particularly in a society such as Russia's, where citizens were hyper-organized under the Soviet regime, instilling a sense of efficacy in individual citizens, rather than a need for organizational membership, is important. Citizens in Russia do want to get involved in community affairs; limiting donor support of that involvement to NGOs that focus on advocacy and potential democratic change in turn limits the impact donors can have on broader populations.

USAID has begun to experiment with broadening their view of civil-society-building activities in Russia. In fall 2002, the Institute for Sustainable Communities, an international development organization based out of Vermont, signed an agreement with USAID to implement a four-year, $3.8 million program to operate in the Russian Far East. Titled the Russian Far East Civic Initiatives Program (not to be confused with the earlier, but different, Save the Children Civic Initiatives Program), the program tries to broaden its influence by including a component to foster community involvement.[35] In this proposal, existing resource centers will be used as the engine behind fostering citizen involvement, despite the fact that, in the past, most have been oriented toward providing services to NGOs. By early 2003, ISC was still in the process of choosing resource centers with whom to partner. We do not yet know whether this verbal support for increased citizen involvement will result in actual greater participation. However, efforts to expand beyond the narrow realm of NGOs are a step toward broadening donors' focus on civil society.

Smaller Is Better

In order to match Russian needs, donors need to continue support for small grants programs rather than investing larger amounts in a few prominent, well-connected organizations. While the practice of giving more money to fewer organizations saves many donors from administrative overload, it doesn't match the needs of Russia's NGO community. Thousands of organizations need money for five hundred envelopes, not a brand-new computer. They may need support for a one-time event, rather than money to support an office staff for a yearlong project. While some donor-supported resource centers, such as the Siberian Center, remain committed to providing small, one-time grants to sponsor local initiatives, other centers are learning to mimic donors by complaining that the work is too time consuming to be worth the effort. Facilitating civic initiatives is hard work, and while it is easier to give fewer groups more money, in reality the reverse is needed.

In addition, large grants from a single donor provide disincentives for groups to seek alternative sources of funding. In several interviews, grant recipients expressed confusion at the idea of the need to develop ties with local constituencies given the overwhelming financial benefits of receiving a grant from the West. Reevaluating old partnerships, rather than automatically increasing the funding for a former grant recipient, or even decreasing funding can encourage groups to expand their contacts and find creative solutions to funding dilemmas. As local government administrations begin to provide their own grants to NGOs, many find that they have been out priced by donors; accustomed to higher salaries from Western organizations, Russian NGOs aren't as interested in applying for local sources which promise fewer financial rewards.

In addition to scaling down some grant sizes, donors should reduce the expensive partnership programs between Russian NGOs and large bureaucratized Western development groups in favor of smaller, extended exchanges among grassroots organizations. Establishing partnerships between Western and Russian NGOs does not have to entail granting large sums of money to both partners. Some of the most effective partnerships I witnessed were ones that did not involve financial transactions. Rather, successful partnerships often evolved out of periodic, yet steady contact between similar groups in two countries. Whether through sister-city projects or exchanges of women's sewing circles, developing personal ties, contacts, and even friendships can help cement and train a Russian group much more effectively than an expensive project involving imported trainers. Sometimes, personal ties of friendship cannot be replaced with money and expensive projects. To be realistic, this suggestion asks many implementing development agencies to put themselves out of work; nonetheless, it is crucial if one wants to reshape the way that aid is formulated and implemented.

CONCLUSION

At the beginning of this book, I asked the reader to imagine that a number of civic groups in the United States had received their primary sources of support from abroad. I suggested that this would have implications for how and why groups organized, and ultimately, how civil society worked. However, there is a big difference; the United States is a consolidated (if imperfect) democracy. In the Russian case, given the tenuous political situation, a weakened state, the paucity of civic traditions, the youth of the emerging civic sector, and the lack of domestic financial support for NGOs, aid has the power to play an even larger role in shaping what emerges.

In efforts to build civil society in Russia, scholars and development practitioners often cast domestic NGO leaders as Cinderellas. Although resource-poor, overworked, and underappreciated, they nonetheless were predicted to play a crucial role in Russia's struggle to redefine itself as a democratic society. In turn, as Western donors engaged in an ambitious and self-conscious effort to accelerate civic development, many initially cast themselves in the role of fairy godmother. With the wave of a wand, the strategic placement of grant dollars, a smattering of training, and some much needed translated material on civic development, Soviet citizens would become civic activists. Many involved in the tasks of civic reform thought their task challenging, but surmountable; organizations such as USAID and their project implementers originally envisioned an involvement lasting five to seven years. With the infrastructure in place, social capital, activism, and public spiritedness would all follow.

Six years later, Jenny Hodgson, co-head of the Charities Aid Foundation Moscow office, smiled wryly at the expectations they all held in the beginning. Commenting on the impact of Western training, she said, "if people [Western donors] pull out tomorrow, there will be books, but that's it." Thinking about the course of foreign aid, she mused: "USAID promised Congress, Russia wasn't Africa. Russians said 'we're not Africa,' but we overestimated how quickly we could change things."[36] Echoing this diagnosis, Janelle Cousino, a civic trainer, reflected, "our expectations were way too optimistic." Now, she predicted, "there will not be change for at least twenty years."[37] A program officer who was leaving Russia after working for four years on civic development issues felt that "it's all pretty hopeless. . . . all NGOs think vertically, not horizontally, which they need to do in order to build networks."[38] As donors and Western nonprofit organizations began to evaluate their own performances and results from their work in Russia, many spoke repeatedly of the high expectations with which they had begun and of the realization that they had miscalculated the time needed to provide the necessary infrastructure for civic development to thrive.

Many donors also spoke of the progress they had made, but emphasized that it was difficult to measure the changes, and that they had evolved slowly as a result of sometimes years of work. The same program officer, who felt his efforts were "hopeless," upon reflection, commented that he had gotten tremendous satisfaction from his job when he had been able to offer practical services that did not entail the transferal of money. His last project had involved a trip to Mongolia to deliver books in Russian to nonprofit organizations. Thinking about it, he said, "concrete results make you feel like there is progress."[39] In a separate exchange, another activist argued, "anyone can write an *ustav* and register an organization. That is the easy part. The hard part is conducting effective programs that address the needs of the local communities."[40]

Reflecting on what works and does not work, she added that "The key here is that it [funding] is not about propping up an organization. . . . the most important thing is that the concept become part of the social fabric." Constant monitoring combined with mentoring, finding innovative and dedicated activists, and the proverbial blood, sweat, and tears helped sustain her organization through growing pains over the years.

Funding to develop civil society has the potential to play a critical role in the long and difficult process of civic and democratic development. To date, it has helped numerous activists all over Russia to develop their organizations and implement projects on a variety of compelling topics. It has kept groups alive that would have faltered in the face of public and state indifference, or sometimes, hostility. Its main impact has been in fostering the development of a nonprofit sector. However, the way that donors have thought about, designed, and implemented civil society aid needs to be substantially rethought. Donor policies have tended to overinstitutionalize a select group of NGOs, create problems of long-term sustainability for the sector, concentrate power into a small number of activists, and further isolate groups from their own hypothetical target populations. Designing strategies that will create a more broad-based, more inclusive civic community, broadly defined, is the challenge of the next decade.

Research Methodology

This research is based on twelve months of fieldwork I conducted in Russia in 1998–99. I employed original survey research, interviews with Russian NGO activists and representatives from Western aid agencies, professional job experience with three foreign foundations involved in distributing aid and advice to Russian NGOs, and the literature and newsletters of various organizations from Russia's third sector. In addition, I returned to Russia in fall 2002 for a three-month follow up visit.

Survey Research

Doing a mail survey in Russia may seem counterintuitive. Many Russians, when I initially approached them with the project, spent much time regaling me with the myriad ways in which I would probably fail in my endeavor. Logistically, the mail is consistent in its constant unreliability. Structurally, Russian society is not analogous to the more sophisticated systems of the West. Russia lacks the consumer society of credit cards and subscriptions, which produce endless mailing lists, pleas for help, and unsolicited requests. Many Russians, as well as fledgling nonprofit groups, are unused to the concept of unsolicited mail, especially mail from an unknown researcher asking for help. If anything, women's groups took a strange delight in advising me against the mail survey, shaking their heads in sage pessimism while telling me that groups in Russia just would not "understand" why they should respond to a survey from someone they did not know. In addition to having little practice in filling out surveys, Russian groups, I was told, were still too "suspicious" of a strange Westerner sending out a solicitation for help.

Despite the obstacles and the warnings, I settled on a mail survey because the gaps in our knowledge of civic groups and of survey research in general in Russia are alarmingly large. Russian and Soviet studies have long been the domain of extremely thorough qualitative work, which has involved extensive field research stretching over several years. It is only in the 1990s that scholars have embarked on quantitative research. However, the quantitative bent has tended toward using the public opinion survey. Thus, although surveys were becoming more frequent, they were often phone-polling calls or face-to-face interviews with randomly selected Russian citizens.[1] In addition, at the time I was conducting my own work research into the civic sector remained the domain of funding agencies working in Russia.[2]

The idea of the survey came from a desire to bridge several bodies of literature. Although much of the qualitative work was exquisite in its attention to detail, nuance, and feeling, it was nonetheless constrained by the geographical range of the researcher. Often it could adequately capture the mood, trend, and feeling of a particular place, time, and locale, but it was difficult to make comparisons with areas not covered by the researcher. On the other hand, the quantitative data that touched on democratization issues often were geared toward catching the mood of the general public and I wanted to focus on civic groups.

As I explain in chapter 1, I chose to focus on women's groups because they represent a significant portion of NGO activism overall and because foreign funders have targeted women's groups and improving the status of women in Russia as a primary mission within the goal of building civil society. In addition, donors have often focused their aid sectorally, on particular movements, such as those advocating greater respect for human rights or environmentalism. Although no two social movements are exactly alike, the women's movement was an ideal candidate to serve as a case study through which to explore the NGO sector as a whole. I defined "women's group" broadly; groups that protected and promoted women's interests were counted as women's organizations.[3]

Compiling a reliable list of women's groups also involved a considerable number of trials and tribulations. Although several national-level women's groups had tried to compile information on one another, the movement was still fragmented and diverse, with many groups operating in isolation from one another.[4] It is difficult to assess exactly how many women's groups are currently active; some estimates optimistically place the number at over 2,000, although only approximately 600 women's groups are registered with the Ministry of Justice.[5]

The most complete listing of women's groups in Russia arose out of a project to publish a guide on women's groups in Russia led by three women's NGOs.[6] The directory was a collaborative project (funded by USAID) among Natasha Abubikirova and Marina Regentova of Feminist Alternative, Tatiana Klimenkova of the Moscow Center for Gender Studies, Elena Kotchkina of the Gender Expertise Analysis Project of the Moscow Center for Gender Studies, and Tatiana Troinova of the Women's Information Network. The first of its kind, this book was the most comprehensive listing of women's organizations to date in Russia, and the database was even larger. Drawing from the database, I collected 379 "usable" addresses.[7]

This, however, does not represent the totality of women's groups in Russia. For example, the Union of Russian Women (the successor to the Soviet-era women's councils) supposedly has ninety-four departments; I located twenty-nine addresses. Similarly, the Movement of Russian Women has fifty-nine regional departments; only three had actual contact information.[8] In addition, rural, religious-oriented, or culturally oriented women's groups are underrepresented, although they are also elusive to track. Thus, this is not a random sample of women's groups; I used the most accurate and extensive listing to date, given the lack of consistent, reliable data about women's groups.

I sent mail surveys to 379 women's organizations across Russia in June 1998. The survey was four pages long and consisted of forty-one questions (135 total variables) covering a variety of topics: (1) basic informational questions, (2) questions on membership and leadership of the organization, (3) questions on resources, (4) questions regarding the activities and goals of the group, and (5) questions on networking and communication with other sectors of society. Respondents were given choices and asked to check off answers rather than write lengthy essays in response to openended questions. This, however, did not prevent organizations from sending lengthy letters explaining their answers or from sending me more detailed information about their organization, thus providing me with invaluable insight into and details about individual organizations and their attitudes.

I gathered questions from several sources. I looked at other survey research done on social movements and interest groups in the West. I wrote many questions similar to those in surveys by Jack Walker,[9] Russell J. Dalton,[10] Mario Diani,[11] and by two doctoral dissertation students.[12] In addition, I looked over the short, open-ended survey that the compilers of the database had distributed to Russian women's groups in 1997.[13]

When I originally wrote the survey, I was drawing primarily from surveys distributed to organizations in Western, industrialized countries. However, I wanted to ensure that the survey I had written was appropriate for the Russian context. Therefore, I worked with a focus group of five women's groups.[14] After translating the survey questions into Russian, they helped me rework the survey and reacted to the questions. It was elating, as well as disheartening, to absorb the multitude of reactions to a survey written for Western NGOs. Although I adjusted many of the questions, there was a fine line between adapting questions to particular criticisms and keeping questions general enough so that they would not exclude a large number of organizations. In addition, as a researcher, I did not want to make the question "too Russian" because I also was curious to see which questions did not translate well (conceptually), and why. As a result, many questions were changed, although many were also left as is as the survey went through several metamorphoses.[15]

Questions that I had thought to be straightforward, yes/no questions ended up provoking hours of debate. For example, the question "Does your organization have a computer" entailed hours of vigorous discussion. What if an organization did not "own" the computer but knew someone who would allow them access? What if they did not have a computer for their NGO work but used their computer at their day job? Many of the questions I had thought were quite simple to answer ended up being scrapped due to the overwhelming "what if" factor. Other questions, which inquired about income levels or annual budgets were deemed "too sensitive" by some people and were also discarded. Likewise, activists treated questions that asked groups their "opinions" or asked them to indicate a political preference or attitude very gingerly.[16] The focus group also did not like the pressure of choosing between subtle gradations, such as "somewhat," and "very." As a result, the categories were collapsed from a five-point range into three-point range: not often, often, and very often.

After many months of revising and negotiation, I sent out 379 surveys in June 1998. After lengthy discussion, I sent the surveys out "cold." Several Russians argued that since survey research was relatively unknown, sending an advance warning would simply confuse groups further. In addition, given the fabled unreliability of the Russian mail system, I was still entertaining the possibility that the letters, and the surveys, would simply never reach their destination. However, much to my surprise, over the following two months I received 144 answers.[17]

The follow-up survey for nonrespondents was scheduled to go out in August 1998; however, in August the economy crashed. The short-term result was that many post offices refused to send mail. Consequently, I delayed resending surveys to see if the situation would improve. Thus, there was a greater time lag between mailing the two surveys than I had originally planned. I sent nonrespondents a second survey in December, and I received an additional forty-two surveys.[18] Despite the delays, incorrect addresses, and erratic mail, the survey had a response rate of 52 percent. Groups from the regions and smaller cities were more likely to respond than groups in the larger cities, such as Moscow and St. Petersburg; only 24 percent of respondents were from cities larger than 2 million (Moscow and St. Petersburg), even though they made up 36 percent of my mailing list. Thus, the answers from the larger cities are underrepresented.[19]

I was interested in comparing organizations that had received outside assistance with those that had not. Curiously, when listing their resources, some groups did not perceive that the money had come from a foreign source. Several foundations have offices in Moscow and have Russified names. For example, the Eurasia Foundation was Fond Evrasii, the Ford Foundation was Fond Forda, and so on. For those few groups, I noted their answer but placed them within the category of aid recipients because they had identified groups based in the United States. A few groups also had not received a grant, but had received an invitation from a Western foundation or NGO to come to the United States for an all-expense-paid workshop, seminar, or other session for an extended period. I also counted these as foreign funding. Contributions from individual foreigners were not counted, however, because they did not represent an actual organized entity and, in addition, were charitable donations and not part of a larger application process that the Russian group had to pursue.

INTERVIEWS

In addition to surveys, I conducted over 100 interviews with NGO activists, women's group leaders, and representatives from various foundations and funding sources in order to fill out the narrative of funding and democratization.

When interviewing NGO activists, I tried to keep an even balance between interviewing funded and unfunded groups. I also tried to interview a broad range of NGOs; I made an effort to interview Westernized NGOs as well as groups with a more conservative stance. I had noticed from the surveys that many organizations were hesitant to provide information that reflected their opinions or views. Thus, the interviews provided a valuable forum for organizations and individuals to explain their behavior and rationale for decision making, both for funders and activists.

With a few exceptions, I chose to interview only one person from each organization; usually this was the leader of the group. Because most groups were small, and had formed in the previous 5–8 years, the leader was the best source of information in terms of recounting group history, organization, goals, and activities. Most leaders were also in charge of ensuring the organizational survival of their group; thus, they were the most qualified to discuss funding issues.

In my interviews with foreign foundations, I tried to interview a broader range of actors. I usually interviewed the head of the local office and then interviewed various program officers who were involved in different aspects of civic development. I also interviewed many freelance consultants who moved from foundation to foundation. It is nearly impossible to keep track of all of the foreign foundations and nonprofit organizations currently active in Russia; as a result, I interviewed a sample of international donors. I interviewed program officers from private foundations, such as the Charities Aid Foundation, Eurasia Foundation, Ford Foundation, MacArthur Foundation, Soros/Open Society Institute; Western government agencies such as USAID and the British Embassy; and smaller Western nonprofits, such as Project Harmony and Connect. Thus, although the list of foreign donors with whom I spoke is not exhaustive, it is a well-rounded sampling of the different kinds of Western donor organizations working in Russia.

The interviews lasted anywhere from fifteen minutes to two hours and were conducted in a wide variety of areas—offices, apartments, park benches, even on public transportation. I used a standard list of openended questions that I had prepared ahead of time; interviewees were given the sheet of questions and often the interview would turn into a discussion of a particular subset of questions, depending on the opinions and views of the person interviewed. I interviewed some people more than once; over the course of the year, I often ran into interviewees multiple times.

In addition, I also sat in the back of the room at many local NGO seminars, conferences, and gatherings in order to simply observe and hoped that my presence would intrude as little as possible on the natural workings of the third sector.

WORK EXPERIENCE

In order to understand the dynamics and issues facing foreign funders themselves, I also worked as a consultant for three foreign agencies in Russia: the Eurasia Foundation, the Ford Foundation, and the National Democratic Institute for International Affairs. For the Eurasia Foundation, I evaluated their grant work related to facilitating a civic community in Russia. I traveled to various regions in Russia to evaluate NGO grant performance. This usually consisted of a quick two-day stay to meet with a series of NGOs in order to assess the impact of a particular grant on the recipient NGO and on the surrounding community.

For the Ford Foundation, I served in a similar capacity, although this time I was in charge of evaluating all Ford Foundation grant work with women's organization in Russia from 1992 to 1999. This work also involved extensive travel to Russia's regions; during my tenure, I visited a wide array of geographical regions, including Pskov, Murmansk, Irkutsk, Petersburg, Petrozavodsk (Republic of Karelia), Novocherkassk, Rostov, and Naberezhniye Chelny (Republic of Tatarstan). In addition to interviewing most of the Ford Foundation's grantees, I also broadened my circle of contacts. I interviewed women's groups that had not received a Foundation grant and women's groups that had never received any Western grant aid in order to better understand the dynamics and effects of grant making. Last, I spoke with program officers from other foundations who also have targeted women's groups, such as USAID and the MacArthur, Soros, and Eurasia Foundations, in order to better assess where the Ford Foundation's work complemented other projects targeting women's NGOs.

I also worked as an assistant to the director of the Moscow office of the National Democratic Institute for Foreign Affairs (NDI). My work consisted of setting up and evaluating seminars conducted for the Russian NGO community. This also involved travel to cities NDI had targeted; my job was to interview as many contacts as I could establish in the local NGO community in order to assess their needs. I was also responsible for writing proposals for potential seminars for Russian civic groups. If the proposals were approved by the Washington, D.C., office, I was then responsible for writing up the report after the training was over, detailing the results and accomplishments of the seminar. In addition, I was responsible for writing the internal year-long assessment of NDI/Moscow's work for the Washington D.C. office.

This invaluable opportunity allowed me an inside glimpse into the rules of funding that a thirty-minute interview would not provide. In addition, it allowed me to travel to a variety of cities outside Moscow and introduced me to a wide swathe of the civic community beyond women's NGOs. I was able to meet with groups that had received Western assistance, as well as groups that relied solely on domestic sources of support. The wide geographical distribution of cities, as well as their differing sizes, helped guard against an overly Moscow-centric point of view. As people in Russia's regions love to tell travelers, "Moscow is not Russia." Thus, I tried to ensure that I spoke with as many people as I could outside of Russia's capital city.

Of course, the reception I received as an employee of an agency that distributes aid was much different than the one I received as a curious graduate student from a university "somewhere in the middle of the United States," as I often described it to Russians. As a graduate student with little to offer in return for their time, many NGO leaders were not particularly enthused about spending time with me; as an employee of a funding agency, I was granted entrée into the NGO community, albeit one whitewashed of blemishes that might be damaging to future funding potential. Thus, the interviews I draw on reflect the fact that I was operating with different personas. NGOs, in turn, presented varying personalities depending on whether I was a graduate student or a consultant for a donor organization. I do not believe, however, that in either of my two roles was I granted access to a "truer" view of the Russian third sector; rather, I saw different facets that in the end allowed me to present a more nuanced and detailed picture of NGO development in Russia.

LITERATURE

I also collected literature from various civic groups in order to obtain additional background on their organizational goals, activities, and guiding philosophies and to gain a greater perspective on the organizations' development over time. I compiled shelves of individual organizations' newsletters, bulletins, journals, publications, personal research, and so on. I also subscribed to the newsletter of the Agency of Social Information, a Moscow-based organization dedicated to collecting and distributing information about the activities of the third sector across Russia as a whole.

A P P E N D I X   B

The Survey

This appendix lists the English translation of my 1998 survey of women's organizations.[1] Please see appendix A for more information on the design and distribution of the survey. Yes/No options, scales, and answer blanks have been omitted.

Women's Organizations in Russia and the NIS

This survey is very easy to fill out. Please read the questions and the various answers that follow below. Choose the answer that best represents your view. If given the option, please write in the answer where appropriate. If you do not want to answer a particular question, you may simply move on to the next question. Individual answers to the survey are completely confidential.

1. What is the official name of your organization?
2. Please write the month and year when your group was founded.
3. Please write the month and year when your group registered.
4. Did your group exist before 1989?
5. Is your group based on a previously existing organization or is it an entirely new organization?
   a. If your organization is based on an older organization, was this organization the product of a merger of older groups or associations?
   b. If your organization is based on an older organization, did this organization originally grow out of or split off from a parent group?
6. Does your organization have an office?
7. Does your organization have a fax?
8. Does your organization have electronic mail?
9. Does your organization have a web page?
10. Does your organization have an office?
    a. If yes, how did you obtain it?
       i. Through members' personal connections
       ii. Rental
       iii. From public agencies
       iv. From other voluntary organizations
       v. Other (please specify)
    b. If no, then where do you meet?
       i. Restaurant or café
       ii. Public building
       iii. Personal apartment or home
       iv. Other (please specify)

The following section of the survey asks questions about the leadership and membership of your organization.

11. Does your organization have any paid staff?
    a. If yes, how many are full-time employees?
    b. If yes, how many are part-time paid employees?
12. How many volunteers does your organization have?
13. About how many members do you have in your group?
    a. Less than 10   d. 30–39
    b. 10–19   e. 40–49
    c. 20–29   f. More than 50
14. What was your membership five years ago?
    a. Larger than current size
    b. Approximately the same size as today
    c. Smaller than the current size
15. Does your organization have membership fees?
16. How many directors have led your organization since its founding?
17. How long has the current director served in his or her position?

In their initial states, many organizations receive financial grants or other forms of assistance to help get them established. In addition, in order to accomplish goals, groups need material resources, such as money, to survive. The following questions ask about your group's sources of income.

18. In general, how has the budget changed over the past 3–5 years?
    a. Increased, despite inflation
    b. Decreased, accounting for inflation
    c. Kept pace with inflation
    d. Other (please specify)
19. Does your organization currently receive any of the following sources of funding for your group?
    a. Membership fees
    b. Fees for services provided by your organization
    c. Grants and subsidies from the Russian government
    d. Grants and subsidies from local administrations
    e. Grants and subsidies from regional administrations
    f. Grants and subsidies from foreign foundations (for example, Soros Foundation, Eurasia Foundation, Ford Foundation, etc.)
    g. Grants and subsidies from foreign governments (for example, TACIS, USAID, or embassies of foreign governments)
    h. Grants and support from other foreign nongovernmental organizations
    i. Grants and support from other Russian nongovernmental organizations
    j. Support from Russian businesses
    k. Support from foreign businesses
    l. Funding from an international branch/chapter of your organization
    m. Funding from a national branch/chapter of your organization
    n. The work of volunteers and enthusiasts
    o. Other source (please specify)
20. Which three sources were most important in 1997?

21. If your organization received a grant or subsidy from a foreign foundation or organization, did you receive aid from any of the following organizations?
    a. MacArthur Foundation
    b. Ford Foundation
    c. IREX
    d. Eurasia Foundation
    e. USAID
    f. TACIS
    g. Soros Foundation
    h. Global Fund for Women
    i. Frauen-Anstiftung
    j. NIS-US Women's Consortium
    k. Other (please specify)
    l. No forms of foreign funding were received

22. If you have received foreign grants and subsidies, which of the following activities did these grants fund?
    a. Funding for travel abroad for conferences, training, workshops
    b. Funding for domestic conferences, training, workshops
    c. Funding for salaries
    d. Funding for your organization's newsletter
    e. Information about proposed laws going through the political system
    f. Protests
    g. Office equipment, such as computers, Xerox machines
    h. Books, literature
    i. Other (please specify)

23. How much time and energy does your organization spend on finding funding?
    a. 10%
    b. 25%
    c. 50%
    d. 75%
    e. Practically all the time

The following section of the survey asks about the goals and activities of your group.

24. Different groups have various political, economic, and social goals. If your organization works on women's issues, please indicate the importance of the following goals to your group. [Indicate importance: very important, important, not very important, not applicable.]
    a. Educate the public about women's issues
    b. To change existing laws on women's issues
    c. To provide services to women
    d. To increase women's access to political power
    e. To increase women's access to economic power
    f. Other goal (please specify)

25. If you provide services to the general population as well, please indicate the importance of the following goals to your group. [Indicate importance: very important, important, not very important, not applicable.]
    a. Defense of the rights of workers within a particular profession
    b. Defense of the rights of Russians of different nationalities
    c. Defense of the environment
    d. Economic development of Russia
    e. Development of religious life in Russia

    f. Development of the political system in Russia
    g. Development of cultural life in Russia
    h. Protection of the welfare of the poor
    i. Protection of children
    j. Protection of the disabled
    k. Other (please indicate)

26. Who makes decisions in your organization?
    a. The director makes the decision
    b. The board makes the decision
    c. We make the decision collectively
    d. Other (please specify)

27. Given your goals, please indicate how often your organization engages in the following activities. [Indicate frequency: very often, often, not very often, the organization does not engage in such activity.]
    a. Participation in the work of government commissions and advisory committees
    b. Contacts with civil servants or ministers
    c. Contacts with members of parliament
    d. Contacts with leaders of political parties
    e. Efforts to mobilize public opinion through disseminating information
    f. Organizing demonstrations, protests, strikes, or other direct actions
    g. Legal recourse to the courts or judicial bodies
    h. Contacts with people in the media
    i. Contacts with other women's organizations
    j. Contacts with other voluntary organizations besides women's groups
    k. Organizing conferences and workshops for specialists in your field
    l. Organizing conferences and workshops for interested citizens or other nonspecialists in your field
    m. Publishing newsletters, magazines, journals, monographs, or books
    n. Working for passage of needed legislation at the local, regional, or national level
    o. Working to ensure the election of political leaders sympathetic to the goals of your organization
    p. Conducting or organizing research on the problems of your field
    q. Fund-raising
    r. Applying for grants
    s. Making efforts through mailings, personal contacts, or other means to increase membership of the organization
    t. Building the identity of your members
    u. Other (please specify)

28. In your opinion, how effective are elections and working with the existing parties as a method for your group to use in influencing policies your group advocates?
    a. Very   c. Not very
    b. Somewhat   d. Hardly at all

The following questions ask about your communication with other groups.

29. How often do the following media sources report on your activities? [Indicate frequency: very often, often, not very often, never.]
    a. Local newspaper
    b. Local radio station
    c. Local TV
    d. National newspapers
    e. National TV
    f. Other (please specify)

30. In the past five years, how have contacts between your group and the following organizations changed? [Indicate dynamic: increased, stayed the same, decreased, not sure.]
    a. Local news
    b. Local radio station
    c. Local TV
    d. National newspapers
    e. National TV
    f. Local administration
    g. National government
    h. Political parties
    i. Other women's groups
    j. Other women's groups abroad
    k. Other voluntary associations besides women's groups
    l. Other (please specify)

31. Do you participate with other organizations in a coalition, forum, or federation?

32. Often groups interact with other groups in sharing information, resources, and services. Do you communicate with other women's organizations?

33. If yes, do you give any of the following resources to other women's organizations?
    a. Funding
    b. Articles, pamphlets, newsletters
    c. Information about proposed laws going through the political system
    d. Information about upcoming workshops or seminars
    e. Information about upcoming protests
    f. Office equipment
    g. Other (please specify)

34. If yes, please indicate two or three organizations, with which you cooperate the most.

35. Have you worked previously for another women's organization?

36. What is your position with this organization?
    a. President/chair/leader
    b. Vice-president
    c. Secretary/treasurer
    d. Other (please specify)

37. What is your sex?

38. What is your age?
    a. 17–24
    b. 25–29
    c. 30–39
    d. 40–49
    e. 50–59
    f. 60–64
    g. 65 and older

39. How much formal education have you completed?
    a. Grade school or less
    b. Some high school
    c. High school graduate
    d. Some college
    e. College graduate
    f. Graduate school

40. What is the size of the city in which your organization operates?
    a. Under 100,000
    b. 100,000–249,999
    c. 250,000–499,999
    d. 500,000–999,999
    e. 1–2 million
    f. Over 2 million

If there is something that is not covered in this survey that you would like to add, explain, or discuss, please write in the space provided below.

Thank you very much for filling out the survey. Please use the enclosed postage-paid envelope to return your questionnaire as soon as possible.

A P P E N D I X   C

Groups Interviewed and Conferences

Russian Organizations

Irkutsk
  Angara (Albina Shirobokova)
  Crisis Center for Women (Lyudmila Svistunova)
  International Center "Woman in Management" (Zoya Matunina)
  Radio Pik (Olga Psareva)
  Union of Ust-Ilimsk Women-Entrepreneurs (Tatiana Riaboshapka)
  University (Vera Karnaukhova)

Moscow
  Anika: Committee of Women-invalid and Civilian Participants of the Afghan War
    (Lyubov Yakovleva)
  ANNA Crisis Center for Women/"No to Violence" Association of Crisis Centers
    (unnamed volunteer)
  Ariadne (Valentina Konstantinova)
  Association of Businesswomen (Lyudmila Konareva)
  Association of Russian Women with University Education
  Association of Women in the Film Industry (Margarita Belyakova)
  Association of Women Journalists
  Center of Support of Women's Initatives (Vera Balakireva)
  Committee of Soldiers' Mothers (Ida Kuklina, Valentina Melnikova)
  Conversion and Women (Lyudmila Kalinichenko)
  Department of the Women's Movement of the History Museum (Anna
    Averyanova)
  Documentation Center and Women's Archives

East-West Innovation Fund (Galina Grishina)
FALTA: Feminist Alternative (Natasha Abubikirova)
Feminist Orientation Center (Marina Liborakina)
Gaia
Gender Expertise Project (Lena Kochkina)
Goluba (Marianna Vronskaya)
Information Center of the Independent Women's Forum (Elizaveta Bozhkova)
Irida (Mariia Esmont)
Memorial
MOLLI: Moscow Society of Lesbian Literature and Art (Larisa Ponarina, Lyudmila Ugolkova)
Moscow Center for Gender Studies (Zoia Khotkina, Marina Maliutina, Olga Voronina)
Moscow City Committee on Social and Interregional Relations (Eleonora Luchnikova)
Moscow-Helsinki Group (Lyudmila Alekseeva)
NEWW: Network of East West Women (Irina Doskich)
NIS-US Women's Consortium (Elena Ershova)
Panorama (Alexander Verkhovsky)
Romashka: Foundation in Support of Women's Entrepreneurship (Olga Romashka)
Syostri (Tatiana Shornikova)
Women for Social Democracy (Olga Shadrina)
Women's Information Network (Tatiana Troinova)
Women's League
Women of Russia (party activist)
Union of Women of Russia (Marina Gordeeva)

Murmansk
Children's House of Creation (Svetlana Parshkova)
Congress of Women of the Kola Peninsula (Irina Fogt, Lyubov Shtyleva)
"Family" (Kalistvena Gonchareva)
Raduga (Magarita Abdurakhmanova)
Severyanka (Galina Filatova)
Shelter
Valentina (Valentina Dikayeva)
Women's Club of Murmansk State Technological University (Lyudmila Bayeva)

Naberezhniye Chelnii
Femina (Elena Mashkova)
Union of Women (Gulzada Rudenko)

Nizhnii Novgorod
Novgorod Women's Parliament (Irina Urtaeva)

Novocherkassk/Rostov
Aksinya
Center of Social Rehabilitation and Youth
Committee of Soldiers' Mothers of the Don (Elena Zyubrovskaya)
Women of the Don (Valentina Cherevatenko)

Petrozavodsk
  Karelian Center for Gender Studies (Larisa Boichenko)
  Society of Wives of Petrozavodsk Garrison Officers (Farida Fadeyeva)
  Union of Women

Pskov
  Crisis Center (Stella Petrova)
  Independent Social Women's Center (Natalya Vasilyeva)

St. Petersburg
  European University at Saint Petersburg (Anna A. Temkina)
  "Mama" (Olga Voronina)
  St. Petersburg Psychological Crisis Center for Women (Natalia Khodyrova)
  St. Petersburg Center of Gender Problems (3 volunteers)
  "Vera" Social-Psychological Center (Vera Savelicheva)

Western Donors

  American Bar Association/Central and East European Law Initiative (Kristen
    Hansen, Diane Post)
  Citizens Democracy Corps, Inc. (Susanne Jalbert)
  Charities Aid Foundation (Jennifer Hodgson)
  Connect US-Russia (Susan Hartman)
  ECHO (Sarah Lindemann)
  Eurasia Foundation (Lyubov Alenichova, Bernadine Jocelyn, Alexei Kolotvin,
    Julia Timofeeva, Andrei Vakulenko)
  Ford Foundation (Michele Dash, Chris Kedzie, Mary McAuley, Irina Yurgina)
  Institute of International Education (Lisa Hayden)
  International Institute of Women, Law, and Development (Gabrielle Fitchett,
    Larisa Ponarina)
  IREX: International Research and Exchanges Board (Larisa Flint, Sarah Polen,
    Jonathon Snydal)
  Johns Hopkins University/Center for Communication Programs (Michele A.
    Berdy)
  "Know How" Fund of the British Embassy (Barbara Woodward)
  MacArthur Foundation (Susan King, Tatiana Zhdanova)
  Magee-Women's Hospital (Pamela M. Deligiannis)
  National Democratic Institute of International Affairs (Janelle Cousino, Natasha
    Miramonova)
  Network of East-West Women (Galina Venediktova)
  Soros Foundation (Larisa Fyoderova)
  USAID (Faith Galetshoge, Karen Greene, Brooke Isham, Lisa Petter)

Conferences Attended

  Democracy Round Tables (USAID/Moscow)
  Round Table series sponsored by ABA/CEELI (Moscow)
  Environmental/Human Rights Coalition Conference (Moscow)
  Interregional Festival "Women's Theme—2" (Tatarstan)

Russian Association of Crisis Centers
Ninetieth Anniversary of the First All-Russia Women's Congress

A P P E N D I X   D

Donor Organizations

Institution[1]	Activities aimed at NGO development
Academy for Educational Development (AED)	Supports programs and NGOs worldwide that address social problems such as health, education, youth development, and education through research, training, policy analysis, innovative programs and management.
American Bar Association (ABA)/Central and East European Law Initiative (CEELI)	Advances the rule of law in the world by supporting the legal reform process in Russia. Provides training and workshops to NGOs seeking to establish ties and advocate within the justice system.
American Russian Center (ARC)	Trains entrepreneurs, business managers and government leaders through grants from USAID and other U.S. agencies. Promotes the transition of the Russian Far East to democracy and a free marketeconomy.
Canada-Russia Partnership Fund	Supports small-scale technical cooperation projects between Canadian and Russian institutions within the framework of democratic development. The Gorbachev Foundation in Moscow is a principal partner.
Canadian Feed the Children	Works in partnership with communities worldwide to develop and implement programs that meet locally identified needs. Also supports the needs of overseas partner programs by procuring and shipping supplies such as medicine, medical equipment, food and clothing.

Canadian International Development Agency (CIDA)	Promotes security and stability in CEE by supporting good governance, democracy and adherence to international norms, transition to market economies, trade and investment links, and nuclear safety.
CEC International Partners (CECIP)	Works specifically with artists, art managers, and museums to facilitate partnerships in the arts and cultural sector to pursue common goals, address issues of mutual concern, and achieve positive, enduring change.
Center for Citizens Initiatives (CCI)	Works specifically to provide training to Russian business leaders, managers, and entrepreneurs. Supports improvement of the Russian food supply, small business initiatives, urban environment projects, and philanthropic projects.
Center for Civil Society International (CSI)	Supports the growth of civil society by publishing materials both in print and electronically to strengthen citizen organizations worldwide working for civil rights, democratic institutions, social assistance, and economic reform.
Citizens Democracy Corps (CDC)	Works through the U.S. private sector and enlists U.S. volunteers to develop private businesses in the NIS and CEE. Promotes the transition to free market economies, promotes the creation of job opportunities, and supports a variety of democratic institutions.
Citizens Networks for Foreign Affairs	Provides technical assistance centers in Krasnodar, Stavropol, and Rostov to help more than 150 Russian grassroots organizations become more effective. (No website available.)
Counterpart International	Works with government agencies, businesses, and affiliate NGOs to develop services, businesses, and local NGO capacity and institute innovative agriculture and forestry programs. Focuses on humanitarian assistance, civil society, environment and conservation, enterprise development, health and child survival, and food security.
Doctors without Borders/Médecins sans Frontières (MSF)	Delivers emergency aid to victims of armed conflict, epidemics, and natural and human-made disasters, and to others who lack health care due to social or geographical isolation. Works with Russian NGOs on HIV/AIDS education, tuberculosis, and health care for the homeless.

Earth Island Institute (EII)	Supports environmental projects to manage nuclear fuels and waste, conserve energy, and reduce toxins and pollutants in the environment. Promotes activist networking and NGO development. Projects include Baikal Watch and the Center for Safe Energy.
Ecologists Linked for Organizing Grassroots Initiatives and Action (ECOLOGIA)	Provides information and training for grass roots environmental groups and citizens who can then make educated decisions about the environment, human health, and sustainable development. Promotes environmental management for small enterprises.
Eurasia Foundation	Funds programs that build democratic and free market institutions. Focuses its grant making in Russia on efforts that promote small business associations, facilitate public oversight of local government, and develop community-based philanthropy.
Ford Foundation	Works with Russian organizations to strengthen democratic institutions and develop of civil society. Promotes equity and access to justice for all, with particular regard to the most disadvantaged groups within society. Supports higher education, policy research, culture, and media.
Freedom House (FH) /National Forum Foundation (NFF)	Supports the expansion of democracy, civil society, human rights, the rule of law, independent media, political and economic freedom, and U.S. engagement in international affairs. The democratization training programs of the NFF were incorporated into FH in 1997.
Heartland International	Designs, implements, and manages political, economic, and social development projects, as well as international exchange programs, such as the Community Connections program. Also provides professional training and exposure the U.S. free market economy.
Henry M. Jackson Foundation	Works to promote human rights in Russia, and "assist groups that are involved in Russia's transition to democracy." Supports organizations including the Panorama Information and Research Center and the Interregional Foundation for Civil Society.
Infoshare International/ AIDS Infoshare Russia	Networks with partner associations across Russia to provide Russian citizens and organizations

with the tools they need to fight HIV/AIDS and
STIs. Also conducts seminars on NGO
management and development for NGOs
working in the field of HIV/AIDS.

Institute for Democracy
in Eastern Europe (IDEE)

Promotes democracy in CEE and the former
Soviet Union by supporting democratic
movements. Established a Network of
Independent Journalists and its Centers for
Pluralism program in Russia to foster civic
development and cross-border cooperation.

Institute for Sustainable
Communities (ISC)

Provides training, technical assistance, and
financial support to communities globally to
address environmental, economic, and social
challenges. Programs in Russia include the
Replication of Lessons Learned (ROLL) and the
Targeted Grants Program (TGP).

International Research
and Exchanges Board
(IREX)

Works with universities, NGOs, organizations,
foundations, governments, and corporations to
strengthen democracy in transitioning societies.
IREX's Russia programs, such as ProNGO, span
academic exchanges, U.S.-Russian partnership
building, NGO development, and professional
training.

International Republican
Institute (IRI)

Strengthens democratic ideals and institutions
through the National Endowment for Democracy.
Programs support civic responsibility, NGOs, the
legislative process, parliamentary training,
participation, federalism, and organizing
political parties and elections.

Initiative for Social
Action and Renewal in
Eurasia (ISAR); formerly
Institute of Soviet
American Relations

Strengthens the ability of citizens and NGOs in
Eurasia and the United States to influence
decision making, advance social justice, foster
civil society, and promote environmentally sound
stewardship of Earth's resources through a
unique grass roots approach to activism.

International Center
for Not-for-Profit Law
(ICNL)

Assists in the creation and improvement of laws
and regulatory systems that permit, encourage,
and regulate the not-for-profit sector in
countries worldwide. Conducts training and
research, including a comprehensive study of the
current laws governing NGOs in Russia.

League of Women Voters
(LWV) (Education Fund)

Encourages informed and active participation
of citizens in government and to increase
knowledge of major public policy issues. Works

	to improve political skills of women to encourage participatory democracy and civic education through conferences in Russia.
(John D. and Catherine T.) MacArthur Foundation	Supports research, policy development, dissemination, education, training, and practice. Targets aid to Russia through the Initiative in the Russian Federation and Post-Soviet States program. Promotes law, society, human rights, environment, peace, and security.
(Charles Stewart) Mott Foundation	Supports global initiatives, including NGOs throughout CEE and Russia that promote civil society by developing their own programs that strengthen the nonprofit sector; citizen rights and responsibilities; ethnic relations; and political, economic, and social transitions.
National Democratic Institute (NDI)	Uses volunteer experts to provide practical assistance to civic and political leaders advancing democratic values and institutions. Russian programs focus on political party building, civic organization, election processes, developing legislation, and local governance.
National Endowment for Democracy (NED)	Provides grants to NGOs such as IRI and NDI to facilitate civic development. Strengthens the bond between indigenous democratic movements abroad and the people of the United States, based on a common commitment to representative government and freedom.
Network of East-West Women (NEWW)	Links women advocates in more than forty countries to share resources, knowledge, and skills to promote tolerance, democracy, nonviolence, health, and respect for the institutions of a civil society. Coordinates projects, committees, training workshops, and informational exchanges.
NIS-US Women's Consortium/Winrock International (WI)	Increases women's participation in democracy by strengthening the organizational capacity of NIS women's NGOs and their leaders. Conducts training, seed grants, and communications/networking programs for women's NGOs in Russia and Ukraine.
Open Society Institute— Russia (OSI)	Dedicated to building and maintaining the infrastructure and institutions of an open society. Strengthens the media, rule of law, local

governments, business community, education, public health, community development, women's rights, culture, and regional cooperation in Russia.

Pacific Environment and Resource Center

Seeks to protect biodiversity around the northern Pacific Rim through the empowerment of citizens. (No website available.)

Planned Parenthood of Northern New England (PPNNE)

Provides in Russia technical assistance, educational, medical, and managerial training to reproductive health-care professionals. Works with Russian NGOs to develop program management, strategic planning, sexuality education and training, marketing, and fund-raising.

Project Harmony

Empowers individuals to create healthier communities through international informational exchanges and training programs. Implements professional, Internet, education, and grassroots community development programs.

Project Kesher

Supports women's grassroots organizing in the NIS that is grounded in spirituality, feminism, and civic justice. Trains women as advocates for change in civil society, feminism, and Jewish life. Organizes Jewish community building and women's leadership workshops.

Sacred Earth Network (SEN)

Empowers people and environmental activists to work in defense of the biosphere through its two major programs, the Northern Eurasia Environmental Assistance Program and the Metamorphosis Project: Restoring Our Inner and Outer Ecology.

Save the Children

Launches relief and community development programs to assist countries in transition and ensure self-sufficiency. Spearheaded the Emergency Humanitarian Assistance Program in the Causasus and the Civic Initiative Program in Russia.

United Way International (UWI)

Builds community capacity worldwide through volunteerism and philanthropy. Provides resources, training, and small grants for NGOs. Supports programs in health and human services, childhood and university education, literacy, and the arts.

United States Agency for International Development (USAID)	Supports long-term, equitable economic growth and the advancement of U.S. foreign policy objectives. Works with private and indigenous organizations, universities, businesses, international and federal agencies, and other governments. Russian programs focus on building private enterprise, economic infrastructure, citizen participation, the environmental, rule of law, human rights, and social services.
Voluntary Organizations Initiative in Central & Eastern Europe/Eurasia (VOICE International)	Strengthens civil society by supporting the formation, independence, and diversity of NGOs in CEE and the NIS. Works with groups in the civic sector, publishes materials, and provides technical assistance that enables such organizations to operate more self-sufficiently.
Whirlwind Wheelchair International (WWI)	Teaches wheelchair riders in developing countries to design, build, and repair their own wheelchairs. Also enables riders and builders to create businesses for the manufacture and distribution of wheelchairs to others.

Notes

Chapter 1. Introduction

1. As I use the term, "civil society' does not include political organizations, parliaments, or economic firms and associations. See Jean L. Cohen and Andrew Arato, *Civil Society and Political Theory* (Cambridge, Mass.: MIT Press, 1992), ix.

2. Juan J. Linz and Alfred Stepan, *Problems of Democratic Transition and Consolidation: Southern Europe, South America, and Post-Communist Europe* (Baltimore: Johns Hopkins University Press, 1996).

3. Although Robert Putnam is not the only person to write about social capital, his work has significantly revived the concept. See Robert D. Putnam, with Robert Leonardi and Rafaella Y. Nanetti, *Making Democracy Work: Civic Traditions in Modern Italy* (Princeton: Princeton University Press, 1993); Putnam, "Bowling Alone: America's Declining Social Capital," *Journal of Democracy* 6.1 (1995): 65–78; Putnam, *Bowling Alone: The Collapse and Revival of American Community* (New York: Simon & Schuster, 2000).

4. For a dissenting view on the connection between the vibrancy of a civil society and the health of a democracy, see Sheri Berman, "Civil Society and Political Institutionalization," *American Behavioral Scientist* 40 (March–April 1997): 562–74; Berman, "Civil Society and the Collapse of the Weimar Republic," *World Politics* 49.3 (1997): 401–29.

5. Thomas Carothers, "The End of the Transition Paradigm," *Journal of Democracy* 13.1 (2002): 5–21; Larry Diamond, *Developing Democracy: Toward Consolidation* (Baltimore: Johns Hopkins University Press, 1999).

6. United States Agency of International Development (USAID), "History of USAID Democracy and Governance Activities"; available from http://www.usaid.gov/democracy/office/history.html. Accessed 01/24/03.

7. For example, see Laurence Whitehead, "The Imposition of Democracy: The Caribbean," in *The International Dimensions of Democratization: Europe and the Americas*, ed. Laurence Whitehead (New York: Oxford University Press, 1996); Larry Diamond, *Promoting Democracy in the 1990s: Actors and Instruments, Issues and Imperatives* (New York: Carnegie Corporation of New York, 1995).

8. Westminster Foundation for Democracy, "About WFD"; available from http://*www.wfd.org.* Accessed 7/2/02.

9. USAID, "Democracy and Governance"; available from http://*www.usiad.gov/democracy/.* Accessed 8/5/02.

10. USAID Center for Democracy and Governance, *Improving Democracy Promotion FY 2000* (Washington, D.C., May 2001), i.

11. USAID, "Broad-Based Economic Growth"; available from http://www.usaid.gov/economic_growth/. Accessed 6/24/02.

12. The other programs broke down in the following manner: civil society funding was followed by support for governance programs (30 percent), rule of law (21 percent), and political processes programs (12 percent). Statistics gathered from USAID Center from Democracy and Governance, available from http://www.usaid.gov/pubs/cbj2002/cent_prog/global/dg.

13. Helmut Anheier, Marlies Glasius, and Mary Kaldor, "Introducing Global Civil Society," in *Global Civil Society 2001,* ed. Helmut Anheier, Marlies Glasius, and Mary Kaldor (Oxford: Oxford University Press, 2001).

14. For example, see Giuseppe DiPalma, *To Craft Democracies: An Essay on Democratic Transitions* (Berkeley: University of California Press, 1990); John Higley and Richard Gunther, eds., *Elites and Democratic Consolidation in Latin America and Southern Europe* (Baltimore: Johns Hopkins University Press, 1992); Guillermo O'Donnell, Philippe C. Schmitter, and Laurence Whitehead, eds., *Transitions from Authoritarian Rule,* 4 vols. (Baltimore: Johns Hopkins University Press, 1986).

15. Marina Ottaway and Thomas Carothers, eds., *Funding Virtue: Civil Society Aid and Democracy Promotion* (Washington, D.C.: Carnegie Endowment for International Peace, 2000).

16. Loren Renz, Josefina Samson-Atienza, Trinh C. Tran, and Rikard R. Treibner, *International Grant Making: A Report on US Foundation Trends* (Washington, D.C.: Foundation Center in cooperation with the Council on Foundations, 1997).

17. Figures from Thomas Carothers, *Aiding Democracy Abroad: The Learning Curve* (Washington, D.C.: The Carnegie Endowment for International Peace, 1999), 51.

18. Organization for Economic Co-operation and Development (OECD), *Creditor Reporting System: Aid Activities in CEECs/NIS 2001.5* (2001), 13.

19. USAID Bureau for Europe and Eurasia and Office of Democracy and Governance, "2001 NGO Sustainability Index: Russia," in *The 2001 NGO Sustainability Index for Central and Eastern Europe and Eurasia;* available from http://www.usaid.gov/regions/europe_eurasia/dem_gov/ngoindex/2001/index.htm. Accessed 5/31/02.

20. Soros Foundation, *Soros Foundation 2000 Annual Report* (New York, 2000).

21. Data compiled from the Eurasia Foundation annual reports (Washington D.C., 1993–2001).

22. John D. and Catherine T. MacArthur Foundation, *The John D. and Catherine T. MacArthur Foundation Initiative in the Independent States of the Former Soviet Union: Grants Approved from 1991 through June 1998* (Moscow, 1998).

23. Figure calculated from the Charles Stewart Mott Foundation website; available from http://www.mott.org. Accessed 7/1/02.

24. Don Pressley, "Forword," in *Lessons in Implementation: the NGO Story: Building Civil Society in Central and Eastern Europe and the New Independent States,* USAID Bureau for Europe and Eurasia and Office of Democracy and Governance (Washington, D.C., October 1999), v.

25. Ibid., xi.

26. In fact, the organization spent much of the time I was visiting attempting to straighten out its financial situation with its bank, which had frozen its accounts.

27. Sarah E. Mendelson and John K. Glenn, eds., *The Power and Limits of NGOs: A Critical Look at Building Democrcy in Eastern Europe and Eurasia* (New York: Columbia University Press, 2002), 6–7.

28. Amanda Bernard, Henny Helmich, and Percy B. Lehning, *Civil Society and International Development* (Paris: North-South Centre of the Council of Europe/Development Centre of the Organization for Economic Co-operation and Development, 1998); Carothers, *Aiding Democracy Abroad*; John Clark, *Democratizing Development: The Role of Voluntary Organizations* (West Hartford, Conn.: Kumarian Press, 1990); Michael Cox, G. John Ikenberry, and Takashi Inoguchi, eds., *American Democracy Promotion: Impulses, Strategies, and Impacts* (New York: Oxford University Press, 2000); Deborah Eade, ed., *Development, NGOs, and Civil Society* (Oxford: Oxfam Press, 2000); Michael Edwards and David Hulme, eds., *Beyond the Magic Bullet: NGO Performance and Accountability in the Post-Cold War World* (Kumarian Press, 1996); Michael Edwards and David Hulme, *NGOs, States, and Donors: Too Close for Comfort?* (New York: St. Martin's Press, 1997); John Farrington and Anthony Bebbington with Kate Wellard and David J. Lewis, *Reluctant Partners: Nongovernmental Organizations, the State and Sustainable Agricultural Development* (New York: Routledge, 1993), 1–28; Jude Howell and Jenny Pearce, *Civil Society and Development: A Critical Exploration* (Boulder: Lynne Rienner Publishers, 2002); Ottaway and Carothers, *Funding Virtue*; Alison Van Rooy, ed., *Civil Society and the Aid Industry* (London: Earthscan Publications, 1998).

29. Diamond, *Promoting Democracy in the 1990s*, vi.

30. Diamond, *Developing Democracy*, 272.

31. Ottaway and Carothers, *Funding Virtue*, 298.

32. Nancy Lubin, "U.S. Assistance to the Newly Independent States: When Good Things Come in Small Packages," in *The International Dimension of Post-Communist Transitions in Russia and the New States of Eurasia*, ed. Karen Dawisha (Armonk, N.Y.: M. E. Sharpe, 1997).

33. For example, see Thomas Carothers, *Assessing Democracy Assistance: The Case of Romania* (Washington, D.C.: Carnegie Endowment for International Peace, 1996); Sarah E. Mendelson, "Democracy Assistance and Political Transition in Russia: Between Success and Failure," *International Security* 25.4 (spring 2001): 68–106; Mendelson and Glenn, *Power and Limits of NGOs*.

34. Margaret E. Keck and Kathryn Sikkink, *Activists beyond Borders: Advocacy Networks in International Politics* (Ithaca: Cornell University Press, 1998).

35. For more on the global civil society argument, see Anne Marie Clark, Elisabeth J. Friedman, and Kathryn Hochstetler, "The Sovereign Limits of Global Civil Society: A Comparison of NGO Participation in UN World Conferences on the Environment, Human Rights, and Women," *World Politics* 51 (October 1998), 1–35; Helmut Anheier, Marlies Glasius, and Mary Kaldor, eds., *Global Civil Society 2001*, (Oxford: Oxford University Press, 2001).

36. Keck and Sikkink, *Activists beyond Borders*, 188.

37. Brian H. Smith, *More than Altruism: The Politics of Private Foreign Aid* (Princeton: Princeton University Press, 1990).

38. Ottaway and Carothers, *Funding Virtue*, 301.

39. See Valerie Sperling, *Organizing Women in Contemporary Russia: Engendering Transition* (Cambridge UK: Cambridge University Press, 1999), 220–56; Mendelson and Glenn, *Power and Limits of NGOs*. In addition, see James Richter, "Evaluating Western

Assistance to Russian Women's Organizations," in *The Power and Limits of NGOs: A Critical Look at Building Democracy in Eastern Europe and Eurasia*, ed. Sarah E. Mendelson and John K. Glenn, 54–90 (New York: Columbia University Press, 2002).

40. See Valerie Sperling, "Foreign Funding of Social Movements in Russia," Memo no. 26 (Cambridge, Mass.: Harvard University, Program on New Approaches to Russian Security Policy Memo Series, January 1998); Robert Sharlet, "Bringing the Rule of Law to Russia and the Newly Independent States: The Role of the West in the Transformation of the Post-Soviet Legal Systems"; Lubin, "U.S. Assistance."

41. Marina Ottaway and Theresa Chung, "Debating Democracy Assistance: Toward a New Paradigm," *Journal of Democracy* 10.4 (1999): 99–113.

42. Diamond, *Developing Democracy*, 253.

43. Sperling, *Organizing Women in Contemporary Russia*, 220–56.

44. Pauline Jones Luong and Erika Weinthal, "The NGO Paradox: Democratic Goals and Nondemocratic Outcomes in Kazakhstan," *Europe-Asia Studies* 51.7 (November 1999): 1267–85.

45. James Richter, "Promoting Activism or Professionalism in Russia's Civil Society?" Memo no. 51 (Cambridge, Mass.: Harvard University, Program on New Approaches to Russian Security Policy Memo Series, November 1998).

46. For comparative perspectives, see Howell and Pearce, *Civil Society and Development*, 177–228; Ottaway and Carothers, *Funding Virtue*; Van Rooy, *Civil Society and the Aid Industry*.

47. Finn Tarp and Peter Hjertholm, eds., *Foreign Aid and Development: Lessons Learnt and Directions for the Future* (New York: Routledge, 2000).

48. Clifford Gaddy and Barry Ickes, "Russia's Virtual Economy," *Foreign Affairs* 77.5 (September/October 1998): 53–68.

49. For a quick, accessible overview of the "Who lost Russia?" debate, see John Lloyd, "The Russian Devolution," *New York Times Magazine*, 15 August 1999, 34.

50. Janine Wedel, *Collision and Collusion: The Strange Case of Western Aid to Eastern Europe 1989–1998* (New York: St. Martin's Press, 1998).

51. Stephen F. Cohen, *Failed Crusade: America and the Tragedy of Post-Communist Russia* (New York: W.W. Norton, 2000).

52. Anders Aslund, who defended privatization policies as being beneficial overall, expressed one of the few voices of relative optimism; see Anders Aslund, *Building Capitalism: The Transformation of the Former Soviet Bloc* (New York: Cambridge University Press, 2001).

53. Wedel, *Collision and Collusion*, 45–82.

54. For example, when I perused the job listings in the Civil Society International email list, the Initiative for Social Action and Renewal in Eurasia (ISAR), a nonprofit organization involved in civic development, offered a salary range of $27,000–29,000 for a program officer and the Center for Citizens Initiatives offered a yearly salary of $26,000–29,000 to a potential candidate to run one of their programs.

55. For example, see Mendelson and Glenn, *The Power and Limits of NGOs*.

56. For example, see Jonathan Steele, *Eternal Russia: Yeltsin, Gorbachev, and the Mirage of Democracy* (London: Faber and Faber, 1994), xv.

57. Stephen White, *Political Culture and Soviet Politics* (New York: St. Martins, 1979). Richard Tucker also broadly concurs with this continuity thesis, in *Political Culture and Leadership in Soviet Russia* (New York: W.W. Norton, 1987).

58. For more on the issue of "habits of the heart," see Stjepan G. Mestrovic, with Slaven Letica and Miroslav Goreta, *Habits of the Balkan Heart: Social Character and the Fall of Communism* (College Station: Texas A&M Press, 1993).

59. Ada Finifter and Ellen Mickiewicz, "Redefining the Political System of the USSR: Mass Support for Political Change," *American Political Science Review* 84.4 (December 1992): 859–62.

60. Robert Brym, "Re-evaluating Mass Support for Political and Economic Change in Russia," *EuropeAsia Studies* 48.5 (1996), 757.

61. Ronald Inglehart demonstrates this movement in cultural values, in *Culture Shift in Advanced Industrial Society* (Princeton: Princeton University Press, 1990) and in *Modernization and Postmodernization: Cultural, Economic, and Political Change in 43 Societies* (Princeton: Princeton University Press, 1997).

62. James L. Gibson, "The Resilience of Mass Support for Democratic Institutions and Processes in the Nascent Russian and Ukrainian Democracies"; Jeffrey W. Hahn, "Changes in Contemporary Russian Political Culture," in *Political Culture and Civil Society in Russia and the New States of Eurasia*, ed. Vladimir Tismaneanu (Armonk: M. E. Sharpe, 1995).

63. Moshe Lewin, *The Gorbachev Phenomenon* (Berkeley: University of California Press, 1988).

64. Nicolai Petro, *The Rebirth of Russian Democracy: An Interpretation of Political Culture* (Cambridge, Mass.: Harvard University Press, 1995).

65. David Hume, quoted in Putnam, *Making Democracy Work*, 163.

66. Mancur Olson, *The Logic of Collective Action* (Cambridge, Mass.: Harvard University Press, 1965).

67. Mancur Olson, *The Rise and Decline of Nations: Economic Growth, Stagflation, and Social Rigidities* (New Haven: Yale University Press, 1982), 18.

68. Ibid., p. 24.

69. Alexander Motyl, *Sovietology, Rationality, Nationality* (New York: Columbia University Press, 1990), 37.

70. Ibid., 38.

71. Edward M. Mueller and Karl-Dieter Opp, "Rational Choice and Rebellious Collective Action," *American Political Science Review* 80.2 (June 1986), 184.

72. Elinor Ostrom, *Governing the Commons: The Evolution of Institutions for Collective Action* (New York: Cambridge University Press, 1990).

73. Putnam, *Making Democracy Work*, 163–85.

74. For an exhaustive treatment of possible solutions to the collective action dilemma, see Mark Irving Lichbach, *The Rebel's Dilemma* (Ann Arbor: University of Michigan Press, 1995); Lichbach, *The Cooperator's Dilemma* (Ann Arbor: University of Michigan Press, 1996).

75. Despite the academic debate over whether Russians conditioned under a system of socialism can act rationally according to traditional Western free market expectations, I maintain that Russians are able to tailor means to ends and able to choose a mean best suited to those ends. Simply put, I have not met a Russian whose thought processes were so alien from my own that I was left perplexed by his or her behavior. Many Russians did not like the new capitalist/free market way of thinking associated with rationality, but this did not mean they could not recognize what would best advance their interests in their new environment.

76. In fact, Jerry Hough and Michael Armascot argue that the failure of economic reform in Russia was the product, not of Russian culture or history, but of the logical consequences of rational men responding to the incentive system created by economic reform. Jerry F. Hough and Michael H. Armacost, *The Logic of Economic Reform in Russia* (Washington, D.C.: Brookings Institution, 2001).

77. Ottaway and Chung, "Debating Democracy Assistance," 99–113.

78. Judith Tendler's analysis in 1981 of seventy-five evaluations of NGO projects done in the late 1970s points out that funders often stress quantifiable data while overlooking qualitative issues. See Tendler, *Turning Private Voluntary Organizations into Development Agencies: Questions for Evaluation,* AID program evaluation discussion paper no. 12 (Washington, D.C.: USAID, 1982), 127, 131–32.

79. Richter, "Promoting Activism or Professionalism."

80. Women in Russia is a well-researched field. A few works include Sue Bridger, Rebecca Kay, and Kathryn Pinnick, *No More Heroines? Russia, Women and the Market* (New York: Routledge, 1996); Mary Buckley, ed., *Post-Soviet Women: From the Baltic to Central Asia* (New York: Cambridge University Press, 1997); Rebecca Kay, *Russian Women and Their Organizations: Gender, Discrimination and Grassroots Women's Organizations, 1991–96* (New York: St. Martin's Press, 2000); Hilary Pilkington, ed., *Gender, Generation and Identity in Contemporary Russia* (New York: Routledge, 1996); Anastasia Posadskaya, ed., *Women in Russia: A New Era in Russian Feminism* (New York: Verso Press, 1994); Linda Racioppi and Katherine O'Sullivan See, *Women's Activism in Contemporary Russia* (Philadelphia: Temple University Press, 1997); Wilma Rule and Norma C. Noonan, eds., *Russian Women in Politics and Society* (Westport: Greenwood Press, 1996); Sperling, *Organizing Women in Contemporary Russia.*

81. Geertz, Clifford, *The Interpretation of Cultures: Selected essays* (New York: Basic Books, 1973).

Chapter 2. Civic Traditions and Trends in Contemporary Russia

1. For a more complete definition of democratic consolidation, see Juan A. Linz and Alfred Stepan, *Problems of Democratic Transition and Consolidation: Southern Europe, South America, and Post-Communist Europe* (Baltimore: Johns Hopkins University Press, 1996), 5.

2. However, Marcia A. Weigle provides a fascinating account of the emergence of civic groups in the post-Gorbachev era, in *Russia's Liberal Project: State-Society Relations in the Transition from Communism* (University Park: Pennsylvania State University Press, 2000), 333–79.

3. Linz and Stepan, *Problems of Democratic Transition and Consolidation,* 7.

4. This number includes independent civic associations, as well as labor unions and political parties. United States Agency for International Development (USAID), *2001 NGO Sustainability Index for Central and Eastern Europe and Eurasia,* 5th ed. (Washington, D.C., March 2002), 133. The Charities Aid Foundation Russia office estimates that there were 300,000 NGOs in 2002, although they do not specify what they mean by NGO or identify the source of this information; available from www.cafonline.org/cafrussia/default.cfm (accessed 6/24/02). Finally, the civic activist Alexander Nikitin estimates that there are over 350,000 registered NGOs and 90,000 active NGOs, in a speech given at the Center for Strategic and International Studies, Washington, D.C., December 13, 2001.

5. For example, Alexander Nikitin estimates that as few as 25 percent of groups are active. Ibid.

6. For example, see USAID, *The NGO Sustainability Index for Central and Eastern Europe and Eurasia for 1998–2001,* available from www.usaid.gov/regions/europe_eurasia/dem_gov/ngoindex/index.htm (accessed 1/29/03); Weigle, *Russia's Liberal Project.*

7. Michael W. Foley and Bob Edwards, "The Paradox of Civil Society," *Journal of Democracy* 7.3 (1996): 38–52.

8. Weigle, *Russia's Liberal Project*, 30.

9. Larry Diamond, *Developing Democracy: Toward Consolidation* (Baltimore: Johns Hopkins University Press, 1999) 239–50.

10. Linz and Stepan, *Problems of Democratic Transition and Consolidation*, 14.

11. Weigle, *Russia's Liberal Project*, 36.

12. Larry Diamond outlines thirteen functions of civil society in *Developing Democracy*, 239–50.

13. Ernest Gellner, *Conditions of Liberty: Civil Society and Its Rivals* (New York: Allen Lane Penguin, 1994), 3–4.

14. Vladimir Tismaneanu and Michael Turner, "Understanding Post-Sovietism: Between Residual Leninism and Uncertain Pluralism," in *Political Culture and Civil Society in Russia and the New States of Eurasia*, ed. Vladimir Tismaneanu (Armonk: M. E. Sharpe, 1995), 4.

15. Robert D. Putnam, *Making Democracy Work: Civic Traditions and Trends in Modern Italy* (Princeton: Princeton University press, 1993), 167–75.

16. Linz and Stepan, *Problems of Democratic Transition and Consolidation*, 9.

17. Larry Diamond, in Doh Chull Shin, "On the Third Wave of Democratization: A Synthesis and Evaluation of Recent Theory and Research," *World Politics* 47 (October 1994): 135–70.

18. Adele Lindenmeyr, *Poverty Is Not a Vice: Charity, Society, and the State in Imperial Russia* (Princeton: Princeton University Press, 1996), 223–4.

19. Paul Legendre, *The Non Profit Sector in Russia* (Moscow: Charities Aid Foundation, 1998), chap. 3.

20. Quoted in M. Steven Fish, *Democracy from Scratch: Opposition and Regime in the New Russian Revolution* (Princeton: Princeton University Press, 1995), 30–1.

21. Legendre, *Non Profit Sector in Russia*, chap. 2.

22. For example, see Hannah Arendt, *The Origins of Totalitarianism* (New York: Harcourt, Brace, and World, 1966); Carl J. Friedrich and Zbigniew K. Brzezinski, *Totalitarian Dictatorship and Autocracy* (New York: Praeger, 1956).

23. Thomas M. Nichols, "Russian Democracy and Social Capital," *Social Science Information* 35.4 (1996), 631. Also, see Linz and Stepan, *Problems of Democratic Transition and Consolidation*; Michael E. Urban, with Vyacheslav Igrunov and Sergei Mitrukhin, *The Rebirth of Politics in Russia* (New York: Cambridge University Press, 1997); Putnam, *Making Democracy Work*, 183.

24. For a more detailed discussion of dissident civic groups in the pre-Gorbachev era, see Nicolai Petro, *The Rebirth of Russian Democracy: An Interpretation of Political Culture* (Cambridge, Mass.: Harvard University Press, 1995), 112–48.

25. Interview with Nadezhda L. Shpitalnaya, November 15, 2002, Novosibirsk.

26. See Robert G. Darst, "Environmentalism in the USSR: The Opposition to the River Diversion Projects," *Soviet Economy* 4.3 (1988): 223–51; Murray Feshbach and Alfred Friendly, Jr., *Ecocide in the USSR* (New York: Basic Books, 1992); Marshall I. Goldman, *The Spoils of Progress: Environmental Pollution in the Soviet Union* (Cambridge, Mass.: MIT Press, 1972); Nicolai N. Petro, "'Project of the Century': A Case Study of Russian National Dissent," *Studies in Comparative Communism* 20.3–4 (1987): 235–52; Philip R. Pryde, *Environmental Management in the Soviet Union* (Cambridge, U.K.: Cambridge University Press, 1991); Barbara Jancar-Webster, *Environmental Management in the Soviet Union and Yugoslavia: Structure and Regulation in Federal Communist States* (Durham: Duke University Press, 1987).

27. See Douglas R. Wiener, *A Little Corner of Freedom: Russian Nature Protection from Stalin to Gorbachev* (Berkeley: University of California Press, 1999).

28. For example, see Gerald Easter and Anne Gruber, "The Dynamics of Change in Contemporary Soviet Society," in *Toward a More Civil Society? The USSR under Mikhail Gorbachev*, ed. William G. Miller (New York: Harper and Row, 1989). See also Frederick Starr, "Soviet Union: A Civil Society," *Foreign Policy* 70 (spring 1988): 26–41.

29. For example, George Breslauer's model of welfare-state authoritarianism presents a more flexible analysis of the Soviet system than totalitarian theory, acknowledging a level of corporate pluralism within the political system and a commitment to minimal levels of security. See George Breslauer, "On the Adaptability of Soviet Welfare-State Authoritarianism," in *The Soviet Polity in the Modern Era*, ed. Erik Hoffman and Robbin Laird (New York: Aldine, 1984).

30. Ibid., 86–91.

31. Ibid., 29.

32. Ibid.

33. Quoted in Weigle, *Russia's Liberal Project*, 97.

34. Fish, *Democracy from Scratch*, 32.

35. Quoted in ibid., 34.

36. Petro, *Rebirth of Russian Democracy*, 134.

37. Weigle, *Russia's Liberal Project*, 79–80.

38. Ibid., 103.

39. Fish, *Democracy from Scratch*, 30–51. Fish looks primarily, however, at the growth of "political" organizations, groups that were directly involved in trying to influence the direction and scope of *perestroika*.

40. Maggie Christie, "Constraints on Russia's NGO Sector" (USAID/Russia, June 1996), attachment D.

41. Section 5 of the code specifically addresses noncommercial organizations, including consumer cooperatives, social and religions organizations (or associations), foundations, institutions, and associations of organizations.

42. Christie, "Constraints on Russia's NGO Sector."

43. See Weigle, *Russia's Liberal Project*, 75–139.

44. Ibid., 80.

45. Lisa Petter, "USAID/Russia NGO Sector Analysis" (Moscow: USAID, 1997), 6.

46. *Facts and Figures: Russia's Non Profit Sector*; available from http://www.cafonline.org/cafrussia/r_fact.cfm. Accessed 9/22/99.

47. USAID, "Russia", in *2001 NGO Sustainability Index*.

48. Petter, "USAID/Russia NGO Sector Analysis," 6.

49. Nikitin (speech given at the Center for Strategic and International Studies, Washington, D.C., December 13, 2001).

50. Woodford McClellan, *Russia: The Soviet Period and After* (Upper Saddle River: Prentice Hall), 320–21.

51. Lev Jakobson, Boris Rudnik, and Sergei Shishkin, "Governmental Economic Policy and Development of the Third Sector in Russia" (paper presented at the International Society for Third Sector Research (ISTR) International Conference, Mexico City, 18–21 July 1996), 1.

52. Russian Centre for Public Opinion and Market Research (VCIOM) public opinion poll (November 1998).

53. Jakobson, Rednik, and Shishkin, "Governmental Economic Policy."

54. Ronald Inglehart, *Culture Shift in Advanced Industrial Society* (Princeton: Princeton University Press, 1990).

55. Survey 20. In order to keep answers confidential survey responses were assigned numbers.

56. A study of central Russian NGOs categorized 38 percent of NGOs as "social defense" organizations. Physical and sports organizations made up another 38 percent; creative, scientific cultural, and educational groups represented 20 percent of the NGO sphere; and public organizations accounted for 4 percent of NGO activity. This categorization excludes political groups, labor organizations, and religious groups. Legendre, *Non Profit Sector in Russia*, chap. 2.

57. Survey 8.

58. Letter 3.

59. Letter 1.

60. Mary McCauley, "The Big Chill: Civil Society in Russia in a New Political Season," in *Ford Foundation Report* (winter 2001). Available at www.civilsoc.org/resource/ffw2001.htm. Accessed 6/24/02.

61. Fred Wier, "Russia's Fledgling Civil Society," *Christian Science Monitor*, 30 July 2002, 6.

62. Inglehart, *Culture Shift in Advanced Industrial Society*; Ronald Inglehart, *Modernization and Postmodernization: Cultural, Economic and Political Change in 43 Societies* (Princeton: Princeton University Press, 1997).

63. Legendre, *Non Profit Sector in Russia*, chap. 2.

64. As of 1997, 15,000 groups existed in Moscow and 7,000 in Petersburg. Ibid.

65. In theory, the judicial authorities were responsible for registration. In practice, the Ministry of Justice of the Russian Federation and the justice departments of the federation subjects, as a rule, registered only public associations, one form of nonprofit organization. Registration for other NGOs took place at either regional government registration chambers or at local administrations. Until 1997, legal entities registered with the local government. In 1997, the regional authorities decided to unify the registration system and to open a branch of the regional registration chamber in each *raion*. Approximately one-third of all local administrations refused to respect this decision and hand over responsibility.

66. Anna Badkhen, "City Refuses to Register Rights Group," *Moscow Times*, 21 August 1999.

67. Charities Aid Foundation Russia, Facts and Figures: Russia's Non Profit Sector.

68. Legendre, *Non Profit Sector in Russia*, chap. 2.

69. Survey 12.

70. Survey 24.

71. Dershem and Patsiorkovski, "Needs and Capacity Assessment," 31.

72. Interview with Jenny Hodgson of Charities Aid Foundation, quoted in "Charities Suffer from Crisis and Mistrust," *Moscow Tribune*, 1 December 1998, pp. 1–2.

73. Results from a Charities Aid Foundation survey of the nonprofit sector in Russia, reported in Legendre, *Non Profit Sector in Russia*, chap. 2.

74. Ibid.; "Charities Suffer from Crisis and Mistrust."

75. Catriona Logan, "Civil Society Development in Russia's Regions" (MA thesis, University of Washington, 1998).

76. The effect was that banks and businesses avoided claiming charitable contributions because a $3 donation could mean that there had been $100 profit, and hence $97 taxable. Christie, "Constraints on Russia's NGO Sector."

77. YUKOS, "Sponsorstvo i Blagotvoritel' nost," available at www.yukos.ru/sponsor.shtml. Accessed 1/29/03. Also, correspondence with Sarah Lindemann-Komareva, February, 1, 2003.

78. Interros, "O Vladimire Potanine," available from www.stipendia.ru/potanin/. Accessed 1/29/03.

79. Fund for International Nonprofit Development "Partners and Grantees," available at www.find-usa.org/partners.html, accessed 2/12/03.

80. "Berezovsky Gives $25 Million to Promote Civil Liberties in Russia," *US Newswire* 15 December 2000.

81. John Varoli, "In Russia, Charity Rides on Corporate Soldiers," *New York Times,* 7 July 1999, sec. C, p. 4.

82. Legendre, *Non Profit Sector in Russia,* chap. 2.

83. Quoted in Logan, "Civil Society Development in Russia's Regions," 47.

84. Larry Diamond, "Toward Democratic Consolidation," *Journal of Democracy* 5.3 (July 1994), 5.

85. Interview with Janelle Cousino, July 23, 1998, Moscow.

86. Legendre, *Non Profit Sector in Russia,* p. 14.

87. In this survey conducted in 1994 by the sociological service Monitoring (1,007 people interviewed), 30 percent of the respondents did not offer assistance to anyone. Almost are half of the respondents helped their parents, just over one-fifth helped their friends, and 30 percent gave money directly to the needy. In contrast, only 3 percent of respondents supported charitable work or charity in general. See "Attitudes toward Charity in Russia: The Business Community and the General Population" (unpublished paper, Charities Aid Foundation, Moscow).

88. Civic Initiatives Program Education Development Center, "Attitudes towards Public Organizations in Russia" (unpublished paper, Moscow, August 1995).

89. In reply to direct questions, less than 5 percent of Russians said that they belonged to a sports, music, or arts club; housing or neighborhood association; or political party. However, by reinterpreting respondents' answers to include monthly church attendance and labor membership as voluntary organization, the number rises to 21 percent. Richard Rose, "Getting Things Done in an Anti-Modern Society: Social Capital Networks in Russia" (Centre for the Study of Public Policy, University of Strathclyde, 1998).

90. Data drawn from Marc Morje Howard, "The Weakness of Postcommunist Civil Society," *Journal of Democracy* 13.1 (2002), 159, fig. 1.

91. *Chronicle of Philanthropy,* 2 May 1998, 1.

92. D. Dokuchaev, "Fond Sporta—Natsionalny, a Prinadlezhit Edinitsam," *Izvestiya,* 5 June 1997.

93. Charities Aid Foundation Russia, Facts and Figures: Russia's Non Profit Sector. Accessed 9/22/99.

94. Quoted in a study conducted by the Russian NGO Interlegal, Nina Yu. Belyaeva, "Charity of Strangers?: Philanthropy in the Russian Commercial Sector" (Moscow, 1995), 2.

95. These results are from an analysis sponsored by Charities Aid Foundation Russia. Anna Sevort'yan, "Rezul'taty Issledovaniya Sovremennovo Sostoyaniya i Perspektiv Sotrudnichestva mezhdu Regional'noi Vlast'yu i nko," (Charities Aid Foundation Russia, n.d.), 2.

96. Civic Initiatives Project Educational Development Center, "Attitudes towards Public Organizations in Russia."

97. Dershem and Patsiorkovski, "Needs and Capacity Assessment."

98. Interview with Janelle Cousino, July 23, 1998, Moscow.

99. Personal correspondence, March 30, 1999.

100. USAID, "Russia."

101. Sarah Lindemann-Komarova, "How I Learned What I Know" (unpublished paper).

102. Petter, "USAID/Russia NGO Sector Analysis." Also, from my own experiences, many groups complained bitterly about the futility of working with political parties and the local administration. They felt that politicians viewed them solely in instrumental terms and abandoned them rather quickly after elections.

103. Grigoriy Osterman, "Grazhdanskiy Forum v Otsenkakh Pressy"; available from http://www.smi.ru/01/11/22/43205.html. Accessed 9/20/02.

104. Georgy Satarov, "Russia's Government Launches Dialog on Civil Society Issues," *Russia Journal* 4.24 (June 22–28, 2001); available from http://www.russiajournal.ru/printer/weekly4798.html. Accessed 9/9/02.

105. "Civic Forum Held. Now What?" *Current Digest of the Soviet Press*, 19 December 2001, 1.

106. Anatoly Kostyukov, "Civil Society Lines Up for Display to the President: An Interview with Yabloko Leader Grigory Yavlinsky," *Obschaya Gazeta*, 22–28 November, Transcript From Johnson's Russia List, Nov. 26, 2001, #5565, story #3.

107. Wier, "Russia's Fledgling Civil Society."

108. Yevgenia Rubtsova, "Berezovsky Tries to Organize Liberal Opposition," *Noviye Izvestiya*, 15 December 2001, p. 2.

109. Aleksandr Dugin, "The Perspective of Civil War in Russia: Interview to Radio 'Utrennaya Volna'" (Ekaterinburg, November 25, 2001); transcript available from http://utenti.lycos.it/ArchivEurasia/dugin_ruv011125.html. Accessed 8/20/02.

110. "Vladimir Zhirinovsky: Grazhdansky Forum: Proobraz Rossyskovo parlamenta v budushchem" (November 29, 2001); available from http://www.Strana.ru. Accessed 9/4/02.

111. Sarah Lindemann-Komarova, "My Civic Forum: An Attempt to Control?" in Johnson's Russia List, #6238, 13 May 2002.

112. "Vladimir Putin: States Are Judged by the Level of Individual Liberty. Excerpts from President Vladimir Putin's speech at the Civil Forum," *Vremya Novosti*, 22 November 2001. Addendum. Transcript From Johnson's Russia List, Nov. 22, 2001, #5560–5561, entry #4.

113. Georgy Satarov, "Russia's Government Launches Dialog on Civil Society Issues," *Russia Journal* 4.24 (June 22–28, 2001); available from http://www.russiajournal.ru/printer/weekly4798.html. Accessed 9/9/02.

114. Zinaida T. Golenkova, "Civil Society in Russia," 40.1 (January–February 1999), 17.

115. For example, see Barrington Moore, Jr., *Social Origins of Dictatorship and Democracy* (Boston: Beacon Press, 1966); Ivan Szelenyi, *Socialist Entrepreneurs: Embourgeoisement in Rural Hungary* (Madison: University of Wisconsin Press, 1988). Dietrich Rueschemeyer, Evelyne Huber Stephens, and John D. Stephens argue that the working class also has played a role and can continue to play a role in civil society development, in *Capitalist Development and Democracy* (Chicago: University of Chicago Press, 1992).

116. Tatiana Maleva, "The Gordian Knot of Social Problems: Post-Crisis Distortions" (Carnegie Moscow Center briefing, September 1999).

117. Sheri Berman, "Civil Society and Political Institutionalization," in *Beyond Tocqueville: Civil Society and the Social Capital Debate in Comparative Perspective*, ed. Bob Edwards, Michael Foley, and Mario Diani, 32–42 (Hanover, N.J.: University Presses of New England, 2001).

Chapter 3. Constructing Civil Society

1. Gabriel A. Almond and Sidney Verba, *The Civic Culture: Political Attitudes and Democracy in Five Nations* (Princeton: Princeton University Press, 1963); Robert D. Putnam, *Making Democracy Work: Civic Traditions in Contemporary Italy* (Princeton: Princeton University Press, 1993).

2. Westminster Foundation for Democracy, "Civil Society Development"; available from http://www.wfd.org. Accessed 7/8/02.

3. Maggie Christie, "Constraints on Russia's NGO Sector" (unpublished paper, USAID Russia, 1996).

4. Janine Wedel, *Collision and Collusion: The Strange Case of Western Aid to Eastern Europe 1989–1998* (New York: St. Martin's Press, 1998).

5. See Michael Edwards and David Hulme, "Introduction: NGO Performance and Accountability," in *Beyond the Magic Bullet: NGO Performance and Accountability in the Post-Cold World War*, ed. Michael Edwards and David Hulme (West Hartford: Kumarian Press, 1996).

6. Thomas Carothers, *Aiding Democracy Abroad: The Learning Curve* (Washington, D.C.: Carnegie Endowment for International Peace, 1999), 214.

7. Helmut Anheier, Marlies Glasius, and Mary Kaldor, "Introducing Global Civil Society," in *Global Civil Society 2001*, ed. Helmut Anheier, Marlies Glasius, and Mary Kaldor (New York: Oxford University Press, 2002), 4.

8. As quoted in Michael Edwards and David Hulme, eds., *Beyond the Magic Bullet: NGO Performance and Accountability in the Post-Cold World War* (West Hartford: Kumarian Press, 1996), 2.

9. Carothers, *Aiding Democracy Abroad*, 209.

10. Jude Howell and Jenny Pearce catalog this transformation in greater depth, in *Civil Society and Development: A Critical Exploration* (Boulder: Lynne Rienner, 2001), 89–102.

11. USAID, "Democracy and Governance"; available from http://www.usaid.gov/democracy/. Accessed 5/29/02.

12. USAID, "The NGO Sustainability Index"; available from http://www.usaid.gov/regions/europe_eurasia/dem_gov/ngoindex/index.htm. Accessed 4/8/02.

13. Howell and Pearce, *Civil Society and Development*, 97.

14. The Ford Foundation has funded the Civil Society and Governance Programme, based at the Institute of Development Studies at the University of Sussexs more information is available from http://www.ids.ac.uk/ids/civsoc/. Accessed 2/7/03.

15. CIVICUS website, http://www.civicus.org. Accessed 9/10/2002.

16. Goran Hyden, "Civil Society, Social Capital, and Development: Dissection of a Complex Discourse," *Studies in Comparative International Development* 32 (spring 1997): 3–30.

17. "Social Capital for Development"; available from http://www.worldbank.org/poverty/scapital. Accessed 2/7/03.

18. In fact, it has been the single largest bilateral donor in Russia, followed by Germany, the United Kingdom, and Norway. USAID, "Russia"; available at http://www.usaid.gov/pubs/bj2001/ee/ru/index.html. Accessed 5/29/02.

19. USAID, "History of USAID Democracy & Governance Activities." Available from http://www.usaid.gov/democracy/office/history.html. Accessed 8/5/02.

20. USAID FY 1998 Congressional presentation, Washington, D.C.

21. USAID, "Russia: FY 2001 Program Description and Activity Data Sheets"; available from http://www.usaid.gov/pubs/bj2001/ee/ru/ru_ads.html. Accessed 5/29/02.

22. Howell and Pearce, *Civil Society and Development*, 94.

23. Alison Van Rooy and Mark Robinson, "Out of the Ivory Tower: Civil Society and the Aid System," in *Civil Society and the Aid Industry*, ed. Alisen Van Rooy (London: Earthscan, 1998), 60.

24. Lisa Petter, "USAID/Russia NGO Sector Analysis" (Moscow: USAID, 1997), 6.

25. For more details on USAID methodology, please see USAID Bureau for Europe and Eurasia and Office for Democracy and Governance, *The 2001 NGO Sustainability Index for Central and Eastern Europe and Eurasia* 5th ed. (March 2002); available from http://www.usaid.gov/regions/europe_eurasia/dem_gov/ngoindex/2001/index.htm. Accessed 5/31/02.

26. Interview with Faith Galetshoge, Brooke Isham, and Lisa Petter, November 13, 1998, Moscow.

27. This practice evolved in the late 1960s and 1970s and was a result of two developments. First, in 1967 the U.S. Congress passed Title 9 of the Foreign Assistance Act. This amendment drastically expanded USAID's grant funding for U.S. NGO activities to increase foreign popular participation in and acceptance of development projects in recipient countries. In 1973, Congress further strengthened this with more amendments that stipulated that NGOs were the most effective channels for foreign assistance. The second development occurred in the 1970s. USAID, like many other administration departments, was constrained by personnel limits. As a result, it started contracting out grants to NGOs in order to spend its budget. See Sarah J. Tisch and Michael B. Wallace, *Dilemmas of Development Assistance: The What, Why, and Who of Foreign Aid* (Boulder: Westview Press, 1994), chap. 3.

28. For example, in 1998, USAID's Citizen's Participation program for Russia contracted out grant money to the following U.S. nonprofit organizations: IRI, Free Trade Union Institute, International Foundation for Electoral Systems, NDI, Initiative for Social Action and Renewal in Eurasia (ISAR), Save the Children Federation, United Way, Helping Hand, Internews, Russian/American Press and Information Center, USIA, and Moscow School of Political Studies. USAID/Russia "USAID/Russia Activity Descriptions as of March 31, 1998." (Moscow, Russia, 1998).

29. USAID, "Russia: FY 2001 Program Description and Activity Data Sheets."

30. Westminster Foundation for Democracy, *What We Do*; available from http://www.wfd.org/wfd.asp?sn=what_we_do&pg=sector. Accessed 7/8/02.

31. Canadian International Development Agency (CIDA), "Russia: Current Projects"; available from http://www.acdi-cida.gc.ca/CIDAWEB/webcountry.nsf/. Accessed 7/2/02.

32. All have offices in Moscow, with the exception of the Mott Foundation, which operates its Russia program from their Prague office.

33. Charities Aid Foundation Russia, "Introduction"; available from www.cafonline.org/cafrussia/default.cfm. Accessed 6/24/02.

34. John D. and Catherine T. MacArthur Foundation, "The John D. and Catherine T. MacArthur Foundation Initiative in the Independent States of the Former Soviet Union: Grants Approved from 1991 through June 1998" (Moscow, 1998).

35. Charles Stewart Mott Foundation, online grant database; available from http://www.mott.org. Accessed 7/1/02.

36. Soros Foundation, "Open Society Institute: Russia"; available from http://www.soros.org/natfound/russia/. Accessed 6/24/02.

37. Ford Foundation, online grant database; available from http://www.fordfound.org. Accessed 6/29/02.

38. During 1993–2001, the Eurasia Foundation made more than $43 million in grants. Figures until 1998 were drawn from "USAID/Russia Activity Descriptions"; subsequent data compiled from Eurasia Foundation, online grant database; available from http://www.eurasia.org. Accessed 6/24/02.

39. IREX has overseen two partnership programs worth more than $34.5 million, and CIP has disbursed more than $14 million in grant money. "USAID/Russia Activity Descriptions."

40. Leonid Polishchuk, "Russian Civil Society: Report for the World Bank" (College Park: Center for Institutional Reform and the Informal Sector, University of Maryland, 1997).

41. CIVICUS, "About US"; available from http://www.civicus.org/main/server_navigation/skeletons/Civ. . ./navigation.cfm?navID=2460. Accessed 9/19/02.

42. See Civic Initiatives Program (CIP), "The Civic Initiatives Program"; available from http://www.openweb.ru/cip/eng/init-e.html. Accessed 1/23/03.

43. Petter, "USAID/Russia NGO Sector Analysis," 4.

44. USAID, "Agency Objectives: Civil Society"; available from www.usaid.gov/democracy/civ.html. Accessed 2/10/03.

45. Westminster Foundation for Democracy, "Civil Society Development."

46. For example, the Charles Stewart Mott Foundation focuses on the support of the nonprofit sector and citizen engagement in order "to contribute to democratic pluralistic societies in Central/Eastern Europe and Russia." Charles Stewart Mett Foundation website.

47. Mercy Corps International website, http://www.mercycorps.org.

48. Initiative for Social Action and Renewal in Eurasia (ISAR) website, http://isar.org.

49. This is a critique that Thomas Carothers makes of democracy aid in general, beyond the Russian case. See Carothers, *Aiding Democracy Abroad*, 211–13.

50. Ibid., 211.

51. Soros Foundations, "Open Society Institute: Russia."

52. "YUKOS and Eurasia Foundation Launch $1.15 Million Development Partnership," in *Impact Russia* (Summer 2002), 1.

53. Marina Ottaway and Theresa Chung, "Debating Democracy Assistance: Toward a New Paradigm." *Journal of Democracy* 10.4 (1999): 99–113.

54. Charites Aid Foundation Russia, "CAF Russia: NGO Services"; available from http://www.cafonline.org/cafrusia/default.cfm&page=ngoservices.

55. Christie, "Constraints on Russia's NGO Sector."

56. CIP, "Civic Initiatives Program."

57. Ibid.

58. Margot Mininni, "Making a Difference: Early Interventions at the Grassroots," *Give and Take* 1 (September 1998); available from http://www.isar.org/archive/GT/GT1Mininni.html. Accessed 2/10/03.

59. Information available at the IREX website, under programs and projects, "Quick links to IREX activities: Russia," www.irex.org/links/russia.htm. Accessed 7/2/03.

60. ISAR, available from http://www.isar.org/isar/rfe.html. Accessed 2/10/03.

61. For example, the ISAR Far East office in 2002 funded groups that provided social services, such as disability assistance in addition to the popular Western funding

topic violence against women. The Ford Foundation in 1998 also began to shift toward funding more groups that provided social services in addition to their ongoing commitment to human rights groups.

62. "Spisok Finalistov Konkursa Universal'nikh Resursnikh Tsentrov." List provided by Lyubov Alenicheva, Eurasia Foundation, July 1998.

63. This list was taken from the schedule of September 2002 posted on the website for the Southern Russia Resource Center, based in Krasnodar, Russia. See "Programmi Grantov YuRRTs"; available from http://www.srrc.ru/srrc/grants/index.html. Accessed 8/8/02.

64. International Research and Exchanges Board (IREX). "The Promoting and Strengthening Russian NGO Development Program (Pro-NGO); available from http://www.irex.org/programs/pro-ngo/index.html.

65. Stewart Chisholm, "Report to USAID on IREX's Progress with the SPAN Grant" (n.d.). IREX, Moscow.

66. Fred Hiatt, "Grass-roots Aid Works Best in Russia," *Washington Post*, February 12, 1995, p. A1.

67. One organization posted information on 143 donors active in funding various projects in Russia. EcoLine, "Spisok Angloyazichnikh Nazvanii Istochnihov Finansirovaniya v Alfavitnom Poryadke"; available from http://www.cci.glasnet.ru/funds/REPORTS/ALPHAE.HTM. Accessed 8/5/02.

68. Based in Togliatti, Russia, the Togliatti Fund is designed for representatives from local government, business, and NGOs interested in developing local philanthropy. Charities Aid Foundation Russia, "CAF Russia: Donor Services"; available from http://www.cafonline.org/cafrussia/default.cfm?page=donorservices. Accessed 6/24/02.

69. For example, MacArthur Foundation field offices have to clear any grant over $50,000 with the home office in Chicago. The Ford Foundation field offices have to write a report on every grant to the New York headquarters.

70. Hiatt, "Grass-roots Aid Works Best in Russia," p. A1.

71. Although U.S. official economic assistance was less in 1998, in terms of real dollars, than in any of the previous fifty years, foreign assistance repeatedly came under fire by an increasingly conservative Congress. Congress, in turn, was supported in its arguments by the perceptions of the U.S. public. Americans believed U.S. foreign economic assistance programs were as much as twenty times greater than they actually were, and public support for "protecting and defending human rights in other countries" was down 24 percent since 1990. Poll quoted in M. Holt Ruffin, Alyssa Deutschler, Catriona Logan, and Richard Upjohn, *The Post-Soviet Handbook: A Guide to Grassroots Organizations and Internet Resources* (Seattle: University of Washington Press, 1999), 3.

72. Interview with Lisa Petter, November 13, 1998, Moscow.

73. Ibid.

74. Thomas O. Melia, "Retreats with Partners" (Memo, September 23, 1998).

75. Interview with Jon Snydal, September 2, 1998, Washington, D.C.

76. NDI works in Moscow, St. Petersburg, Nizhnii Novgorod, Chelyabinsk, Ekaterinburg, and Krasnodar. IRI works in Moscow, St. Petersburg, Arkhangelsk, Murmansk, Rostov, Voronezh, Perm, and Yaroslavl'.

77. Interview with John Snydal, September 2, 1998.

78. Ibid.

79. Ibid.

80. Interview with Janelle Cousino, July 23, 1998, Moscow.

81. Interview with John Snydal, September 2, 1998, Moscow.

82. USAID, "Results of Questionnaire for USAID/Implementing Partners in Russia," 1998, Moscow.

83. Interview with John Snydal, September 2, 1998.

Chapter 4. Women's Organizations and Foreign Aid

1. Also, Project Harmony, a development NGO based in Vermont, runs the Domestic Violence Community Partnership Program to develop the capacity of Russian, Ukrainian, and Georgian communities to work in coalitions to reduce domestic violence. Project Harmony, "Domestic Violence Community Partnership"; available from http://www.projectharmony.org/dvcp. Accessed 7/8/02.

2. International Research and Exchanges Board (IREX), "Regional Empowerment for Women"; available from http://www.irex.org/programs/reiw/index.htm. Accessed 7/1/02.

3. Soros Foundation, "Women's Programs"; available from http://www.soros.org/netprogram/women.html. Accessed 6/28/02.

4. Examples, in addition to those listed, are the Global Fund for Women and the Charles Stewart Mott Foundation.

5. Examples are USAID, TACIS, the British embassy, the Canadian embassy, CIDA, and the northern European embassies. In addition, several groups had developed ties with a department of the German Green Party (Frauen-Anstiftung) and had received financial assistance; however, that department has since been reorganized.

6. Examples are the MacArthur Foundation; ISAR; the Institute of International Collaboration of Germany; the Heinrich Boll Foundation; the Center for Citizen's Initiatives; the Liberty Road Association; the Austrian Foundation Karitas; Women, Law, and Development; and various sister city projects.

7. Westminster Fund for Democracy, "Women's Political Participation"; available from http://www.wfd.org/wfd.asp?sn=what_we_do&pg=sector&ps=sp_women&ty=Sec&SC=WO. Accessed 7/8/2002.

8. USAID, Bureau for Europe and Eurasia Office of Democracy and Governance, "Lessons in Implementation: The NGO Story. Building Civil Society in Central and Eastern Europe and the New Independent States" (Washington, D.C., October 1999) 24.

9. Ibid., 22–25.

10. In addition, groups that won a competition from a Western or international agency to travel to a sponsored seminar are categorized as funded. Very few groups, however, qualified under this specification.

11. In her interviews with forty women's groups in Moscow, Valerie Sperling also finds that just over one-half had received a foreign grant. See Valerie Sperling, *Organizing Women in Contemporary Russia* (Cambridge: Cambridge University Press), 228. A separate study finds that 63 percent of women's groups had received assistance from the West; see Natalia I. Abubikirova, Tatiana A. Klimenkova, Elena V. Kotchkina, Marina A. Regentova, and Tatiana G. Troinova, *Spravochnik: Zhenskiye Nepravitelsvenniye Organizatsii Rossii i SNG* (Moscow: Aslan, 1998), 16.

12. For a more extensive treatment of women's lives under the Soviet era, see Linda Racioppi and Katherine O'Sullivan See, "Women's Activism in Historical Context," in *Women's Activism in Contemporary Russia*, ed. Linda Racioppi and Katherine O'Sullivan

See (Philadelphia: Temple University Press, 1997). See also Lynn Attwood, *The New Soviet Man and Woman: Sex Role Socialization in the USSR* (Bloomington: Indiana University Press, 1990); Sue Bridger, *Women in the Soviet Countryside: Women's Roles in Rural Development in the Soviet Union* (New York: Cambridge University Press, 1987); Genia K. Browning, *Women and Politics in the USSR: Consciousness Raising and the Soviet Women's Groups* (New York: St. Martin's Press, 1987); Mary Buckley, ed., *Perestroika and the Soviet Woman* (New York: Cambridge University Press, 1992); Gail W. Lapidus, *Women in Soviet Society: Equality, Development, and Social Change* (Berkeley: University of California Press, 1987).

13. Some excellent sources are Sue Bridger, Rebecca Kay, and Kathryn Pinnock, *No More Heroines? Russia, Women, and the Market* (London: Routledge, 1996); Linda Racioppi and Katherine O'Sullivan See, eds., *Women's Activism in Contemporary Russia* (Philadelphia: Temple University Press, 1997); Sperling, *Organizing Women in Contemporary Russia;* Rebecca Kay, *Russian Women and Their Organizations: Gender, Discrimination and Grassroots Women's Organizations, 1991–1996* (New York: St. Martin's Press, 2000).

14. James Richter, "Citizens or Professionals." Unpublished paper, 1998.

15. See Tatiana Mamanova, "Introduction: The Feminist Movement in the Soviet Union," in *Women and Russia: Feminist Writings from the Soviet Union,* ed. Tatiana Mamanova (Boston: Beacon Hill Press, 1984).

16. See Sperling, *Organizing Women in Contemporary Russia,* 98–145.

17. Lidia Skoptsova, Gien Tuender-de Haan, Patricia Weijer, and Anne van de Zande, eds., "Vtoroi Nizavisimii Zhenskii Forum, Dubna, Rossiya 1992" (program manual, 1992).

18. For example, the conference program was published by Foundation Women's Activities, based in the Netherlands.

19. See Ludmilla Rzhanitsyna, "Women's Attitudes toward Economic Reforms and the Market Economy" in *Women in Contemporary Russia,* ed. Valentina Koval (Providence: Berghahn Books, 1995), 35–36. The widespread anecdotal evidence of discrimination in the job market, in which businesses advertised for women under the age of twenty-five without inhibitions or "complexes," are infamous.

20. The semifree elections for the newly created Congress of People's Deputies of 1989 shows just how symbolic these quotas were—women's representation tumbled to 15.7 percent. However, even this was a windfall; the Soviet Women's Committee was allotted seventy-five seats. See Carol Nechemias, "Equal Players or Back to the Kitchen?" in *Russian Women in Politics and Society,* ed. Normac Noonan and Wilma Rule (Westport: Greenwood Publishers, 1996), 26. The 1999 figure is from Olga Papkova, "In Russia the Word 'Power' Is of Masculine Gender," *Woman Plus* 4 (2000). Available at http://www.owl.ru/erg/womanplus/2000/femina.htm. Accessed 8/8/2002.

21. The authors of the *Spravochnik* estimate that 9 percent of groups have a specifically feminist orientation, whereas two-thirds of groups are involved in what they term "social rights issues." See Abubikirova et al., *Spravochnik.*

22. Survey 111.

23. Survey 20.

24. Survey 115.

25. Survey 78.

26. Survey 84.

27. Survey 181.

28. Survey 165.

29. Survey 153.
30. Survey 90.
31. Survey 20.
32. Letter 3.
33. Survey 186.
34. Survey 29.
35. Letter 1.
36. Survey 17.
37. Survey 15.
38. Survey 172.
39. Abubikirova et al., *Spravochnik*, 325–40.
40. Elena Gapova, "When Western Assistance Overlooks Cultural Values in FSU Gender Program," *Give and Take* (Summer 2000), 1–2. Available at http://www.isar.org/isar/archive/GT/GT8gapova.html. Accessed 7/3/02.
41. Survey 178.
42. Survey 95.
43. For example, as was the case with Survey 19.
44. Survey 1.
45. Survey 63.
46. Survey 15.
47. Survey 27.
48. Survey 17.
49. For example, this was the response of Surveys 32, 51, and 62, among others.
50. Survey 32.
51. Survey 180.
52. Survey 20.
53. Survey 24.
54. Interestingly, funded groups also did not perceive their grant-writing activities as "fund-raising"; 35 percent of funded groups also reported that they did not engage in such activity.
55. Survey 100.
56. Letter 1.
57. Survey 129.
58. Survey 155.
59. Survey 59.
60. Survey 27.
61. Survey 31.
62. Survey 51.
63. Survey 33.
64. Survey 51.
65. Survey 121.
66. Many are simply personal home numbers.
67. However, only 38 percent of unfunded groups that had an office paid rent on their office, which implies that many of them used their personal apartments as office space; 58 percent of funded groups pay rent.
68. Survey 62.
69. Survey 135.
70. Richter, "Citizens or Professionals," 2.
71. Survey 99.
72. Letter 4.

73. Survey 23.

74. Survey 28.

75. Survey 35.

76. Survey 61.

77. Survey 129.

78. Robert D. Putnam, with Robert Leonardi and Rafaella Y. Nanetti, *Making Democracy Work: Civic Traditions in Modern Italy* (Princeton: Princeton University Press, 1993).

79. It was somewhat surprising to find that 42 percent of groups said that they shared information about protests, because only 6 percent of groups admitted organizing demonstrations "often" or "very often."

80. Survey 21.

81. Survey 20.

82. Survey 84.

83. Survey 84.

84. Survey 15.

85. Survey 61.

86. Letter 3.

87. Letter 6.

88. Ibid.

89. A possible explanation for this difference could be that many of the groups that had formed before the 1990s were remnants of the old Soviet-era women's organizations; these groups were much more likely to rely on local administrations for their sources of support.

90. Survey 24.

91. Survey 109.

92. Survey 106.

93. Survey 31.

Chapter 5. Women's Organizations and the Ford Foundation

1. I was unable to evaluate the community development and self-employment grants; because this was a new area of grant activity, none of the grants had started as of 1998.

2. James Richter, "Evaluating Western Assistance to Russian Women's Organizations," in *The Power and Limits of NGOs: A Critical Look at Building Democracy in Eastern Europe and Eurasia*, ed. Sarah E. Mendelson and John K. Glenn, 54–90 (New York: Columbia University Press, 2002).

3. Valerie Sperling also discusses this trend, in *Organizing Women in Contemporary Russia: Engendering Transition* (Cambridge: Cambridge University Press, 1999), 244–49.

4. See Rebecca Kay, *Russian Women and Their Organizations: Gender, Discrimination, and Grassroots Women's Organizations* (New York: St. Martin's Press, 2000), 187–209; James Richter, "Evaluating Western Assistance"; Sperling, *Organizing Women in Contemporary Russia*, 220–56.

5. See Kay, *Russian Women and Their Organizations,*187–209; Sperling, *Organizing Women in Contemporary Russia*, 220–56.

6. This is a critique that has been made of many aspects of civil society aid, across movements and across countries; see chapter 1.

7. "The Ford Foundation/Moscow Office" (pamphlet, Moscow, 1998).

8. Specifically, it has offices in Nairobi, Kenya; Cairo, Egypt; Johannesburg, South Africa; Windhoek, Namibia; Lagos, Nigeria; Beijing, China; New Delhi, India; Jakarta, India; Manila, Philippines; Hanoi, Vietnam; Bangkok, Thailand; Rio de Janeiro, Brazil; Mexico City, Mexico; Santiago, Chile; and Moscow, Russia. *1997 Ford Foundation Annual Report*, New York, 1998.

9. "Ford Foundation/Moscow Office."

10. Interview with Chris Kedzie, September 1, 1998, Moscow.

11. Elizabieta Matynia of the New School for Social Research prepared a report on the status of women in Poland, Hungary, the Czech Republic, and the Slovak Republic; Colette Shulman wrote a report on Russia. "Recommendation for Grant Action," September 8, 1994, New York, unpublished paper.

12. Ford Foundation, memorandum, December 7, 1995, New York.

13. Ibid.

14. Ibid., 7.

15. Although the NIS-US Women's Consortium in 1998 links over ninety organizations across Russia, at the time the grant proposal was written, only fourteen of its organizations had email. Thus, the consortium sought to ease communication problems by providing modems and training to thirty-five member organizations that already had computers.

16. Interview with Mary McCauley, October 27, 1998, Moscow.

17. Interview with Chris Kedzie, July 13, 1998, Moscow.

18. However, this requirement was becoming more flexible; the Moscow office worked with organizations to help them translate their proposals into English if they themselves did not possess the requisite language skills. Ford Foundation, "Checklist for Grant Recipients" (Moscow, n.d.).

19. Interview with Mary McCauley, October 27, 1998, Moscow.

20. Interview with Chris Kedzie, July 13,1998.

21. Ibid.

22. Ibid.

23. For example, the Ford Foundation worked with the human rights organization Memorial since the early 1990s.

24. Interview with Chris Kedzie, Moscow.

25. Quoted in Larisa Flint, "Evaluation of NEWW in Russia: A Project of the Network of East-West Women in Partnership with Moscow Center for Gender Studies" (unpublished evaluation, World Learning, December 1995).

26. Interview with Irina Yurgina, Moscow

27. This is mentioned in Flint, "Evaluation of NEWW in Russia"; however, I did not follow up to see if it is true.

28. Interview, St. Petersburg Center for Gender Studies.

29. This was the complaint of Elena Ershova of the NIS-US Women's Consortium and Larisa Boichenko of the Karelian Center for Gender Studies.

30. Sperling, *Organizing Women in Contemporary Russia.*

31. This was the experience of one women's group in Petrozavodsk.

32. There is also self-selection at work here. Most traditional women's groups did not apply for foreign funding. Mainstream charitable organizations, however, complained that they were unable to get access to funds when other (feminist) groups were able to get them.

33. Interview with Natasha Mirimanova, March 16, 1998, Moscow.

34. See, for example, Sarah Henderson, "Importing Civil Society: Western Funding and the Women's Movement in Russia" (paper presented at the 1998 Annual Meeting of the American Political Science Association, September 1998); Sarah E. Mendelson and John K. Glenn, "Democracy Assistance and NGO Strategies in Post-Communist Societies" (Washington DC: College Endowment for International Peace, 2000).

35. Interview with Larisa Flint, August 11, 1998, Moscow.

36. Interview with Lyubov Alenichova, July 3, 1998, Moscow.

37. E-mail correspondence with Lyubov Alenichova, September 3, 1998.

38. Archives. Database. Library was a multiyear project funded by Frauen-Anstiftung, a German organization and was designed to document the women's movement in Russia. The organization eventually revoked funding for the program when the project disintegrated as a result of fighting over funding.

39. Interview with Elena Ershova, July 21, 1998, Moscow.

40. Ibid.

41. Interview with Irina Doskich, Moscow, December 9, 1998.

42. Interview with Gabrielle Fitchett, August 26, 1998, Moscow.

43. E-mail correspondence with Sarah Lindemann, November 9, 1998.

44. Interview with Elena (last name unknown) September 28, 1998, Pskov.

Chapter 6. The Paradox of Externally Promoting Civil Society

1. Interview, May 6, 1998, Moscow.

2. Charles Stewart Mott Foundation, *2001 Facts on Grants: Civil Society* (Flint, MI: Charles Stewart Mott Foundation, 2002), 52.

3. This is part of IREX's Prevention of Trafficking in Women and Girls Program.

4. Funded by the Moscow office of ISAR, available from www.isar.org/isar/Russia.html#programs.

5. James Richter, "Citizens or Professionals," unpublished paper, 1998, 1.

6. Interview with Caryn Wilde, October 1, 2002, Moscow.

7. Interview with Caryn Wilde, October 1, 2002, Moscow.

8. E-mail correspondence, November 9, 1998.

9. E-mail correspondence, January 2, 1999.

10. This sentiment came up repeatedly in the answers to my survey. Group after group bemoaned the fact that they didn't have a computer, didn't know how to write a grant, and had no idea where to start in formulating requests to foreign foundations.

11. Interview with Jon Snydal, September 2, 1998.

12. Interview with Larisa Flint, August 11, 1998, Moscow.

13. E-mail correspondence, May 11, 1999.

14. Interview with Jenny Hodgson, date unknown, Moscow.

15. E-mail correspondence with Lyubov Alenicheva, July 1998.

16. Round Table on Budget Transparency, Stavropol, October 2003.

17. Interview with Andrei Vakulenko, date unknown, Moscow.

18. E-mail correspondence, November 9, 1998.

19. Interview with Elena Kotchkina, July 25, 1998, Moscow.

20. Ibid.

21. E-mail correspondence, November 9, 1998.

22. Ibid.

23. E-mail correspondence, January 3, 1999.

24. Ibid.

25. John E. Squier, "Henderson on Civil Society," Johnson's Russia List #7053 8 February 2003.

26. E-mail correspondence, May 10, 1999.

27. S. N. Eisenstadt and Luis Roniger, *Patrons, Clients, and Friends: Interpersonal Relations and the Structure of Trust in Society* (New York: Cambridge University Press, 1994).

28. Claus Offe, "Cultural Aspects of Consolidation: A Note on the Peculiarities of Postcommunist Transformations," *East European Constitutional Review* 6, no. 4 (Fall 1997), 67.

29. James Richter, "Civil Society or the Third Sector?" *Give and Take* 4 (April 1999); available from http://www.isar.org/isar/archive/GT/GT4Richter.html.

30. Jim Richter discusses foreign aid's role in facilitating civil society's external and internal functions, "Promoting Activism or Professionalism in Russia's Civil Society?" Memo no. 51 (Cambridge, Mass.: Harvard University Program on New Approaches to Russian Security Policy Memo Series, November 1998).

31. Interview with Kacey Wardle, April 17, 2000, Boulder, Col.

32. Thomas Carothers and Marina Ottaway, "The Burgeoning World of Civil Society Aid," in *Funding Virtue: Civil Society Aid and Democracy Promotion*, ed. Marina Ottaway and Thomas Carothers (Washington, D.C.: Carnegie Endowment for International Peace, 2000), 15.

33. Sarah E. Mendelson, "Conclusion: The Power and Limits of Transnational Democracy Networks in Postcommunist Societies," in *The Power and Limits of NGOs: A Critical Look at Building Democracy in Eastern Europe and Eurasia*, ed. Sarah Mendelson and John K. Glenn (New York: Columbia University Press, 2002), 239–40.

34. Alexis de Tocqueville, *Democracy in America* (Garden City, N.J.: Anchor Books, 1969), 513.

35. Institute for Sustainable Communities, "What's New—Story 16." Available at http://www.iscvt.org/wnstory16.html. Accessed 2/18/03.

36. Interview with Jenny Hodgson, date unknown, Moscow.

37. Interview, July 23, 1998, Moscow.

38. Interview with John Snydal, September 2, 1998.

39. Ibid.

40. Johnson's List, May 26, 1999, Sarah Lindemann's response to Paul Goble.

Appendix A. Research Methodology

1. For example, some survey research in the areas of civic networks has been done by James L. Gibson, "Social Networks and Civil Society in Processes of Democratization" (paper presented at the August 1997 Annual Meeting of the American Political Science Association); Richard Rose, "Getting Things Done in an Anti-Modern Society: Social Capital Networks in Russia" (Centre for the Study of Public Policy Research, University of Strathclyde, 1998). In addition, the New Russia Barometer, also run by Richard Rose, produces quarterly reports on public opinion in Russia.

2. For example, USAID produced two reports on NGOs in Russia based on interviews. See Maggie Christie, "Constraints on Russia's NGO Sector" (Moscow: USAID, 1996); Lisa Petter, "USAID/Russia NGO Sector Analysis" (Moscow: USAID, 1997). Save

the Children, operating under a USAID grant, sponsored an evaluation of the Civic Initiatives Project. See Larry Dershem and Valeri Patsiorkovski, "Needs and Capacity Assessment of the Third Sector in the Central Russia: Kaluga, Yaroslavl', Smolensk, Tula, Tver', Vladimir, Ryazan', and Moscow Oblasts" (unpublished report for the Save the Children Foundation, Moscow, August 20, 1997). The World Learning Project and Save the Children have also sponsored several studies. All are based on a face-to-face interview format with surveys given and filled out on location.

3. In fact, several of the women's groups surveyed filled out the survey, but wrote that they did not consider themselves to be women's groups. This happened most often with the Committee of Soldiers' Mothers and with a few environmental groups.

4. Previous attempts to catalogue women's groups on a systematic basis include a German-funded project called Archives. Data. Library (ADL). Funding, however, was discontinued after several years. The project (and the information) then split into three separate organizations. Also, the Second Independent Women's Forum in Dubna, Russia, published a directory of participants, the most extensive listing of women activists in Russia at the time.

5. In the introduction to *Spravochnik*, the authors estimate that there are 2,000 women's organizations in Russia. There is no reliable data, however, to confirm that number. The 2000 estimate is based on the estimate that "every subject of the Russian Federation has, on average, 10 to 30 such organizations. . . ." Natalia Abubikirova, Marina Klimenkova, Elena Kotchkina, Tatiana Regentova, and Tatiana Troinova, *Spravochnik: Zhenskiye Nepravitelsvenniye Organizatsii Russii I SNG* (Moscow: Aslan, 1998), 9.

6. Tatiana Troinova provided me access to the database and was invaluable in her assistance to me in sending out the survey.

7. Some organizations had incomplete contact information. I also did not send surveys to women's groups in the republic of Chechnya; mail delivery was irregular at best, nonexistent in reality. Also, several groups listed in the directory were either temporary organizations that revolved around the lifespan of a grant project or for all intents and purposes defunct. I was able to weed out several of the defunct Moscow groups using my own knowledge. In addition, several entries in the directory were under the umbrella of one overarching group. Thus, I chose to send one survey to the group as a whole rather than to survey the various parts. For example, The Congress of Women of the Kola Peninsula runs several projects, that are not separate legal entities but instead are simply different activities of the same organization; yet they had several entries in the database.

8. My own attempts to get mailing lists from these women's organizations were fruitless.

9. Jack Walker, *Mobilizing Interest Groups in America: Patrons, Professions, and Social Movements* (Ann Arbor: University of Michigan Press, 1991).

10. Russell J. Dalton, *The Green Rainbow: Environmental Groups in Western Europe* (New Haven: Yale University Press, 1994). Please contact the author for copy of the survey he used.

11. Mario Diani, *Green Networks: A Structural Analysis of the Italian Environmental Movement* (Edinburgh: Edinburgh University Press, 1995).

12 I thank Laura Brunnell (University of Colorado) for sharing her survey of women's groups in Poland and Jonathan Squier (University of Michigan) for sharing his survey of Moscow NGOs.

13. This is the survey that the authors of the *Spravochnik* sent to women's groups in order to compile their guide. See Abubikirova, Klimenkova, Kotchkina, Regentova, and Troinova, "Zhenskiye Organizatsii v Rossii" in *Spravochnick: Zhenskiye Nepra-*

vitelsvenniye Organizatsii Russii I SNG, ed. Abubikirova et al., (Moscow: Aslan, 1998).

14. I thank Zoya Khotkina of Moscow Center for Gender Studies, Tatiana Troinova of Women's Information Network, Liza Bashkova of the Independent Women's Forum, Lyubov Yakovleva of Anika, and Marianna Vronskaya of Goluba. One additional unnamed woman declined to cooperate, citing instrumental reasons. Because I was a young researcher from the United States, she felt any contacts I might have would not be useful enough for her to help me out.

15. I thank once again Zoya Khotkina of the Moscow Center for Gender Studies for spending numerous late nights in her office reworking the questions.

16. Many felt they were not "qualified" to contribute their opinions. Others wanted to know why their opinion was important.

17. In addition, sixteen surveys were returned to me marked "return to sender: address unknown."

18. In the second batch, six were returned with the label "return to sender." Also, I received four surveys for which I had already received a response; these were, consequently not counted.

19. Overall, this corresponds with a general feeling of weariness with Western academics in Moscow. Many women's groups in Moscow complained that they were tired of Western academics coming through for a few weeks, collecting research, using them as guinea pigs, and then leaving to write an article on them. Perhaps this weariness with always being under scrutiny (and always doing favors without feeling there was a return) explains some of the underrepresentation of Moscow groups.

Appendix B. The Survey

1. This appendix does not include the cover letter sent out with the survey. For a copy, please contact the author. Originally, I had planned to send the survey out to organizations in the former Soviet republics for whom I had contact information. However, the logistics of including a stamped envelope that would cross national borders turned out to be too complex for me to handle and, as a result, I abandoned that plan. I had already printed up the survey, so the title remained.

Appendix D. Donor Organizations

1. List compiled from M. Holt Ruffin, Alyssa Deutschler, Catriona Logan, and Richard Upjohn, *The Post-Soviet Handbook: A Guide to Grassroots Organizations and Internet Resources* (Seattle: Center for Civil Society International and University of Washington Press, 1999) and from the Civil Society International email list.

Index